THE ASIAN ELEPHANT
A NATURAL HISTORY

J.C. DANIEL

NATRAJ PUBLISHERS

© J.C. Daniel

First Published 1998
Second Edition 2009

ISBN: 978-81-858-123-5

Published by Mrs.Veena Arora, for Natraj Publishers,
Publications Division, and printed at Gay Printers, New Delhi

Acknowledgment

"The author and publisher thank : the Bombay Natural History Society for permission to use E P Gee's photographs; Mr M K Harikrishnan for permission to use Mr M Krishnan's photographs, Dr A J T Johnsingh, Mr Krupakar Senani, Dr Hemant Datye for permission to use their photographs of elephants.

They thank Ms. P.A. Kohli for editorial assistance."

To
Ajai, Siva, Ramesh, Hemant
and
'Doc' Krishnamurthy

Table of Contents

Preface   7-8

1.   **Past and Present Distribution**   9-17

    1.1   Historical

    1.1.1   Moghul Period

    1.1.2   Early British Period

    1.2   Madhya Pradesh

    1.3   Present Distribution

    1.3.1   Altitudinal Distribution

    1.4   Indian Sanctuaries and
              National Parks holding elephants

2.   **Populations in the Past and Present**   18-27

    2.1   Moghul Period

    2.2   British Period

    2.2.1   Uttar Pradesh

    2.2.2   Orissa

    2.3   Present Population

3.   **Colour and Size**   28-38

    3.1   Colour

    3.2   Size

    3.3   White Elephant

4.   **Tuskers and Tusks**   39-61

    4.1   Siamese

    4.2   Burmese

    4.3   Indian

4.4   Abnormal

4.5   Aborted

4.6   Multiple

4.7   Tusker Tracks

4.8   Makhnas

5.   Habits   **62-83**

5.1   General

5.2   Speed

5.3   Stride

5.4   Swimming and Water Requirement

5.5   Vocalisation

5.6   Vision

5.7   Smell

5.8   Sleep

5.9   Play

5.10   Food

5.11   Salt lick

5.12   Home Range

6.   Behaviour   **84-115**

6.1   Social Organisation

6.1.1 Lone or Solitary Bulls

6.2   Combat between Bulls

6.3   Rogue elephants

6.4   Mother, Calf and "Aunty"

6.4.1 Protection of Calf

6.4.2 Seeking assistance

6.5   Demonstration and mock charge

6.6   Tame and Wild Elephants

6.7 Intelligence

6.8 Reaction to Earthquake

7. **Breeding**   116-144

7.1 Sexual Maturity

7.2 Calving interval

7.3 Breeding in Captivity and Gestation

7.4 Musth

7.5 Mating

7.6 Redirected Sexual Activities

7.7 Birth in the wild

7.8 Twin and Triple Calves

8. **Growth**   145-156

9. **Age**   157-163

10. **Disease**   164-168

11. **Death, Natural and un-natural**   169-190

12. **Elephant and Tiger**   191-195

13. **Man and Elephant**   196-233

13.1 Encounters

13.2 Elephant Capture

13.2.1 Pit Traps

13.2.2 Mela Shikar

13.2.3 Kheddah

13.3 Care and Management of Captive Elephants

14. **Hunting**   234-291

15. **Conservation and Future of the Indian Elephant**   292-302

References   303-306

PREFACE

Probably the most well known among the wild animals of India is the elephant. Only a very small fraction of the population of over 900 million Indians may have seen it in the wild, but almost everyone has seen domesticated ones at some time or other. The elephant is deeply interlinked with man in India in his religious and cultural heritage. In spite of this close association, amounting often to veneration, the elephant has now, quite often, become to the people who live in the vicinity of its habitat, one of the most destructive species of wildlife.

Curiously enough, even though the elephant has been a part of human history in India from time immemorial, and treatises such as Palakapyas Hastayurveda (Treatment of Elephants) have been written in the past, scientific enquiry into the ecology of the elephant in India was not undertaken till the late seventies of this century. The elephant had, however, been the subject of serious scientific enquiry in countries adjoining India, particularly Sri Lanka and Malaysia. Nevertheless, there is an abundance of natural history notes published in the *Journal of the Bombay Natural History Society* from the time the elephant's value as an adjunct to forestry practices was recognised. It had always been a ceremonial as well as a transport animal and in the past used in wars. To the sportsman the hunting of proscribed rogues was the acme of sport. Their observations and the observations of those who managed elephants in captivity provides a wealth of information on the habits and behaviour of the Indian Elephant.

The earlier natural history notes are the offshoot of the primary interest, which was hunting, of such naturalist sportsmen as R.C. Morris, W.S. Thom, Phythian-Adams, and of capture and management by such exemplary forest officials as A.J.W. Milroy, N.L. Bor, F.W. Champion, P.D. Stracey, E.A. Smythies, and of domestic elephants by G.H. Evans of Burma who wrote the classic book "The Treatment of Elephants in Disease and Health".

I have also referred extensively to the research by the scientists of the Bombay Natural History Society undertaken during the eighties of this century, particularly during the nine years from 1983 when Ajai Desai, N Sivaganesan and Ramesh Kumar studied the elephants of the Mudumalai and adjoining sanctuaries and national parks with Dr V Krishnamurthy as Co-ordinator. A subsidiary project on an isolated population at Dalma Wildlife Sanctuary in Bihar was undertaken by Hemant Datye who had been trained at Mudumalai. The scientific programme was under the general guidance of A J T Johnsingh, and received advice as consultant from Chris Wemmer of the Smithsonian Institution, U.S.A. The project originally conceived by me was funded by the Fish and Wildlife Service of the U.S.A. I was the Principal Investigator.

I have not referred here to the earlier studies by R. Sukumar whose pioneering efforts have been reported elsewhere. From the *Journal* I have, however, quoted extensively from M. Krishnan's natural history notes, which are without doubt the best writing on the subject.

I have also collated the available information from the *Journal of the Bombay Natural History Society* and have arranged them in sequential order. The information is slightly lopsided, based as it is on the field of interest of the major contributors, which was hunting.

I have concluded with current thinking on the conservation and management of the Asian Elephant, a species threatened with gradual extinction throughout its existing range.

J.C. Daniel

Chapter 1

PAST AND PRESENT DISTRIBUTION

1.1 Historical

The Indian Elephant, considering its past and present distribution in Asia, should be correctly termed the Asian Elephant. The elephant occurred over an enormous area in the past, stretching from the Tigris and Euphrates Valleys of present day Syria and Iraq up to the Yellow River in China in the east and Sumatra (Indonesia) in the south east. The Pharaohs of Egypt hunted them in the Euphrates valley. Considering the fact that a canopy forest is an essential requirement for the elephants' existence, it gives an idea of the conditions prevailing in the Euphrates and Tigris valleys approximately 6000 years ago, compared to the present day aridity of those regions. Much of the information available on the past status of the Middle East habitat of the elephant is largely conjectural but probably accurate. There is sufficient evidence, however, to conclude that West Asia had a very wet climate up to 400-500 B.C. (1) and even up to the first century AD, and that the elephant occurred in areas which are now semideserts and deserts as D K Lahiri Choudhury very succintly puts it (106).

"The loss of forests has been going on since the days of the Indus Valley civilization (c. 2500-1500 B.C.). If an elephant distribution map for ancient India were made, it would probably cover all of India: from the present Thar Desert in the west to the evergreen forests of north-eastern India, from the Himalayan foothills in the north to Cape Comorin in the south, with scattered patches of human settlements along the fertile river valleys.

"The Aryan invasion that came from the northwest and spread along the Ganges Valley caused what was probably the first major crack in the compact elephant habitat, which was to separate the southern from the northern population permanently. In the course of time, elephants gradually retreated like the forest from the west, away from human population and the land that could no longer sustain them "

9

1.1.1 Moghul Period

Though the elephant was very much a part of the Indian empires which existed from the time of recorded history, either as a part of the war machine or as a domestic animal of religious and cultural significance, precise information on the distribution of the elephant is available only from the memoirs and writings of the Moghul Emperors of the 16th and 17th centuries A.D. (2). The Emperor Babur (1526-30) notes in his memoirs that the elephant "inhabits the district of Kalpi and the higher you advance thence towards the east, the more do the elephants increase in number. "His grandson, Akbar, who ruled from 1556 to 1605 describes an elephant-capturing hunt in the forests of Narwar, and his son, Jahangir, (1605-1627) describes a similar hunt in Dohad in the Panchmahals. Kalpi (26°39'N, 77°54'E), is in present day Rajasthan, Narwar (25°39'N, 77°16'E) in present day Madhya Pradesh; and Dohad (22°50'N, 74°16'E) in Gujarat represents the westernmost distribution of the population in the peninsula during the 16th and 17th centuries and thus provides an indication of the extent of loss of habitat up to that period. Nowadays there are no elephants, except isolated northern herds in U.P., west of 84° longitude which runs roughly through Bihar in the Central Peninsula, and none at all north of 16° latitude in Western India.

1.1.2 Early British Period

The elephant is now restricted to the forests in the hills of the peninsula that can hold elephants being the only areas, even here suitable forests that had elephants in the recent past do not hold them now, as noted by Burton (3) while recording evidence of the past occurrence of elephants in Madhya Pradesh where there are none now. Burton gives an interesting account of the havoc done by a tame tusker run wild in Madhya Pradesh in mid-nineteenth century. Burton states:

1.2 Madhya Pradesh

A copy of the illustrated pamphlet, 'The Doings and Destruction of the Most Murderous Rogue' by Colonel Arthur Bloomfield of the Indian Army is in the Library of the Nagpur University and listed, Class B 63 No.748. The pamphlet was printed by H B Crisp, High Street, Samundham (Norfolk). The date is not given in the transcribed copy of it -- about 13,000 words - made by Mr. Joseph Fernandez, botanist, of Nagpur and given to the writer of this note. Its handwritten copy is now bound and added to the Society's Library.

'Historical records, and names of places such as "Hathi-Doh" or Elephant Pool, indicate that in times past elephants were found in many parts of the Central Provinces, but that is no longer so; (Dunbar Brander). So remarks Bloomfield in his pamphlet dealing with the period 1868 onwards: 'There are in the Central Provinces no wild elephants anywhere except the Matin and Uprora Zemindaries of the Bilaspur District some 250 miles from these (Balaghat) jungles. This elephant therefore, hard pressed for companions, was said to pass most of his time with two wild buffaloes, which sometimes, so the rumours were, he used to chastise in his displeasure."

It was in 1868 that Captain Bloomfield, when Deputy Commissioner of the Balaghat District, first came in contact with this animal which up to that time had not been destructive. He relates that the animal escaped between the years 1830-1840 from its master at Ellichpur in western Berar, and eventually found its way some hundreds of miles to the east to the wild and hilly forests of the Balaghat.

It was not until three years later that the elephant began to pull down huts and kill the people. Between January 27 and February 17, 1871, he was in the Mandla District and originally reported to have killed 21 (6 men, 8 women and 7 children). The pamphlet gives the official reports which relate that not only did the brute tear the victims into pieces but devoured parts of the scattered corpses. He no doubt commenced this series of attacks in a state of musth, for during the seven months of the hot weather and rainy season following, nothing was either heard or seen of the animal. With the approach of the cold weather, however, he again became musth, and destructive to the houses, stores of grain, fields and jungle people. That the reported devouring of portions of his victims was widely credited is gathered from Bloomfield's narrative. 'On the afternoon of the 2nd November (in camp) in walked F.A. Naylor, the District Superintendent of Police, and said, "That man-eating elephant that killed so many people in the Mandla District in the beginning of the year, has appeared in this District and killed and partly devoured a man near Behir". "All right", I said "We must stop his fun, and start as soon as possible." Then began the exciting and dangerous hunt through

11

dense and hilly forests which ended on the afternoon of the 7th November beyond the village of Kaswara. The final scenes, are graphically related. The weapons used were 12 bore breech-loading rifles taking 5 to 6 drams of powder, and spherical-faced solid lead conical bullets weighing 6.5 to the lb. or 1077 gm.

The animal was in perfect condition, his skin glossy black and under it a thick coating of fat. The tusks were 41 inches long.

The pamphlet is not just a dull narrative, but contains much of interest concerning the country, the hills and forests, the jungle tribes, their dwellings and way of life. Baigas they were, and it is clear that without the brave and willing aid of these simple people the two Europeans would not have been able to penetrate those difficult forests and come up with the elephant. The Government reward of Rs.200 seems somewhat niggardly for the destruction of such a beast as this. The money was distributed among the Baigas.

During the days of the hunt the monster killed a number of people and pulled down houses. The villages and hamlets of Jagla, Limoti, and Godari provided victims; and during the night of November 3/4 ten people were killed in the hamlets of Nandar, Markapahar, Mate, Kesa, Dhatta and Daidi.

"Thus ended the career of what Sir Samuel Baker of African fame told me was the worst rogue elephant he had even heard of. I think I can certainly claim for him the proud position of being "The Record Monster" whose atrocities will seldom or never be equalled.

Mahesh Rangarajan ("Fencing the Forest". Oxford University Press, 1996) states that Mahmud Khalji (1436-39) Ruler of Malwa accepted gifts of captive elephants from the forests of Bandhavgarh. He adds that during Akbar's reign elephants were abundant in the districts of Hoshangabad, Garh and Bajagarh, and in the late 16th century elephants were common in Chanderi, Rassir, Hoshangabad and Handia. Human settlements in the passes of Rajpipla and Dohad in the 17th century cut off the population of elephants in central India from those of western India. In the mid-19th century elephants occurred in Pendra and Matin Zamindaries of Bilaspur, and in Rewah (and Sankalpur,

M Krishnan

Blunt-tusks and sharp-tusks.

A calf, lying down in its mother's path, being hoisted to its legs.

M Krishnan

Lone tusker feeding on submerged grass and sedge.

A tusker and elephant herd at Bandipur

MY Ghorpade

The herd in the water spreading out in a semicircle : note outreaching trunks.

M Krishnan

Calf waiting for its mother after a spell of play with another calf.

Herd of elephants grazing on a hill, near Koyyathotti, Periyar

M Krishnan

Orissa). From an estimated population of about 300 elephants in the Sal and Bamboo forests of Bilaspur zamindaries over 120 elephants were trapped between 1865 and 1867 in Kheddas in the Bilaspur zamindaries. The elephant became a protected species all over India in 1879 but by 1878 there were no elephants in government forests, only in private and feudal forests (Mahesh Rangarajan, op. cit.).

Present Status

A herd of elephants had recently moved back into eastern Madhya Pradesh from Bihar, and had to be tranquilised and domesticated because of the damage they caused to tribal settlements in forested areas.

1.3.1 Present Distribution

The Elephant habitat in India presently ranges from climax evergreen forests to dry thorn forest, swamp and grasslands. Among these the optimum habitats are the moist and dry deciduous forests. The elephant in India now exists in five separate populations distributed as under:

a)   A Northwest Indian population in the forest divisions of Dehra Dun, Bijnor and Nainital districts of U.P.

b)   A Southern population distributed in the Western Ghats in the states of Karnataka, Kerala and Tamil Nadu north of the Palghat gap at latitude 12°N.

c)   A Southern population in the states of Kerala-Tamil Nadu south of the Palghat Gap.

d)   A Central Indian population distributed in Southern Bihar, South Bengal and Orissa.

e)   An Eastern population distributed in North Bengal, Assam and other states in Eastern India. It is possible that the peripheral elements in the east are shared with Burma and Bangladesh.

In north east India elephants do occur in the plains, especially in the riverain jungles of sanctuaries such as the Manas and Kaziranga sanctuaries in Assam.

1.3.2 Altitudinal Distribution

The height up to which they go in the Himalayas has been a point of debate. Molesworth (4) discussing the vertical distribution of animal life as given in the Illustrated London News states:

"Amongst the animals shown, the Indian Elephant is placed at 5000 ft. During the recent Aka expedition, we found elephants on the Bhutan-Tibet boundary at a height of 10,200 ft. It would be interesting to know if they have ever been observed formerly at this height. The elephants seem to ascend from the main valley (5,000') during the hot weather, from which there was a broad well trodden Elephant path to the ridge above. The whole ridge above 8,000' is covered with rhododendrons and with occasional pine trees.

Lesser Rhino were found in the main Valley at a height of over 5,000 ft. I understand that the Lesser Rhino was observed at considerable elevation in Burma, but can find no reference to the exact height."

I have retained the note on the rhinoceros as unusual information on an animal which is now extinct in India.

Responding to Molesworth, E.O. Shebbeare (5) wrote:

"In your current issue Capt. Molesworth asks if elephants have ever before been observed at 10,200 ft elevation. Though I have never seen them myself, a number of people who know the Kalimpong district have told me that elephants are frequently seen on Rechila at high elevations, and the following note in the margin of my copy of the "Fauna of British India" may be of interest. The book originally belonged to the late Mr. Tinne of the Forest Department, and the note is in his handwriting:

"They (elephants) go at all seasons of the year to the top of Rechila and Sathila in British Bhutan, 10,060 ft., to feed on the Maling bamboo, *Arundinaria racemosa*, and I think, to escape the mosquitoes and other pests in the Dooars. I have found fresh tracks at most seasons of the year, even through 2 ft. of snow in April 1907, when the season was unusually late. As the approach to the summit is extremely steep they must have a regular track, probably crossing from side to side of the Neora (narchu) river. From their tracks, they appear to wade into the ponds found at 9,200 ft, but not extensively. They probably also graze on the small grassy meadows which cap Rechila where bamboo and rhododendron grow."

Another confirmatory note on elephants visiting high altitudes is given by H J Elwes (6), who had one of his sheep killed by a tiger! Elwes writes:

"I am able to confirm the late Mr. Tinne's note on this subject, quoted by Mr. Shebbeare. In August, 1886 I made a trip with

Mr. Prestage from Darjeeling up the Rishilah or Rechila with the object of finding a shorter and better route into the Chumbi Valley. For some miles the only path that then existed was made by wild elephants, and our camp below the summit at about 9,000 ft was disturbed in the night by a herd. On the top at about 10,400 feet, the sheep which we had taken with us for food was killed by a tiger, and this is the highest elevation I know of on record for tigers. But I was assured by my friend, the late Mr. C B Clarke, F.R.S., that on one of his botanical expeditions into Eastern Sikkim, he had seen elephants' tracks in the snow at about 12,000 feet, which must have been made by elephants coming from British Bhutan over or round the shoulder of the Richilah."

Elephants have been noted further east at similar altitudes by F N Betts (7) in Arunachal Pradesh. He writes:

"While crossing the Bompu La (9,600') in early September I was surprised to find fresh traces of a number of elephants on the very summit, and to learn that one had actually been encountered on the path a few days before. The Bompu La is in the Se-La Subagency of the North-East Frontier of India lying some 30 miles east of the eastern boundary of Bhutan. The range, whose highest peaks are over 10,000', rises straight from the plains and the southern base is covered in evergreen forest. Above 9,000' this becomes a dense growth of Ringal Bamboo under a cover of Rhododendrons and other evergreens, and it is apparently this bamboo which attracts the elephants only during the summer months since from December to February the Pass is regularly under snow."

The present day world distribution of the Asian Elephant is a fraction of what it was in the past. Apart from the population in India, which incidentally has the largest existing population, elephants occur in Nepal, Bhutan, Myanmar (Burma), Thailand, Laos, Cambodia, Vietnam, Yunnan (China), Malaysia and Sumatra (Indonesia), and Sri Lanka.

1.3.2 Distribution in Indian Sanctuaries

Sanctuaries holding elephants in India are listed below:

Name of PA	Area (km²)	Name of PA	Area (km²)
Andamans	131	**Kerala**	2,158
1. Interviews Island WS	131	26. Chendurny WS	100
		27. Chimmony WS	90
Andhra Pradesh	357	28. Chinnar WS	90
2. Kaundinya WS	357	29. Eravikulam WS	77
		30. Neyyar WS	128
Arunachal Pradesh	3,281	31. Parambikulam WS	285
3. D'Ering WS	190	32. Peechi Vazhani WS	125
4. Itanagar WS	140	33. Peppara WS	53
5. Mehao WS	282	34. Periyar TR	777
6. Namdapha TR	1,807	35. Silent Valley NP	89
7. Pakhui WS	862	36. Wyand WS	344
Assam	1,987	**Meghalaya**	254
8. Barnadi WS	26	37. Balphakram NP	200
9. Garampani WS	6	38. Nokrek NP	49
10. Kaziranga NP	696	39. Siju WS	5
11. Laokhowa WS	70		
12. Manas TR	1,097	**Nagaland**	56
13. Rajiv Gandhi (Orang) WS	92	40. Intanki WS	56
Bihar	5,160	**Orissa**	4,579
14. Dalma WS	193	41. Chandaka Ws	189
15. Palamau TR	767	42. Hadgarh WS	192
16. Singbhum*	4,200	43. Kapilasa WS	126
		44. Kotagarh Ws	400
Karnataka	4,218	45. Kuldiha WS	273
17. Bandipur TR	874	46. Lakhari Valley WS	118
18. Bannerghatta NP	104	47. Satkoshia Gorge WS	
19. Bhadra WS	492	South	478
20. Biligiri Rangan Temple WS	574	48. Satkoshia Gorge WS	
21. Brahmagiri WS	181	North	318
22. Dandeli WS	995	49. Simlipal TR	2,200
23. Nagarhole NP	572	50. Ushakothi WS	285
24. Nugu WS	30		
25. Shettihally WS	396		

Tamil Nadu	2,489
51. Anamalai WS (Indira Gandhi)	890
52. Grizzled Giant Squirrel WS	400
53. Kalakkad-Mundanthurai TR	800
54. Mudumalai WS (Jayalalitha)	321
55. Mukurthi NP	78
Tripura	349
56. Gumti WS	349
Uttar Pradesh	2,711
57. Corbett TR	
58. Sonnadi WS	1,400
59. Dudwa TR	490
60. Rajaji NP	821
West Bengal	950
61. Buxa TR	750
62. Chapramari WS	9
63. Gorumara WS	9
64. Jaldapara WS	216
65. Mahananda WS	66
TOTAL	**28,780**

adopted from Envis Bi-annual Bulletin 1(1) 1998. WII.

In addition, elephants occur in reserved forests adjoining protected areas that form part of elephant ranges, where their protection remains a cause for considerable concern.

Chapter 2

POPULATIONS IN THE PAST & PRESENT

The Conservation Action Plan of the Asian Elephant Specialist Group of the World Conservation Union (IUCN) estimates the total world population of the Asian Elephant as between 37+ to 48+ thousand with a minimum country population of between 50 to 85 in Nepal and a maximum of 20,000 to 24,000 in India.

2.1 Moghul Period

In comparison, according to D.K. Lahiri Choudhury (106), the Moghul Emperor Jehangir (1569–1637), Akbar's son, claimed to have 12,000 largest–size elephants in active army service and another 1,000 to supply fodder to these animals. (Elephants spend most of their waking hours eating; when they are employed in strenuous work throughout the day and cannot collect fodder for their consumption at night, large quantities must be provided for them in camp on their return from duty). Additionally, so it is claimed, there were 100,000 elephants to carry male courtiers, officials, and their attendants, and –– both apparently given the same status –– court ladies and baggage. Even allowing for a certain high–minded imperial exaggeration in these figures, particularly in the figure of 100,000 (the editors of Jahangir's memoirs, finding the figure too high to be credible, tend to attribute it to scribal error), there can hardly be any doubt that the elephant arm of the imperial Mughal fighting forces must have been truly formidable. According to Jehangir, Akbar had 12,000 fighting elephants of the largest class and another 20,000 of lesser size to provide fodder and provender.

The logistics involved in maintaining 100,000 elephants is mind boggling at a daily requirement of 500 lbs of fodder per animal, considering the transport facilities then available, one tends to agree with the scepticism of the editors of Jehangir's memoirs on the number of elephants in the Imperial Stables. It is, however, unlikely that all the 100,000 elephants were stabled at one location and were possibly spread over the entire empire. One could also hazard a guess that forests capable of sustaining elephants were considerably larger than nowadays and, therefore, our judgement of the statement should take that into account.

2.2 British Period

Between the time of the Mughals and the establishment of British rule over India there is a gap in our knowledge on the distribution and population of elephants. But it is apparent, from the fact that they were considered vermin and shot indiscriminately because of the damage they caused to crops, that they were abundant and widespread. It was only the passing of the Elephant Protection Act in 1832 that saved the species from early extinction.

2.2.1 Uttar Pradesh

No population estimates are available till the late seventies of the present century, except in Uttar Pradesh, (the former United Provinces) where F.W. Champion (8) states that, in 1938, they occurred:

"All along the forest belt at the base of the United Provinces' Himalayas, wild elephants are to be found in small numbers and a few also occur in the terai forests of Oudh, as well as in the Zemindari forests of Bijnor and elsewhere. The largest number live in the dense bamboo forests of the Garhwal Bhabar, in the Lansdowne Forest Division, where there are probably about fifty permanent residents, but elsewhere the numbers are smaller and the total head of wild elephants in the whole of the United Provinces probably does not exceed some 250 individuals, divided up into a number of small herds, with numerous semi–solitary tuskers and maknas scattered about in the forest areas. A fairly large herd has recently appeared in the terai forests of the Pilibhit Forest Division, in Oudh, and it is probable that this herd has recently emigrated into British India from the neighbouring forests of Nepal.

In the earlier part of the last century these wild elephants were greatly persecuted by sportsmen, particularly in the neigh-bourhood of Dehra Dun, and it is probable that they were saved from annihilation only by the Elephant Preservation Act of some fifty years ago. This Act prohibits the shooting or killing of elephants entirely, except in the case of proclaimed rogues, and it is a great pity that some of the other species, such as rhinoceros, were not saved from destruction in the same way. Elephant catching operations have taken place a few times since, but certainly not more than 100 have been caught, whereas the number of proclaimed rogues that have been shot could not exceed twenty, yet the number of elephants at present in existence seems remarkably small after fifty years of protection, and it would appear that they are not breeding as prolifically as one would have expected under the circumstances. The number of young calves to be seen is extremely small and it has been suggested that this may be due to in–breeding as the result of segregation from the large number of elephants in Nepal, of which these United Provinces elephants originally formed a part. At one time large stretches of the Nepal terai forests adjoined the forests of the United Provinces and there were then numerous opportunities for wild elephants to pass from one country to the other, but much of the Nepal elephant country has since been opened up for cultivation and few elephants now come over from Nepal to inter–breed with the survivors in the United Provinces. The new herd in Pilibhit already referred to has apparently come from Nepal, and it is to be hoped that these animals will spread over the Province and infuse new blood into what seems to be a dying race.

The ordinary wild elephant of the United Provinces appears to be a very inoffensive individual and does not ordinarily do any harm to mankind, although he is held in terrible awe by the local inhabitants and men working in the jungles. Indeed, in Lansdowne Forest Division —— the main home of the wild elephants —— there has been no casualty from them for the last ten years, although one rogue killed a number of people about the beginning of the Great War, before he was finally shot by the then Divisional Forest Officer, Mr R. St. G. Burke, within a few hundred yards of the Forest Rest House at Kotwara.

These wild elephants are, however, extremely destructive to bamboo forests and also destroy a considerable number of young sal trees, so that some Forest Officers are of the opinion that they should be caught or destroyed in the interests of Forestry. The Balrampur trackers consider that the number of animals at present in the forests is insufficient to justify the heavy expense of 'khedah' operations, and it would indeed be a pity if Government were to allow the few remaining wild elephants in Northern India to be slaughtered for the sake of the very slight increase in forest revenue which might result upon their destruction. One is glad however, to be able to write that there is no immediate prospect of such a calamity occurring."

Comparative data on the population in Uttar Pradesh is available from two censi carried out by V.B. Singh nearly four decades later in 1966 and 1976 in the forests of Uttar Pradesh. Whereas Champion estimated an approximate population of 250 in 1929. V.B. Singh (9) reports that -

"On the basis of the evidence furnished by the data the population of elephants in U.P. has risen to just over 500.

A comparison of the census results carried out in 1967 and 1976 shows that there has been an increase of nearly 130 heads during this period. (The maximum number of elephants as per 1967 census was 380 while that for the 1976 is 507). The maximum number of females during the 1967 census was 180 which should produce at least 30 calves per year. Assuming that the survival percentage is not more than 60%, nearly 18 calves should have been added annually and over a period of 9 years the total increase in the population should have been by about 162. The increase in the population as indicated by the 1976 census is not too far off and, considering the various adverse factors which have acted against their normal living and breeding conditions, can be taken to be quite reasonable. The sex ratio remained stationary. The percentage of young ones stayed at 20% of the total population. Lansdowne Forest Division and Corbett National Park hold more than 2/3 of the total population in the State, and the survival of elephants in U.P. depends on the preservation and development of their habitat in these two areas."

The most recent census of the population of elephants in Uttar Pradesh Forests estimates at 875! (1996), A 66% increase, which seem to be a somewhat optimistic estimate.

2.2.2 Orissa

The only other area from which some historic information is available is Orissa, where H.F. Mooney (10) reported in 1928 that :

"Wild elephants in the province of Bihar and Orissa are entirely confined to the Native States, Angul district and a small area in the west of Singhbhum district. Outside this tract they are nowhere else resident in the province, but do occasionally wander into the adjoining districts of British India at certain times of the year.

The Feudatory States of Orissa (with Angul district) are about thirty thousand square miles in extent; they are very sparsely populated and largely covered in forest. Some of these jungles are very extensive, especially those lying between the Mahanadi river and the main line of the Bengal–Nagpur Railway, and contain vast quantities of bamboo. These forests provide an ideal sanctuary for elephants as both water and fodder are plentiful, while their inaccessibility and dense cover afford an excellent retreat in the hot weather. It is interesting to note that, with the exception of one large herd in the extreme southwest of the area on the borders of Vizagapatam district, elephants are not found permanently south of the Mahanadi, although they occasionally cross it in the rainy season. The jungles south of the river are similar in all respects to those lying north of it and abound in bamboo, but the water supply of the southern States is scanty; this would account for their absence from this tract. An abundant supply of water is essential. Mayurbhanj State with its vast extent of forest–clad hills and perennial streams is the largest sanctuary in Orissa.

It would be extremely difficult to estimate accurately the number of wild elephants in the Feudal States, but there are not less than five hundred, and may be considerably more. The herds seem to contain nine to twelve individuals as a rule; but occasionally they are met in considerably larger numbers, probably due to the temporary fusion of two or more herds. Single animals are frequently seen and appear invariably to be bulls. These males do not, I believe, lead an entirely solitary existence, but associate with the herd when so inclined. It is my experience that they are for the most part the biggest tuskers, so that their absence from the herd is more likely of their own choosing, and not because they have been driven from it. A few old males may through failing strength, be deprived of the leadership of the herd and compelled to lead a solitary life, for a time at least. I have frequently watched herds feeding and have noticed that they usually consist of young bulls, cows and calves; the big tuskers being generally found feeding at some distance from the main herd. It appears to be not unusual to find two such bulls in company.

From February to the break of the monsoon the elephants are located in the heavier jungles, where feeding is good and water abundant, but during the rains they move widely throughout the area and take a heavy toll of the crops during their wanderings. The damage done to paddy and sugarcane is considerable and in a few places this has become a serious menace, land going out of cultivation since the raiyats seldom succeed in reaping a tithe of what they have sown. The problem of reducing the number of elephants is a difficult one; for beyond the limited utility of khedda operations, no effective solution presents itself.

It is accepted as a fact by those with long local experience that elephants have been steadily on the increase in Orissa in recent times. This I believe to be unquestionable. The Elephant Preservation Act applies only in the British district of Angul, but elephants have always been protected in the States by the Rajas. Both Angul and the Feudal States have been the scene of khedda operations for many years past, and from time to time considerable catches are made. Beyond this casualties are very few indeed. The number of elephants trapped during the past ten or fifteen years would not exceed an average of twenty annually. The calves born each year must be in excess of this figure so that kheddas, on their present scale, do not succeed in coping with the natural increase. Last cold weather exceptionally large catches were made, aggregating sixty–nine animals in all.

Mr Champion attributes the slow rate of increase among the wild elephants of the United Provinces to in–breeding. The fact that in Orissa the numbers are considerable and the herds are spread over a larger area might account for their being more prolific. Certainly many of the herds I have seen have contained a good number of calves, which invariably constitute a large proportion of the number trapped.

Casualties from disease and the bullet are not great; perhaps four or five animals each year.

2.3 Present Population

The Project Elephant directorate has issued the following summary table of the elephant population in India in 1996, on the basis of information supplied to them by State Forest Departments and other sources:

POPULATION OF WILD ELEPHANTS IN INDIA
(Figures represent mid-values of the Range of Estimated Population)

States	1985 *AESG Report	1989 +CES Report	% Variation over 1985	1993 GOI Report	% Variation over 1989
SOUTH INDIA					
1. Andhra Pradesh				46	N.A.
2. Karnataka	(5755-7050)	(6750-8850)		(5000-6000) 5500	N.A.
3. Kerala				(3000-4000) 3500	N.A.
4. Tamil Nadu				(2300-2500) 2400	N.A.
Total	6412	6950	+8.39%	11446	+64.09%
EAST INDIA					
5. Bihar		335		(500-600) 550	64.18%
6. Orissa		(1300-2000) 1650		(1500-2000) 1750	6.06%
Total	1635	1985	+21.41%	2300	+15.86$
N.E. INDIA					
7. Arunachal Pradesh		(2000-4300) 3150		(2000-3000) 2500	-20.63%
8. Assam (inc. Nagaland)		3500		(5000-6000) 5500	+57.14%
9. Meghalaya		(2750-3825) 3287		(2500-3000) 2750	-16.33%
10. West Bengal		155		200	+29.03%
11. Tripura		(120-150) 135			N.A.
Total	10468	12227	+16.80%	10950	-10.44%

N.W. INDIA

12. Uttar Pradesh	445	525	+17.97	(750-1000)	875	+66.67%
Total	445	525	+17.97%		875	66.67%
Grand Total (midvalues)	18960	21687	+14.38%		25571	+17.91%

(Project Elephant Directorate)
* Asian Elephant Specialist Group
+ Centre for Ecological Sciences

It is apparent that there is considerable discrepancy in estimation, and the percentage of increase in some populations requires careful reconsideration. On the basis of the gestation period and calving intervals, which are well documented from captive animals, it is possible to obtain a statistically viable population growth rate. There is no doubt that there has been a definite increase in population in Protected Areas, but how far this is due to loss of habitat and compression of populations into protected areas has to be determined. The study of population trends in the different regions of the country requires urgent consideration by State and Central government's and wildlife biologists.

An equally indeterminate assessment of the world population has been put forth by the WCMC and WWF International in 1996. This is quoted below without comments:

Population estimates for the Asian Elephant – 1996

Country	Estimated Numbers	
	Minimum	Maximum
Bangladesh	200	250
Bhutan*	60	150
Borneo (Sabah & Kalimantan)	750	1000
Cambodia	2000	2000 (?)
China	250	350
India**	20000	24000
Indonesia (excl. Kalimantan, i.e. Sumatra)	2500	4500 (?)
Laos	2000	4000 (?)
Myanmar (formerly Burma)	5000	6000
Peninsular Malaysia (i.e. excl. Sabah)	800	1000
Nepal	50	85
Sri Lanka	2500	3000
Thailand	2000	2000 (?)
Viet Nam	250	400
Total	37860	48740

Sources: WWF–International and IUCN's Asian Elephant Specialist Group; 1996.

25

* Bhutan has a seasonal population of 2000 to 3000 – mainly migrant elephants from India.

** India's Project Elephant estimates there are between 17000 and 24000 animals.

Warning: Almost all figures are approximate. Major Population: India has by far the largest remaining population of the Asian Elephant (estimated at near 50% of the total). Within India, about half the elephants are found in the northeastern states, notably Assam, Arunachal Pradesh, and Meghalaya.

Estimated population of wild elephants in different states in 1993

State	Minimum	Maximum
1. Andhra Pradesh	46	46
2. Arunchal Pradesh	2000	3000
3. Assam	5000	6000
4. Bihar	500	600
5. Karnataka	5000	6000
6. Kerala	3000	4000
7. Meghalaya	2500	3000
8. Orissa	1500	2000
9. Tamil Nadu	2300	2500
10. Uttar Pradesh	750	1000
11. West Bengal	200	200
	22796	28346

$$\text{Mean Estimated Value} = \frac{22796 + 28346}{2} = 25{,}571$$

1985 Asian Elephant Group's estimate : 16590 – 21361

Status report of AESG (2985)

1989 R. Sukumar's Estimate

South India	6750 – 8850
Central India	1635 – 2335
N.E. India	8525 – 11930
N. India	725 – 975
Mean Value 22,845	

Mean Estimated Value : 18961

South India	5775 – 7050
Central India	1635 +
N.E. India	8705 – 12231
N. India	445

1985	18961
1989	22845
1993	25571

Chapter 3

COLOUR & SIZE

3.1 Colour

According to M. Krishnan (20):

"The colour of an adult elephant is largely a question of the colour of its skin, for when full-grown the hair on the body is too sparse to influence colour. Some animals have a lighter coloured skin and some much darker skin: in the lighter grey animals there is often a pink tinge to the grey. The colour of a wild elephant however, is exceedingly difficult to judge, because the colour of the animal is so often that of the earth it has been throwing over itself – even a bright red elephant may be seen. Fresh from a bath, before they have dusted themselves with earth or thrown mire over themselves, elephants appear a gleaming black, and the lighter colour of an animal in the herd is then easily noticed. Some animals are definitely and noticeably light grey in colour.

Calves up to the first 6 months of their lives may be covered with brown hair, not in a regular coat but in a loose tomentum. The colour of this hair may be quite light at times, a warm, yellowish grey, and may give the calf a light-coloured appearance. This hair is not retained however, and such calves usually grow up into dark grey animals."

In the opinion of R.C. Morris (88):

"The description of the young of Malayan Elephants having sometimes a thick coat of black, and in part, bristly hair ... in the *Proceedings of the Zoological Society*, 1914,––– may well apply to the young of Indian Elephants also. It just describes the appearance of a two-day old elephant calf I saw, and filmed, a few yards from me, in 1936 –– in the North Coimbatore jungles. I have never seen any other young calf so covered with black 'bristly' hair as this was.

28

The reports of 'white elephants' heard occasionally are based on people seeing such calves. No authentic white elephant (i.e. a notably light–skinned animal, a creamy–grey in colour with some pink in places) has been recorded within the peninsula.

In many adults, especially old bulls, there may be much light pink speckling on the face, trunk and ears: the tip of the trunk is usually entirely pink in such animals. Sometimes a lacing of light pink may form a conspicuous border to the lower edge of the ears."

3.2 Size

It was G.P. Sanderson's considered opinion that "there is little doubt that there is not an elephant of 10' at the shoulder". R.C. Morris (62) writes:

"It is extraordinary that Sanderson should have made such an assertion. The two tallest elephants I have ever seen were two single tuskers, shot by Major Brook Purdon, R.A.M.C., in 1925, and by me in 1928. In each case, the elephant had only one tusk and both were 10' at the shoulder; in fact the first was just over 10'."

Morris (62) further remarks:

"With reference to "Mannlicher's" letter in your issue of April 26, under the caption "Record Elephant", the diameter of the elephant's forefoot (20 1/4") gives the circumference of the foot as 63.6". Twice the circumference of an elephant's forefoot will give the elephant's height – almost to an inch. In the case quoted the height will therefore be 10'7"; so 'Mannlicher" measured his elephant accurately: not an easy matter, for it is very difficult to get an accurate measurement of the height of a fallen elephant, or even a bison. I have shot 2 elephants over 10' height – both, curiously enough, single tuskers.

Sanderson was quite wrong in laying down that a 10' elephant did not exist; others, who should know better, have expressed the same opinions over 10' tiger! I think Sir Victor Brooke's :Celebrated Tusker" might quite possibly have been 11' high (again a single tusker).

Machnas (tuskless males) in S. India are generally of colossal size – in bulk, not necessarily in height."

P.D. Stracey (24) commenting on the size of elephants writes:

"I send you herewith details of some large elephants that have been shot in India within recent years. As long ago as 1886 (vide `The Statesman' of February 23, 1886) the question of the 11' Asiatic elephant was exercising the minds of sportsmen and others, and the late Mr G P Sanderson had not measured any larger than 10'6.5" high at that time. In recent years I have measured two large tuskers, one belonging to the Raja of Gauripore, Assam, which was 10'4.5" at the shoulder and the other belonging to the Maharajah of Gwalior, which is 10'5" at the shoulder. I doubt if there is a larger elephant than this in captivity today, unless it be found among those owned by the Maharajah of Nepal.

But while the existence of a captive 11' elephant is still to be proved, I have no doubt that such elephants exist in the wild State. Very recently an animal found dying in the forests of Kachugaon, Goalpara District, Assam, was measured by a Forest Officer after death, and found to be 11' high. His tusks were as follows:

1. 8'0" long, 1'4.5" thickest mid–girth. Weight 1 md. (=82 lb.)

2. 8'0"long, 1'4–3/4" thickest mid–girth. Weight 1 md. 14 chat-taks (84 lb.)

This elephant, I think, constitutes an all–round record for the Asiatic elephant, and I shall be interested to know of any bigger.

The present Maharajah of Mysore claims to have shot an 11' elephant in his State. This animal, a photograph of which appeared in `The Illustrated Weekly' in 1940, had tusks which weighed 162 lb. all told, though they were little over 6' in length. The present Rajkumar of Gauripur, Assam, shot a makhna (tuskless male) in the Garo Hills of Assam in 1945, the forefoot of which measured 5'6" in circumference. It was not possible to measure the shoulder–height of this animal as it lay in an awkward position.

Coming to elephants below 11' in height, the late Mr P.R. Phukon of Gauhati, Assam, shot a tusker in the Khasi Hills of Assam in 1938 which measured 10'10", Mr Gyles Mackrell shot a tusker in the Haltugaon Forest of Goalpara District which was 10'9.5" in height while I shot one in Kachugaon in 1940 which had a height of 10'8.5"."

Finally M. Krishnan (20) comments on height, measurements and build of the elephant, which are very pertinent to the discussion. Krishnan writes:

"Old Indian Shikar and faunal literature exhibits a tendency, surprisingly unusual in it, to be conservative in estimating the height of an elephant. The build of the animal is such that the height at the shoulder is a less reliable indication of size than with most other animals –– the length and circumference of the body, the thickness of the limbs and trunk, and the relative size of the head and body vary so much with individuals that the indigenous system of classifying elephants into the koomeriah, meerga and dwasala types recognises that animals of all three types may be seen in the same herd. In a large herd of over 50 elephants closely observed (and photographed) there was a striking variety of build and conformation noticed. When it is possible to follow a herd of elephants and watch them for some time, it is not difficult to distinguish between individual members of the herd by their peculiarities of build.

G.P. Sanderson's much–quoted opinion, 'There is little doubt that there is not an elephant 10' at the shoulder in India', was published late in the 19th century. In the section on 'Indian Shooting' by Lt. Col. R. Heber Percy in C. Philipps–Wolley's compilation, Big Game Shooting (London, 1895), this interesting information is provided: 'The skeleton of the well–known Arcot rogue elephant, now in the Madras Museum, measures 10'6", as personally verified.

It is true that a bull elephant over 10'6" high or a cow over 9' is so exceptional that it must be left out of consideration on judging adult size, but though I myself have never seen a 10' elephant, to fix this as a maximum height attained by a big bull is incorrect. I measured 3 undefaced prints of the forefoot of a big bull in the Manas Sanctuary (Assam) and all 3 gave the height at the shoulder at over 10'2".

Incidentally, it is practically impossible to measure the height of a dead elephant: if the animal subsides on its belly, the feet are bent: if it falls on a flank, the sag of the shoulder is so great that the front leg which is uppermost (naturally, the lower leg cannot be measured) may be extended or retracted: a further complication is that this foreleg in death usually slopes down towards the ground (exceptionally, in rigor mortis, the foreleg may remain parallel to the ground, in the corpses of 2 elephants electrocuted by accidental contact with a low–slung high–voltage cable, the upper foreleg jutted out of the body rigidly, well off the ground. Furthermore, without the weight of the body on the legs, the height cannot be measured reliably: in 2 experiments, camp elephants were made to recline on their flanks and keep the foreleg straight out: measurements of the distance between shoulder and sole varied within wide limits and was much in excess of the height of the animal measured when it was standing.

Even with tamed elephants, unless there are necessary facilities for accurately measuring the height when the animal is standing on level ground, measurement of the height of the shoulder may vary considerably. For example, the tusker Kali Prasad, stationed at Manas in February, 1968, was over 10 foot as high as measured by the Range Officer and only 9–foot 9–inches as measured by me.

Provided the elephant is not malformed or exceptionally short–legged, the rule that twice the circumference of the fore-foot will give the height at the shoulder within an inch or so is quite reliable with adult elephants. This is the only way to know the height of a wild elephant. Here, again, care and accuracy in measuring the circumference are essential for reliability. It is the clear, undefaced print of the forefoot that must be measured (as where the animal has turned sharply) and it is often said that this print must be on hard dry ground and not on moist soil, because in soft soil the footprint tends to splay. It does not. The sole of an elephant's foot does not splay in the manner of the pug of a tiger or even the slots of a sambar on wet soil. Of course, in loose sand the imprint is not clear, and the sand pushed out at the periphery leads to errors, and in mud (when the foot is pulled out of the mire at each step) there is never a clean imprint, but it is on moist earth, as on the edges of paddy fields or on bare ground after a rain, that the clearest imprints will be found. I have measured the forefoot print of the same elephant on such moist ground and also on firm ground a few yards away, and it was the print on hard dry ground that gave a circumference greater by an inch: this is because with slightly yielding soil it is not only the cushioned sole of the animal that gives beneath its great weight. The method used by me is to lay a thin, non–stretchable cord, inch by inch, along the inner line marking the circumference, with no sag in the cord: small sharp slivers of wood driven vertically into the periphery of the footprint help in this. The total length of the cord marking the circumference, is then measured. With care this method gives unvarying measurements. The diameter should not be measured for two reasons: first, the forefoot imprint of the elephant is not perfectly circular and therefore the circumference cannot be calculated by multiplying the diameter by 3–1/7; second, even small errors become material in such a calculation for by the time the height of the elephant is computed the diameter, and therefore the error, has been multiplied 6–2/7 times.

As already said, height is only one dimension in assessing the size an elephant. The length of the body varies considerably, especially in big bulls, as also its thickness. A massive bull fully 6" shorter than a leggy, thin animal may easily defeat the latter in a fight.

Weight is a much more reliable indication of size in an elephant than measurements, but naturally it is very seldom possible to weigh such a huge beast, and there are few reliable records. The weight of tamed elephants is no guide, for it is seldom that an elephant in captivity attains the mass and musculature of wild elephants. A very big bull may probably weigh between 4 and 5 tons. The height of a newborn calf varies from about 30" to 36" and its weight is about 200 lb."

3.3 White Elephants

The white elephant is rare enough to be almost a mythical beast. It is venerated in Buddhist countries, a pale coloured animal usually has great value. G.H. Evans (17) writing in 1896 on elephants in Burma says:

"From time immemorial the Burmese and Siamese have regarded the white elephant as a sacred beast. Sir John Bowring states that the reason why this animal is so specially reverenced is "because it is believed that Buddha, the divine emanation from the Diety, must necessarily in his multitudinous metamorphoses or transmissions through all existences, and through millions of aeons, delight to abide for some time in that grand incarnation of purity, which is represented by the white elephant. While the Phongyis (priests) teach that there is no spot in the heavens above, or the earth below, or the waters under the earth, which is not visited in the peregrinations of the divinity, whose every stage or step is towards purification, they hold that his tarrying may be longer in the white elephant than in any other abode, and that in the sacred creature they may possess the presence of Buddha himself". The same author states that these animals have been the cause of many a war, and their possession more an object of envy than the conquest of territory.

The kings of Burma were very proud of the titles of "Lord of the Celestial Elephant" and "Lord of many White Elephants".

The kings of Siam also glory in these pompous titles; in that country everything associated with majesty and rank bears the image of the white elephant. These animals are surrounded with all the adjuncts of royalty, viz. gold umbrellas, etc., – and when they die are accorded a royal funeral. The Burmese, being Buddhists, are naturally kind to all dumb creatures, so that the elephant, in common with other domestic animals, is well cared for"."

In fact, it was believed that the Kings of Siam had a subtle way of putting down members of the court who had annoyed them, by allocating to them the care and maintenance of a white elephant which usually pauperised the man who had been so honoured. Hence, the expression `a white elephant' to anything that may be of great intrinsic value, but cannot be economically maintained.

To be judged a white elephant the animal has to have a number of characteristics as H. Macnaghten (59) reports:

"Considerable interest was shown in Bombay in the statement in a recent Burmese letter to the "Times of India that a white calf had been born to one of the Bombay–Burmah Elephants, and it may be of interest to record what actually happened."

"A female calf born on 6th March 1918 aroused a good deal of excitement by its unusually light colour, and, in view of the importance attached by the Burmese to the birth of a genuine Sinpyudaw, it was thought advisable to submit the claims of the calf to a jury of prominent Burmans on the 7th April.

The points of a Sinpyudaw appears to be as follows:–

1. Twenty toes
2. Pearl eyes
3. Tail "Tah Gah Paik"
4. Red mouth
5. Light coloured and smooth skin

The calf though possessing a rather light skin at birth and pearl eyes failed to fulfil these conditions, having only eighteen toes and a tail that was not up to the requirements. It was. therefore, at once pronounced to be not a genuine sinpyudaw.

The colour has since grown perceptibly darker and on reaching maturity is not like to differ in any way from the ordinary.

The fact that the "whiteness" of an elephant depends as much on the possession of certain points as on its colour may be of interest to your readers, as most people appear to believe in the existence of a milk white animal."

The Borneo Company in Siam, in 1926, according to D.F. Macfie (70) raised :

"Much interest recently in this district by the birth of a supposed white elephant calf to one of the Borneo Company's timber elephants working teak in the Muang Fang Forest, north of Chiengmai. The calf was born on May 6 last, and rumours at once spread among the native population that it had the attributes of a true white elephant, and this reaching the ears of the Chao Luang or Chief of Chiengmai and the Siamese Commissioner here, the calf and its mother, at their request, were brought down to Chiengmai, where the calf was pronounced to be a true 'Chang Peuak' or white elephant by local experts and entered the city in procession with the usual ceremonies. An official from the Royal White Elephant Department in Bangkok was also sent up to inspect the animal and report on it, and I am informed that his verdict supports that of the local elephant 'mors' or experts. The chief 'points' looked for, in such elephants, appears to be (1) a light red skin, the lighter the better, with still lighter coloured patches on belly and inside of legs; (2) white hairs on body and tail; (3) a very light pink palate or roof of mouth; (4) eyes a light bluish–pink colour; (5) white toe nails. The number of toes does not seem to matter materially, but five on each foot, fore and hind, is considered, I believe, a mark of high caste. The calf, with its mother, has been handed over by the Borneo Company to the Chao Luang of Chiengmai to look after, pending the visit of His Majesty the King of Siam to Chiengmai in January next when it will be inspected by. him."

E.S. Simon (71) writing from the Travancore State presently a part of Kerala reported that:

"A cow elephant, captured from the Travancore forests in April 1945, has aroused much interest on account of its colour and other attributes of a white elephant; and it may quite possibly be the first time that an elephant having the characteristics of either partial or complete albinism is observed in India.

This elephant, having a height of 5'11" at the shoulder and whose age is estimated to be 10 years, was caught in a pit at Karippanthode, about 13 miles from Koni, the headquarters of the Central Forest Division. Rao Bahadur T.V. Venkiteswara Iyer, Conservator of Forests, Travancore, examined the animal and, finding that it compared favourably with the Siamese White Elephants, brought her over to the Trivandrum Zoological Gardens for exhibition.

Mahaswari, by which name she has since been known, has a light pink skin with white hairs except at the tip of the tail, and pearl eyes. The white hairs on the head are prominent and in spite of them, the light pink background of the skin, gives the elephant a pinkish grey colour. The usual black colour of elephants is nowhere visible on its body. The mouth and palate are also light pink. There are, as usual in ordinary elephants, eighteen toes, five on each forefoot and four on each hind limb but the toe–nails are of a lighter colour, rather whitish. In all other respects, there is nothing to distinguish it from a normal elephant. She has been under observation for about a year now, and it may be remarked that no change in its colour has taken place during this period.

Simon draws attention to the points noted by Macnaghton and Mr. D.F. Macfie that the "chief points looked for an white elephants to be light red skin, white hairs on body and tail, very light pink palate, eyes of a light bluish pinky colour and white toe–nails. Evidently a milk–white colour is not to be expected; the 'whiteness' of an elephant is therefore determined on the possession of the above 'points'. On the basis of this the Travancore specimen has all the attributes of an albino elephant."

37

What happened to this white elephant, and whether it remained white is not known.

"U Tun Yin (72) on the basis of available records states that early in the present century an albino elephant calf was captured by the Government Kheddah department in the Katha Forest Division. The calf was presented to the Trustees of the Shwe Dagon Pagoda, but died shortly after arrival in Rangoon as a result of over–feeding by pilgrims.

Later in the century, one was captured in the Toungoo Forest Division. The owner, Saw Durmay Po Min. took the albino elephant with one black elephant for exhibition in Europe and America. On the return journey, the elephant died at Calcutta. A photo of this albino elephant is published in 'Wonders of Animal Life' Vol. 3, p. 2,036.

In 1939, a game ranger employed on elephant control in the Ngaputaw Township in the Henzada–Bassein Division, was charged in heavy bamboo jungle by an elephant, which he had to shoot in self defence. The animal on examination, turned out to be an albino. In 1940, a game ranger, operating in the Mayu Hills of Arakan Division, was also compelled to shoot an albino elephant.

Chapter 4

TUSKERS & TUSKS

Tusks are the magnificence of a bull elephant and the most coveted trophy of sportsmen, and now the most lusted after prize of the ivory poacher. To both, size and weight counted.

According to M. Krishnan (20):

"Length of tusks, in adult bulls, especially in old bulls, convey no idea whatever of size. The biggest tusks are carried by bulls whose tusks slope down to the ground, and these are generally thin. Nor does the mere thickness of the tusks reflect size or power, though an animal with horizontally–carried thick tusks, especially when these project about 3 feet from the gums and are evenly curved, is usually stout, long–barrelled and powerful; very long tusks, such as the 'record tusks' cited in literature on elephants, are no indication of the bull is being exceptional in size; on the contrary, such animals are usually average size. Such tusks are a constant embarrassment to their owners, hindering free movement (especially of the head and trunk) and being a serious handicap in fights, sometimes even in feeding. Thin, sharp–pointed, curved tusks are murderous weapons in combat.

Cows, even when adult or old, frequently carry short tusks, projecting a few inches from the lips –– these are called 'scrivelloes' in the ivory trade in India"

4.1 Siamese Tusks
The longest tusks appear to have come from Siam. S.S. Flower (21) writing on the collection in the Royal Siamese Museum, Bangkok states; in 1897:

"In Blanford's "Mammalia of India" and in Rowland Ward's "Great Game of the World" the record tusk of an Asiatic elephant mentioned is the late Sir Victor Brooke's from Mysore, 8' long, 16 5/8" in circumference, and 90 lbs. in weight; therefore the following measurements, which I have taken today of the collection of tusks in the Royal Siamese Museum,

Bangkok, may be of interest. As far as I can ascertain, the tusks are all from Siam; there are two of 9' (2.75 m) and over, five of 8' (2.44 m) and over, twelve of 7' (2.13 m) and over, six of 6' (1.83 m) and over, ten of 5' (1.52 m) and over, five of 4'6" (1.40 m) and over, and numerous shorter ones. The length is measured along the outside curve of the tusk; the large ones being mounted upright in wooden sockets, it is difficult to get the exact length to an inch in many cases, but I have tried to do so, and in case of doubt have taken the smaller measurement. Owing to their being thus mounted I have been unable to ascertain their weight. The thickest tusk is a single one, 7'7" (2.31 m) in length and 20 3/4" (52.7 m) in circumference.

The measurement of the four finest pairs are as follows:

Length	Circumference	
7'4.5" (2.25 m), 7'5.5" (2.28 m)	16 3/8" (42 cm), 16 3/8" (42 cm)	
7'8.5" (2.35 m), 7'8" (2.34 m)	13.5" (34 cm), 13.5" (34 cm)	A massive, even pair
8'3" (2.51 m), 8'4" (2.75 m)	14.5" (37 cm), 11.5" (29 cm)	Points of tusks much worn.
9'0" (2.75 m), 9'10.5" (3.01 m)	15 3/8" (39 cm), 15.5" (39 cm)	A slender, symmetrical pair

The fourth pair belonged to an elephant, said to have been 90 years old, which died in Bangkok some twenty years ago, and I think they must be the record pair for Asia".

The age of the animal from which the longest pair were removed seems to be unusual.

4.2 Burmese Tusks

On Burmese elephants, J.K. Stanford (22) wrote that he :

"Saw a remarkable pair of elephant tusks at Lonhkin recently, in the house of Sinwa Nawng, Duwa of Kansi in the Kachin Hill Tracts of this district. These tusks are said to have been obtained from an elephant which was found dead some eight years ago near Kansi village. This village is on the Uyu, a tributary of the Chindwin in the western part of this district.

One tusk is 79.5" (2.01 m) long and the other measures 77.5" (1.48 m). The girth near the base is 17" (43 cm) and 17 3/4" (45 cm) respectively and at 5" (12 cm) from the tip, the girth is 10 1/4" (26 cm). These tusks are slightly larger than a very fine pair shot by Mr. H.E. Flint, O.B.E., in the Ruby Mines some years ago (which he has in Myitkyina and of which one is 79" (2 m) and the other 69" (1.75 m). The Kansi tusks are extremely dark in colour. I did not get an opportunity to weigh them."

Following up on this note U Tun Yin (23) writes:

"In the Society's Journal 37: 468, J.K. Stanford has given a description of a large pair of elephant's tusks which he saw at Lonkhin, in the house of Kansi Duwa. He did· not get the opportunity to weigh the tusks.

This pair was brought down to Rangoon recently and were found to weigh 180 pounds, when weighed at the airstrip, Myitkina.

The measurements and weight of these, tusks therefore, are:

Length	Girth		Weight	Remarks
R 6'5.5"	17.5"	)		
L 6'7.5"	17"	)	180 pounds	Owner – Kansi Duwa.

For comparison, measurements and weights of some other large pairs of Burmese tusks are given below:"

Extracts from appendix 1 — Burma Game Manual 1929.

Length	Girth	Weight	Remarks
R–8'0"	...	...	Government House, Rangoon
L 8'6"	...	...	(R.W.)
R 7'3"	17.5"	102 lb.	The tusks of the sacred white
L 7'3.5"			elephant from Mandalay Palace. Owner – The Marquis of Waterloo (R.W.)
R 7'9.5"	17.5"	72 lb.	Shot by J N Clough
L 8'6"	17"	74 lb.	Kyaikto District 1896 (I.F.S.B.)
R 6'8"	18.25"	84 lb.	Owner – H. Shaw Dum (R.W.)
L 6'5"	18.25"	82 lb.	
R 6'11"	15.5"	106 lb.	Owner – Gordon Smith (R.W.)
L 6'6"	15.5"		
R 6'7"	17"	110 lb.	Shot by H.E.Flint. Mogok Forest Division.
L 5'9"	17"		
R 6'2.5"	17.25"		Shot by A. Hazlehood. Basein
L 6'1.25"			Forest Division.

1" = 2.54 cm   1' = 30.48 cm

Extract from The Burmese Forest. Vol. V, No.2 – December 1955 (Page 134).

Length	Girth	Weight	Remarks
R 7'11.5"	16.5"	138.6 lb.	A big tusker shot at Hnokeho,
L 7'11"	16.5"		Bhamo Divisiion in 1936 by U Su.

4.3 Indian Tusks

For India P.D. Stracey (56) gives a list of the biggest tusks that he had knowledge of:

"In 1953 the Ruler of Talcher killed a rogue tusker elephant in Dhenkanal, Orissa, which was 11' in height, each tusk weighing 1 md 10 seers and measuring 8'6" in length". (See M. Krishnan's remarks on measuring dead elephants).

In 1952 a very large pair of tusks was found in the Goalpara East Division, Assam, the elephant having died a natural death or having been shot by poachers. One tusk weighed 1 md. 9 seers. 13 chattaks and measured 9'2" in length and 1'5" in girth. The other tusk was found cut short, probably by the people who had concealed both the tusks in the jungle with the obvious intention of stealing them. Though some cut pieces were recovered, it was not possible to ascertain the exact measurements and weight of the mutilated tusk. As the two tusks were obviously symmetrical it may be taken that the cut tusk was of approximately the same length, weight and girth as the complete tusk. The cut tusk was reconstructed with a wooden piece shaped and coloured exactly like the ivory, and the pair was exhibited at the IVth World Forestry Congress at Dehra Dun in December 1954.

While the Ruler of Talcher's pair is the second heaviest pair on record, there are 3 individual tusks on record each heavier than a single tusk of this pair. The uncut tusk of the Assam pair referred to here is the third longest on record. I give below the weights and the measurements of some of the biggest tusks so far as I have been able to ascertain:

No.	Length outside curve	Greatest circumference	Weight	Locality	Owner
1.	9'2	17"	1 md. 9 Srs. 13 ch.	Assam, Goalpara East 1952	Assam Forest Museum, Gauhati
	–do– (?)	–do–(?)	(91 1b, 13ch.)		
			–do– (?)		
2.	8'6"	–"–	1 md. 10 Srs. (92 1b),	Orissa, Dhenkanal 1953	Ruler of Talcher
	8'6"	–"–	1 md. 10 Srs. (92 1b)		

3.	7'3–3/8"	12.5"	102 lb.*	Burma (King Thebaw's sacred	* Record. Marquis of Waterford
	7'3.25"	12 1/8"	97.5 lb.	white elephant)	
4.	–	–	100 lb.	Assam	The late Charles Redde
5.	8'	105"	90 lb.	S.India	Sir Victor Brooke's Collection
6.	8'	16.5"	82 lb.	Assam, Goalpara West, 1946	Assam Legislative Assembly,
	8'	16 3/4"	82 lb. 14 chs.		Shillong
7.	7'8" R.	18 3/8"	79.5 lb.	Coimbatore Jungles, S.India	C.R.T. Congreve (JBNHS, 29:1045)
	7'10" L	19 1/4"	82.5" lb.	1923	
8.	8'9" R	17 1/8"	81 lb.	Assam	Late Lord Lytton
	8'2" L.	17"		81.2 lb.	
9.	7'5" R.	17 1/4"	77 lb.	Mysore	Maharajah of Mysore
	7'4" L.	17"	71 lb.		
10.	7'1.5"	18 1/4"	77 lb.	Assam, Goalpara West, 1910	P.D. Stracey, I.F.S.
	7'3"	18 1/8"	77 lb.		
11.	6'6"	19" *	68 lb.	Mysore	*Record. Major Goring and
	5'8"	16"	68 lb.		C. Theobald.
12.	5'9"	18.5"	65 lb.	Wynaad, South India	W.H. Pitt.
	5'11"	18.5"			

1 md = 92 lb.

Tusker with wide tusks

Hemant Datye

Tusker drinking at the Ramganga: note extensile trunk.

M Krishnan

M Krishnan

The tusker that followed our ground-scent to Sullukatte, Nagarhole

Tusker Feeding - Bandipur National Park

Vivek R Sinha

Tusker on the Road - Corbett National Park

Trained elephants rolling a log

E.P. Gee

Tusker in Musth drinking at forest pool

Vivek R Sinha

Stracey's note drew a response from R.C. Morris (25) who gave measurements and weights "of two pairs of tusks of rogue elephants shot on the Baragur Hills in the Coimbatore District, Madras State, in 1926 and 1929.

1. Shot by R.C. Morris on March 2, 1926, at Kokkuvarai, Madeswaranmalai. Length of right tusk 7'4.5" (weight 63 lb.); length of left tusk 7'7.5" (weight 68 lb.).

2. Shot by Col. F.S. Gillespie and R.C. Morris on February 13, 1929, at Madeswaranmalai (Kokkuvarai). Length of both tusks 8'2" (weights 90.5 and 91 lb.)

It was remarkable that both these fine tuskers were shot in almost the same spot. The first elephant was undersized, due possibly to the fact that it had considerable difficulty in feeding itself, its tusks being crossed within about 18" of its mouth. The tusks of the second elephant were also crossed, but near the tips. Both were vicious rogues, attacking pilgrims proceeding to and from the famous Madeswaranmalai temple. The measurements were sent to, and recorded by, Rowland Ward and the Bombay Natural History Society."

Another record elephant from south India was reported by A.W. John (26):

"The following are the measurements of the tusker elephant I wrote you about :–

Height at shoulder 10'4.5".

	Length	Girth	Weight
Right tusk	6'2"	21"	85 lbs.
Left	6'3"	21"	86 lbs.
			171 lbs.

The above were taken in the presence of witnesses and certified measurements were sent to Rowland Ward. What struck me about the tusks was their girth and symmetry — a perfect pair! As regards height, this is of course difficult to get accurately, but it was taken between uprights, and the least I could make it was 10' 4.5"; taken at the highest point of shoulder, I made it 10'9", but did not think this possible after all Sanderson says about their being no such thing as a 10' elephant. He was 65" round the forefoot. I think there can be no doubt of his being a record for South India. Apparently the Senior Ranee of Travancore thinks so too, for all my offers to purchase the tusks have been refused!"

And finally, G.D.L. Millar's (27) query from Assam.

"Will you kindly let me know the weight of the largest pair of elephant tusks recorded in Assam? I have just shot an extremely large solitary elephant carrying tusks of 7' and 7'1" weighing 115.5 lbs. The tusks are perfectly symmetrical and converge towards the extremities leaving a distance of only 4" between the points making it impossible for the elephant to raise his trunk between them.

I am writing to you because it occurs to me that the weight and length of these tusks may constitute a record for Assam."

The editorial note reads:

"The heaviest recorded tusks of the Indian Elephant is a pair in the possession of H.M. The King: – Length 8'9", and 8'6.5"; weight 161 and 160 lbs. The animal was shot in the Terai. The record for Assam is a pair of tusks in the possession of Lord Lytton:– Length 8'9" and 8'2"; weight 81 and 80.2 lbs. (Rowland Ward, Records of Big Game, 8th edn.)"

There is obviously an error in the weight of the tusks in the possession of the King. There cannot be a 100% difference in the weight of the almost equal sized tusks in the possession of H.M. The King and Lord Lytton!

In Champion's (8) opinion:

"The United Provinces' elephants do not appear to carry very large tusks, and I have never seen one with tusks which I should estimate at over 50 lbs. each. There is, however, said to be one famous tusker, known locally as the 'Palak–danta,' which wanders about in the Reserved and Zemindari forests of the Bijnor District, and this animal is reported to be one of the very finest elephants in India, worth a huge sum should it ever be captured. Once or twice agitations have been made by interested people to have this animal proclaimed a rogue, but fortunately the evidence against him is very weak, and, so far, it has been possible to protect this magnificent creature from an ignominious death at the hands of some local sportsman. I have never had the good fortune to see this beast, or try my camera on him, although I have been in his neighbourhood a number of times and still hope that we may yet meet one day.

Even though large tusks are rare in the United Provinces, the elephants often grow to a large size and two rogues, measuring well over ten feet at the shoulder have been shot within recent years, the details of these two animals being recorded in the current numbers of the "Indian Forester" at the time. Of these, one was shot in the Ramnagar Forest Division in 1914 and measured 10'5" high, the tusks being 6'4", and 6'3.5" in length and each 56 lbs. in weight. The other was much the same size and was shot at about the same time in Haldwani Forest Division."

According to H.F. Mooney (60):

"The bulls seem to carry on the whole, very fair sized ivory in Orissa. The largest pair of tusks I have seen are a pair in the possession of the Maharaja of Mayurbhanj, which measure 8'6" along the outer curve. They are a symmetrical pair of great beauty and are said to have been taken from a tame elephant, which died in captivity. One which I shot in 1925 had tusks measuring 6'0" and 6'6", which weighed 62 and 59 lbs. respectively. These were not at all symmetrical and one was considerably broken at the point. This elephant taped 9'1" at the shoulder, as accurately, as I could measure, the girth of his feet being 55" and 54.5". Another rogue shot in Angul district in 1923 had a single tusk which weighed 62.5 lb. This was a very massive tusk and had a girth at the thickest part of almost 20". A large bull, which was found dead in the same district in March this year, had tusks measuring 6'1" each and weighing 140 lb. the pair. This elephant had a deep wound in his flank, probably inflicted in a fight with another tusker. I have seen a number of tusks weighing between forty and fifty pounds, and I should say as a result of my observations that many elephants have tusks of forty pounds apiece, and not a few carry ivory much in excess of this figure. As far as I am aware, the elephants in Orissa are isolated and are not connected with herds in any other part of India unless perhaps in the extreme south–west of the area, where it borders on the Vizagapatam district of Madras. I believe that a few solitary elephants occur in Ganjam district, but whether or not there is any connecting link between those of Orissa and southern India I do not know and should be interested to learn."

4.4 Abnormal Tusks

G.D.L. Millar (28) reported on an elephant with upturned tusks like the waxed whiskers of a Sergeant Major with the tips pointing heavenwards.

"The tusks were of "a most unusual shape and symmetry. The awkward position in which he wore his tusks is really responsible for his death. This elephant had been doing extensive damage to crops in the Borelli River area, in the Tezpur district of Assam. I was able to follow up that night's tracks and after about 6 miles came upon him, wallowing in a small bheel 200 yards ahead of where I stood. As I was deliberating the best method of approaching him, he winded us and made off at full tilt. I had a very good Miri tracker with me, and after pushing on his trail for an hour or so I thought it was going to be an all–day job, when the tusker foolishly changed his direction and plunged into 'Geruka' jungle. We listened carefully and could then hear him breaking through about a quarter of a mile ahead. We left his tracks and ran as fast as was possible in soft mud along the edge of the Geruka patch to head him off, and we arrived at the other end as the tusker was emerging into the tree jungle just where we were standing. He came out directly facing us, and one barrel from my .470 fetched his brain. Had this elephant kept to the tree jungle he would probably have put many miles between us before pulling up."

R.C. Morris (97) writes:

"I once watched a bull elephant with most abnormal tusks (quite 6 feet long outside and so wide apart that they must have been almost useless to him in a fight) standing on the outskirts of a herd, in which there were two other fine tuskers, and spending his whole time trumpeting loudly. I think he was made to keep his distance from the herd: and was furious!"

Another abnormal tusk was collected by L.L. Reade (29) who wrote:

"The people inhabiting the jungly tract at the northern part of the Khasi Hills, known as Bhois, mainly depend upon rice cultivation for their existence. This they generally cultivate by the system known as 'Jhum cultivation', i.e. burning a patch of jungle and then sowing paddy. They also cultivate other side lines, such as pumpkins, chillies, cotton, Indian corn, etc., but their chief, and in fact only, cereal is rice.

These tracts are frequented by large numbers of wild animals of all sorts and they include such destructive creatures, as wild pigs, deer, sambhar, and finally wild elephants, so the cultivators frequently suffer great losses from their ravages.

Smaller creatures such as pigs, deer, etc., can be frightened off by various stratagems and even a herd of elephants may be made to leave early by means of fires, torches, etc., but when a solitary wild male elephant visits such cultivations, then the matter assumes quite another aspect. Not only will such an animal take no notice of any attempt to drive him away, but he will frequently chase the people about, and anyone caught by him meets with a sure death.

During the course of my tours as a member of the Agricultural Department of the District, I frequently came across depredations committed by rogue elephants and was fortunate enough to bag some of them on various occasions. So far as I was aware, male elephants consisted of tuskers and non–tuskers or Muknas, there being many types of tusks amongst the former class, but recently I shot a rogue tusker, which had most peculiar tusks. One of the tusks (the right) was short and straight with a fleshy protuberance along the length of the tusk, quite unlike any other tusks I have seen. Apparently this tusk is in the nature of a freak as it did not appear to have been broken off."

4.5 Aborted(?) Tusks

R.C. Morris (30), writing on aborted tusks, recounts this story of the collection of such tusks.

"I was recently out after a proscribed rogue elephant and, having had him marked down one morning, I came up to him after a fair tramp and found him browsing on a steep hillside on the edge of a' shola. As I worked round for a good position he entered the shola. The sun was well up and I feared that I would not see him out again till late in the afternoon, so decided to take the best shot I could from the edge of the shola. I took the ear shot but unfortunately must have just missed the brain as, though the shot brought him down (I was using a .450 H.V.), he recovered before I could get in my second barrel and went off with a shrill trumpet. I realized that he was likely to take a short cut across a steep open hillside in order to reach a large patch of evergreen jungle down below, and this proved correct. As he came out into the open below me I fired again but, the elephant travelling at a good pace, the bullet again missed the brain but knocked him clean off his feet and he then did the most amazing roll that could be imagined. He rolled over and over for about 50 yards down the hillside, crashing into the shola down below and would have rolled still further had he not been stopped by a big tree which was nearly uprooted. From the hillside, above I could not see whether the elephant was dead or alive. I had to scramble down to the edge of the shola, and found the elephant had regained its feet and was slowly walking along the elephant path breathing heavily. For a moment I was absolutely astounded as I imagined that the fall would have at least disabled the brute even if my bullet had not done its work. I did not lose much time, after my momentary pause from sheer astonishment, in following up the animal, and after some trouble in carefully tracking him through high grass came up to him again, seemingly none the worse for his roll, and finished him off with a shot behind the ear.

The elephant was a single tusker, that is to say it had only one tusk showing. It was an enormous brute measuring 10' at the shoulder, and had been severely bruised and cut by his roll, his knees and the top of his head suffering the most. This is the second elephant I know of measuring 10' or more, another single tusker shot by Major Brook Purdon three years ago, measured just over 10' This is interesting in view of Sanderson's dictum that a 10' elephant did not exist. On cutting out the tusk of Major Brook Purdon's elephant we decided to see whether there was any growth of ivory on the other side where a tusk should have been. The head was therefore cut in half and we discovered, completely encased in a thin layer of bone, a solid conical block of ivory about 9" long with a girth of about 11" at its base, the base being rounded. There was no sign of any disease having set in or any damage having occupied. This encased block of ivory was not pointing in the right direction but considerably inwards. I decided therefore to find out whether my rogue held any ivory in its head on its tuskless side. Sure enough by cutting his head open I found a similar block of ivory measuring 9" in length with a girth of nearly 14" round the centre of it. The base is also rounded, but with an extraordinary lump of ivory growing out of it. It is most curious, being irregular in shape with a thin ragged wall of ivory sticking out. The block of ivory was encased in this instance also in a thin covering of bone up to where the curious wall of ivory jutted out, and this was embedded in gristle which contained 6 little balls of ivory, two about the size of marbles, two a little smaller, and two about the size of peas. It seems possible therefore that single tuskers, except those that have had the tusk broken of at or just inside the jaw in a fight or by accident, possess this curious block of ivory on their tuskless side.

The question arises, do mucknas (i.e. tuskless males) have a similar growth of ivory?"

4.6 Multiple Tusks

Sir Frank Colyer (31) of the Royal College of Surgeons reported on abnormal multiple tusks and also on Mr. Morris's find, he states that :

"Six small tusks were removed from the 'tuskless' side of a rogue elephant. There was a seventh tusk which it was impossible to extract owing to it being firmly embedded in the bone. They were obtained and presented to the Society by Mr. C.R. Pawsey, ICS, Deputy Commissioner, Mokokchung, Naga Hills, Assam. The specimens have been presented to the Royal College of Surgeons' Museum by the Bombay Natural History Society. In the letter accompanying the gift it was stated that 'the tusks were jammed together and between them a substance described as being like marrow was found. The tusks protruded a distance of 2 or 3" from the opening of the socket". The length and girth of the tusks are as follows:

Tusk	Length	Girth
1	61 cm.	19.0 cm.
2	56 cm.	15.3 cm.
3	42 cm.	12.7 cm.
4	42 cm.	7.0 cm.
5	28 cm.	7.3 cm.
6	26 cm.	7.6 cm.

Sections made through four of the tusks show that they are composed of well formed ivory surrounded by a layer of cement.

Cases of multiple tusks are rare and there are but few records in the literature on pathological ivory. There is a reference in Chapman's 'Travels in the Interior of South Africa' to a male elephant with nine perfect tusks; the tusks were ranged five on one side and four on the other. There is also a specimen in the Royal College of Surgeons' Museum where the tusk is represented by eight 'tusklets'. The tusks vary in length from 37 cm to 23 cm and were to some degree functional as shown by wear on the tissues.

The double tusk is at times due to dichotomy (division in two parts) of the tooth germ; in this tusk there are definite grooves on opposite sides of the tusk.

There are, however, cases of double tusks which seem to arise from the development of an accessory tooth germ such as we see in the extra incisor at times met with in man and other animals. An example of a double tusk, which probably originated in this way, was brought to my notice by a big game hunter in East Africa. One tusk weighed 27 lbs. and was twisted so that it curved downwards and backwards bringing the point between the elephant's knees. At the base of this tusk was another small tusk, the end of which had been broken. A piece of the surrounding bone was present, and one was thus able to obtain an accurate idea of the relation of the one tusk to the other.

There is fairly good evidence for cases of four-tusks on either side. During the month of January 1926 there were several letters published in the 'Times' on the question of four-tusked elephants from the region of the Congo–Divide. One writer, Capt. Tracy Phillips, stated that he stayed a night at the residence of the Vongara–Zande Sultan Ngilima, who described how he had killed a 'four-tusker' during the war. In one letter reference was made to an elephant with four tusks seen by an army officer in the region of the Congo–Divide. The account published in Sudan Notes and Records (Vol. II, 1919, p. 231) is as follows:

"On May 18, 1917, I was out shooting in the district of Sheik Ako Mangara, in the Markaz of Yambio, in the village of Wakila Marbo, on the borders between Tembura and Yambio districts. I met a herd of elephants, which I followed, searching for a good one to shoot. I kept following them until they stopped near a pool of water, where they began to drink and throw mud on themselves. I was hiding behind a tree about 15 yards from them, looking at them, when I saw an elephant with four tusks. The left tusk was the bigger and had the usual direction, but the direction of the small tusk was downwards and came out from under the big one. It was round, and its thickness was about 2.5". The direction of the right tusk was downwards, and the small tusk came from under it in the usual direction, but it was small, like the other one."

It is of interest to note that the natives of the district do not question the existence of four–tusked elephants. Capt. Tracy Phillips makes the suggestion 'that the four–tuskers' of the Uele–Shari may be rarely recurrent types, and something more than mere accidental freaks of Nature. the fact that the condition described was symmetrical is in favour of a developmental origin and it is more probable that the extra teeth arose from accessory tooth germs than by dichotomy of one tooth germ, as in the latter case one would expect to find the teeth on each side simulating one another.

Many cases of multiple tusks are, I feel sure, due to trauma, i.e. produced by injury, a subsidiary tusk as the result of injury is probably brought about as follows:

The injury disorganizes the pulp or formative part of the tooth, the pericementum dips into the pulp, and in this way separates a portion or portions from the main body. The fold gradually extends around the portion thus separated, so as to envelop it completely.

A suggestion has been made that elephants with only one tusk carry on the tuskless side rudiments of a tusk, that is to say, the tooth fails to develop in a normal way. R.C. Morris gave an account of a 'rogue' elephant in which there was on one side a well–formed tusk, and on the other side buried in the bone a block of ivory. He also records a similar case in an animal shot by Major Brook Purdon. The tusk measures 34 cm. in its greatest circumference. The upper surface is irregular in formation, two–thirds of the lower surface. The arrangement of the tissues as they appear in a section is strongly suggestive of injury to the growing tooth. An examination of similar masses removed from the tuskless side of this type of elephant would help to clear up the cause of the condition.

The formation of subsidiary tusks when due to injury would seem to follow a blow which causes the tusk to split in a longitudinal direction. In some cases where the tusk is split in a longititudal manner, necrosis of some of the fragments follows, and a single portion of a tusk retains sufficient vitality to recover. The splinters of the tusk that remain in the bone may still retain their attachment to the periosteum and growth may follow."

R.C. Morris (32) queried Colyer's conclusions, and wrote to the editors. He also quotes Colyer's clarification:

"I write with reference to Sir Frank Colyer's excellent article on Abnormal Turks of Elephants in the Society's Journal. Sir Frank Colyer, who was good enough to show me his collection of abnormal tusks in the Museum of the Royal College of Surgeons in August last year, must be regarded as an authority on the subject, but with all due deference to his opinion regarding the unerupted tusks found on the tuskless side of elephants with single tusks, I still hold that there is just a possibility that his views on the matter may not be correct. In his opinion, these unerupted ivories are caused and developed by a natural process of reformation on the original tusk having been torn out. This may possibly be so, but I still hold to my theory to the effect that the unerupted tusks being still more pronounced in 'Mucknas' which have no tusks. If 'Mucknas' were found to possess similar unerupted ivories, this would rather tend to prove my theory correct. After all, as 'Mucknas' exist, why should not there be single tuskers?"

Sir Frank wrote to me on 26th February 1931 as follows:–

'Let me see if I can make the matter clear. A growing tooth in the jaw is always surrounded by a layer of dense bone. When the tooth erupts there is still a dense layer of bone around the root. If the hard part of the tusk is torn out and the wound does not go septic then the socket fills at first with a blood clot; this is replaced in time by bone, the layer of hard bone disappearing except the portion covering the soft pulp. The soft pulp is in time formed into ivory with a layer of bone around. If the tusk is split so that a portion remains in the socket, suppuration follows, the socket does not fill up, and the layer of hard bone remains."

The discussion continued, and R.C. Morris (35) gives extracts of correspondence he had with Colyer.

Colyer wrote:

'It is a most unusual condition for an animal to have one tooth absent and the other well developed. It does occur in the Narwhal but in that animal it is the normal. The tusk in many Indian elephants seems to be a degenerate organ. Is that not the case? That is, do not a good number of elephants fail to develop tusks? Is it only the females? Have the calves which have shed a tusk been followed up to see if the tusk which develops on the other side is a well–formed and grown tooth? It is most important to settle this question. I take it that in your view, many elephants which have only one developed tusk have at some time possessed another small tusk which was shed in early years. Further you think that masses such as you sent me may really be formed from a tooth germ, which has failed to produce a tusk in the proper way, but has formed a shapeless mass which is retained in the bone. It may be so but, judging from similar conditions which I have seen in other animals, and they are very rare, the mass of hard tissue formed is not tissue which approaches to the structure of the normal tooth.

I have had another good look at the specimen you sent to the Museum, and have discussed the tooth with some of my friends; we still think that it is not an aborted tooth but is the remnants of the formative parts of a tusk which was once in position. If you can prove that elephants which shed one tusk as calves develop really well–developed tusks then you have something to ·support your contention. I had a long talk to Major Powell–Cotton, a Big Game hunter and collector, who has seen plenty of elephant life in Africa. I put the question of the frequency of tusks with severe fractures in a longitudinal direction and he remarked that such conditions were to be expected when one realised the way in which the African elephant used the tusks for breaking trunks of trees, etc."

In reply Morris stated:

"In your letter you put forward two or three queries, and you expressed the opinion that the tusk in many Indian elephants seems to be a degenerate organ, which would certainly seem to be the case as quite a number of male elephants fail to develop tusks, and in Ceylon, of course, tuskers are uncommon. It is my view that many elephants which have only one developed tusk were possibly born with only one tusk, or when their 'milk tushes', as it were, were shed they were replaced by only one instead of a pair of tusks. I had some correspondence on the matter with Mr. Gordon Hundley of Steel Brothers & Co., and one of the Bombay–Burma Trading Corporation men. Both these Companies maintain, as you no doubt know, a large number of elephants, several thousand in fact. Gordon Hundley informed me that calves have been known which developed into single tuskers and referred me to Evan's work on `Elephants and their Diseases'. He also told me an interesting thing; that ivory thieves used to steal whole tusks from a living tusker by repeated blows on the point, after a certain period the tusk so maltreated can be removed or is shed. Also that one type of tusker will 'cut through' a large tusk in a comparatively short time by continually 'knocking' a trunkful of grass against one of his tusks.

Evans in his `Elephants and their Diseases' records a case where an elephant dropped a male calf which grew up with only one tusk. He also states that Selous recorded it. as far from uncommon to meet with one–tusked animals among elephant cows in South Africa, though rarer among the bulls; and when an elephant has only one tusk the bone on the other side is quite solid and shows no sign of a hollow where the hollow ought to be. This has been my experience exactly, and you will recollect my informing you of this myself in regard to Indian single tuskers. Evans goes on to say that 'Males occasionally lose a tusk when fighting or through other injury, but some are born with a single tusk'. Evans disagrees with Sanderson in the latter's statement that the first tushes of a bull elephant are never shed and says that on the contrary the milk tusks are shed between one and two years of age and replaced by the permanent ones."

And there the matter stands.

4.7 Tusker tracks

Tusks being the reason for hunting, elephant hunters with experience apparently could tell from the tracks whether an elephant had worthwhile tusks.

W.S. Thom (18) for instance believed that he could tell the probable size of the tusk from the size of the tracks for as he says he "made a point of never following the tracks of a solitary tusker elephant unless these measured 18 or 20" from toe to heel. I refer only to impressions of the forefeet. There is no mistaking the elongated tracks of an old tusker elephant. The cracks and wrinkles on all four soles of the feet and the large toe nail indentations on the soft ground are also usually clearly defined. The length and thickness of an elephant's tusks may be indicated by the cavities he digs in the soft earth of stream banks as he moves along or by the marks left by his tusks on the ground where he has passed the night".

As Thom has indicated it is possible to distinguish between the tracks of a tusker and a Makhna. On a query raised by J.J. Cameron (34) A.J.W. Milroy, and N.L. Bor, the editors comment:

"There is a statement in Mr. E.L. Walker's `Elephant Hunting and Shooting in Ceylon', p.73, to the effect that a Ceylon Tusker elephant has a slightly oval forefoot, similar to, though not so pronounced as, the hind foot.

I have personally investigated this point, and of four captive tuskers' feet which I have examined I find that this is actually so to some extent.

Tuskers being rare in Ceylon, I have only been able so far to examine four.

I find, however, that this is a difference of approximately an inch in the back-to-front as against the breadth measurement in Ceylon non-tuskers, feet also, and that in the case of the tuskers examined the difference is 2 to 2.5"."

Commenting on the above A.J.W. Milroy writes :-

"I have never taken any measurements to prove that tuskers' forefeet are rather more elongated than those of Mukhanas, because I have always accepted it as a fact.

Experienced natives will generally state without hesitation whether a track in the forest was made by a tusker or a Mukhana, but of course one only occasionally actually comes on the animal itself so they may often be wrong. They have had so many generations of experience however, in the tracking of elephants turned loose to graze, and so many opportunities of seeing the tracks of elephants that have raided their crops, that the probability is that they are not mistaken.

Personally, given a distinct track, I have always been accustomed unconsciously to ascribe it to a tusker or a Mukhana, as the case might be, but I cannot remember to have proved definitely that I was right, though it has never occurred to me till the present moment that there could be any mistake in most cases. I will forward your letter to Mr. N.L. Bor, who will be conducting Kheddahs on a big scale next season, and will ask him to take measurements."

N.L. Bor, Deputy Conservator of Forests, Kohima, Naga Hills, Assam, in reference to the subject wrote:

"I made some measurements last cold weather, and append results. It will be seen that the front–and–back measurements of the feet of tusker and tuskless is greater than the breadth in every case.

I do not think a study of the figures would justify one in laying down a definite rule as to whether the difference in the two measurements is greater in the case of tuskers.

I think it is a misnomer to apply the term oval to a forefoot though the term can be applied correctly to hind feet. The greatest breadth of a forefoot occurs well behind the centre of the foot to back axis."

Bor appended a list of measurements of the forefeet of twenty-nine tuskers and thirty five tuskless (Makhnas) the average difference between the back-to-front and breadth measurements in the tuskers was 1.56", in the Makhnas 1.45". The forefoot in the largest tusker measured 1'7 1.4", back-to-front with a breadth of 1'5.5" the same measurements in the largest makhna were 1'6" by 1'2". Eds."

4.8 Makhnas

W.S. Thom (18) writing on makhnas says :

"Tuskless male elephants, called by the Burmans 'haings' or 'hines' and by Indians 'mucknas' are generally big fellows with powerful trunks. A big muckna is usually feared by the members of any herd to which he may belong, and he is a very dangerous animal when he becomes a rogue and turns solitary. As a rule there is no mistaking the tracks of a 'muckna' or 'haing' for they are generally more circular and less elongated than the forefoot impressions of a tusker. No sportsman ever shoots or is permitted to shoot a female elephant in India or Burma unless compelled to do so in self–defence, simply because, unlike the African species, they carry no tusks"

R.C. Morris (33) quotes Evans, and the opinion of jungle tribes, on the strength of makhnas, and writes:

"Evans in his classical work on elephants mentions instances of mucknas (tuskless males) being feared even by powerful tuskers. This, of course, is well known among the jungle tribes both in India and Burma; mucknas seem to make up in size of body and trunk for the lack of tusks and are generally enormously powerful elephants. In fights between mucknas and even large tuskers, as often as not the tusker will be defeated. Evans quotes a case of a fight between a good–sized tusker and a large muckna which was well known in the Shweli forests of Burma. During the course of the battle the muckna snapped off one of the tusks of its opponent with its trunk. A somewhat similar instance is recorded of a fight between a muckna and a tusker, in which the former was seen to seize and break of one of the tusks of its antagonist.

Chapter 5

HABITS

5.1 General

In M. Krishnan's view (20) much of the daily activities of elephants centre around the two main features of their life, food and water:

"They need quantities of fodder (estimated at about 500 lb. of green fodder per adult) to sustain their great bodies, and half their time is spent in feeding; they are highly gregarious and reassemble periodically after getting split up in the course of their search for food.

Although the largest and most massive land animals, their peculiar build and anatomy enables them to ascend steep slopes, and they are remarkably expert at climbing hills. There are few hills in the south whose tops are not marked by regular, well defined elephant–walks: these are not just the tracks of a herd that has recently passed that way, but the well tamped paths used and re–used by a succession of elephants: these paths always follow the easiest and safest gradients, and an expert engineer planning the best routes up and down a hill cannot do better than follow elephant–paths. It is noteworthy that at times such paths follow the very edges of hilltops, with a sheer fall of a hundred feet or more to one side – elephants are exceptionally sure–footed and apparently never suffer from vertigo."

The ability of elephant to climb rock faces which seem practically impossible have been noticed by R.C. Morris who wrote:

In 1929 while following a rogue elephant on the Baragur Hills, I was amazed to find that the elephant had climbed the face of a small dry waterfall – in a ravine – leaving a good path to do so. Had I not personally verified this I would never have believed it to be possible. Further, there was no apparent reason for the climb – which was quite 12', possibly more."

Evans (17) confirms that, considering their great size, elephants are wonderfully active - climb up and go down steep places in a surprising manner:

As Krishnan (20) notes:

"It is said that the fastest pace of an elephant, as when charging, is a fast walk or shuffle and that the animal cannot run. Even G.P. Sanderson, whose knowledge of elephants was extensive, deep and authentic, and whose authority still sustains many passages in recent books (for example, Ivan T Sanderson's `The Dynasty of Abu') has fallen into the error of supposing that elephants cannot run; he says 'the only pace of the elephant is the walk, capable of being increased to a fast shuffle ... it can neither trot, canter nor gallop. An elephant cannot trot, canter or gallop for the same reason that a man, when running naturally, does not trot, canter or gallop. The anatomy of the elephant is peculiar in that it has no hock as other quandrupeds have, but a true knee, like the human knee, that bends back. Therefore the elephant runs without leaping into the air, but it has two definite, paces the walk and the run.

G.H. Evans (17) believes that the usual pace of elephant is a walk; it is only when annoyed or scared that they take on a faster rate of locomotion, which is a shuffling amble, but the wonderful amount of speed these creature can attain in an incredibly short time is known only to those who have had an enraged monster after them."

5.2 Speed

Writing on the speed of the elephant when going flat out, R.C. Morris (62) states that:

"Personally I consider from my own experience that an Indian Elephant when 'all out' can travel quite 20 miles an hour. I do not think any 'mahout' can make an elephant travel as fast as one in full charge, or in full terrified flight. I once saw a pair of elephants cross a grassy flat, and their speed over this stretch of about 300 yards must have been nearly as great as that of a racehorse."

5.3 Stride

The inability of the elephant to jump has given rise to the elephant trenches, the protective devise against elephant incursion and depredation. Exceptionally, however, elephants do strike across a trench as noted by R.C. Morris (99):

"Three elephants (tuskers) strode, without apparent difficulty, across an elephant trench round a ragi field, in the moonlight. The width of the trench was 5.5'; the stride measured in each case 8'2" from centre to centre of the footprints. Had I not myself seen this occur I would have considered the feat incredible."

In another instance Morris (100) writes:

"This month, on two successive nights, an elephant, in a single stride, crossed and re-crossed an 8' V-shaped trench bordering our raghi farm. From the tracks he would appear to have lurched himself over."

5.4 Swimming and Water Requirement

The ability of the elephant to swim is well known. According to Evans (17):

"They are excellent swimmers. When in deep water the whole body is immersed; only the end of the trunk is kept above water."

According to Krishnan (20):

"A consequence of their great bodily bulk is that they are virtually unsinkable, but they do not ride high in the water. They swim almost submerged, or just below the water, and the advantage of this when surface currents are strong is obvious. G.P. Sanderson records that a batch of 79 tame elephants he despatched across the tidal creeks of the Ganges were in the water for six hours without touching bottom in one swim, and that in the course of this and three other long swims not one was lost. He rightly observes that 'full-grown elephants swim perhaps better than any other land animals'. The very young calves are at times reluctant to take to the water and are pushed in by their mothers or 'aunts'. In the water, young calves are helped by the support and guidance of the trunks of their mothers. G.P. Sanderson observes that older calves sometimes scramble on to the shoulders of their mothers during a long swim, holding on with their legs: I too have observed this. In crossing a broad, swift running river they choose both the point of entry along a path sloping gently down the bank into the water and the point at which they clamber ashore on the bank across the water. They have regular paths for getting into the water and out of it, even into and out of a small forest pool.

Elephants bathe in forest pools and rivers, entering the water carefully, fanning out, and then rolling over in the water, frequently submerging themselves."

Their dependence on water is remarked on by M. Krishnan (20):

"They are not found in places where there is no source of drinking water, for they drink every day though they may not bathe every day. Baths are also indulged in during the rainy season, even when it is raining. A small water–hole may suffice to provide drinking water. They drink by sucking water up their trunk and then squirting it down their throats. The process seems reversible in a small measure. It is well known that, when feeling hot, an elephant will insert the tip of its trunk into its mouth, bring out some fluid and spray it all over itself. This fluid is not water from the elephant's stomach, as it is said to be: it is not acid and does not turn blue litmus red. It is probably saliva.

Elephants draw muddy water up their trunks and squirt it over themselves, muddying the water with a forefoot for this purpose if it is too watery. Water is also squirted in a shower over the back and head, and directed in squirts at the belly and head – a hot elephant cools itself in this manner. Where semi–solid mire is freely available, as at drying pools, it is taken up in lumps in the crook of the tip of the trunk and flung over the back, head and flanks.

A regular wallow is also indulged in: this may be when it is dry and hot, as in summer, or when it is cool, as on an overcast day in September or October.

Dust–baths are usually taken soon after climbing ashore from water, the dust being drawn up the trunk and blown over the head and back. Dust is also sprayed over wounds to cover them. Earth, and salt–earth, is kicked up by the forefoot, and eaten. There appears to be a tendency among gravid cows to eat earth.

Apparently all this dusting and mud–bathing and miresmearing serves to relieve cutaneous irritation or to provide some cutaneous gratification: the way elephants revel in baths, dust–baths, wallows and mud–slinging does suggest such a purpose. Calves under six months do not indulge in dust–baths or squirt mire over themselves because at that age they have not acquired sufficient skill with their trunk to put that most versatile organ to such uses: They wallow in the wet mud however, and in muddy shallow water.

Elephants also rub themselves, both when their bodies are covered with wet mud and when their skins are dry and clean, against the boles of trees. For this purpose a thick tree is chosen, often with a slight lean from the perpendicular, and they rub themselves against the bole on the side on which the bole leans towards the ground: such rubbing trees, covered with mud from about 3' to 9' up their boles, are often to be seen in the neighbourhood of forest pools.

One big bull chose and detached a dry twig while having a mire bath, and then scratched himself over the flanks and back with the twig held in his trunk. Another bull, with maggot-infested gunshot wounds, rubbed himself against a bole to detach the maggots from his wound."

5.5 Vocalisation
M. Krishnan (20) has succintly summarised vocalisations by elephants. He wrote:

"Some of the vocalisations of elephants are well–known, such as trumpeting, squealing, squeaking (the two terms are used to distinguish a louder sound of protest from a weaker and softer sound, usually of pleasure in elephants), roaring (usually indulged in by juvenile elephants of from one to five years, when separated from their mothers in the course of foraging), and a sudden metallic and at the same time tympanic sound made by rapping the trunk shapely against the ground (the sound seems to be produced mainly by the sudden percussion of the column of air in the trunk as it is expelled) which is a sound of apprehension and interrogation – strictly speaking, not all of these sounds are vocalisations, since some are produced not in the throat but in the trunk. Other vocalisations are less well–known and may be briefly set out here. One of these is a plaintive, reiterated 'kook–kook–kook', sounded when the animal suddenly discovers something that annoys it (such as the near presence of a man: it is a sound of protest, but I have also heard it used by an exceptionally burly tusker that was demonstrating to us, while covering the retreat of the herd (which we were following), evidently some form of communication with the herd. Very young calves (under 2 months) come out with a loud, quickly–repeated bark that is very like the barking of a dog (though louder and flatter); a sound that is known to very few mahouts, for it is not uttered by calves in elephant camps. It can be heard only from the calves of wild elephants, and seems to be an expression of exhilaration. Older calves do not indulge in this vocalisation.

A loud, repeated smacking, made with the lips, is commonly employed by the leading adult animals in a herd when the herd is on the move and somewhat uneasy over what lies ahead: an adult cow smelling at the rump of another adult cow was also heard coming out with this smacking sound. Frequently when the herd is grazing in the open (never in cover), the adults converge in a close circle, with their heads facing the centre, and seem to confer together; after such a conference, the animals usually move away steadily in one direction, keeping close together and not in loose formation as when grazing: I have never been able to get sufficiently close to elephants in 'conference' to know whether or not they make any sounds then, but believe they do come out with some soft, low sounds – they certainly do indulge in tactile expressions with their trunks then. Among tame elephants, two cows may be seen standing close together, almost in a huddle, caressing each other with their trunks and coming out with throaty, hardly–audible sounds – this is especially noticeable when two cows that like each other meet after a separation.

Elephants in the herd are sometimes quite noisy, and at such times they are apt to be belligerent, and particularly aggressive towards human intruders. The many vocalisations of a herd are often missed when observing elephants by day (partly, no doubt, because one is then preoccupied with seeing), but in the stillness of the night and when conditions are specially favourable for hearing the sounds made, as when the elephants are grouped around a sheet of water (which acts as a most efficient sounding–board), grunts, grumblings, squeals, squeaks, trumpetings, 'kook–kook–kooks' and softer, less definable sounds may all be heard. A sound which elephants frequently utter when they are alone (maybe in a herd the sound is drowned by the other sounds made by the animals) is a deep, audible sigh, made by the expulsion of air through the trunk – it is the one sound made by an elephant which is otherwise keeping utterly silent, and a sound for which men in elephant jungles must always listen.

Many observers have recorded becoming aware of the presence of wild elephants by hearing their intestinal rumblings -- this, of course, is purely involuntary and no sort of vocalisation, even stretching the term to its widest application. But on occasion, an elephant, while standing still, will come out with a vibrant rumbling sound, low–pitched but clearly audible from some distance, that is a sound made in the throat, though the

A fine tusker with the tusks nearly crossing

Krupakar Senani

Mother elephants scrubbing babies, Periyar

M.Y. Ghorpade

Tusker 'Checking' female - Nagarhole National Park

Vivek R Sinha

Big lone tusker near road to Moolapura, Periyar

M Krishnan

M Krishnan

Tuskers having a mud bath.

Tusker at a Pool at Nagarhole National Park

AJT Johnsingh

flanks also appear to vibrate while it is made. It is a sound difficult to describe, something between a low growl and a throbbing purr. A charging elephant may come on in silence or utter a piercing, malevolent scream."

People who have had long contact with elephants in the field are certain that elephants communicate with each other at a infrasonic level below human hearing capacity. This requires further research in India. Studies are in progress in Africa on this mode of communication."

M. Krishnan (20) comments on other means of communication:

"As in other mammals, communications and expressions of mood and intent are not limited to vocalisations. The attitude of an elephant, the way it stands and moves and the way it holds it head, tail, ears and trunk are all expressive of its emotional state. An elephant in a rage stands very still, without swinging its trunk or flapping its ears – the ears are held flat against the neck. When alarmed and on the point of bolting, the tail is thrown up and the head raised, with the ears fanned out and then folded back, an attitude that serves effectively in visual communication of the alarm to other elephants around.

5.6 Vision

The elephant's vision is said to be poor, but it seems to be much better than reputed. It is true that the animal is not good at picking out stationary human beings inconspicuously clad in dark colours. Against this, (an elephant's inability to see what is right beneath it, such as a man crouching in a bush, is no doubt partly due to the bulge of its cheeks and the base of its trunk), the fact that a great many signals are usually sensed visually must be offset. An old cow returned to the water, at which a younger cow was lingering after the rest of the party had left after drinking, stood on the bank for a moment and then moved off, when the younger animal instantly followed. I have observed this mode of beckoning to a member of the herd that lags behind on a few previous occasions as well. An elephant in cover, wishing to cross an open space to get to cover beyond, inspected the open ground visually and also investigated it by smelling, before crossing it. At times, when it has been apprised by smell of the near presence of a man, an elephant turns round for visual confirmation of its olfactory perception."

A peculiar behaviour was noticed by F.W. Haswell (101), who is not quite certain whether it is related to sight or smell. He was after elephants in the Kale Valley in Burma, and writes:

"Having unfortunately badly wounded one elephant, I was not entitled to shoot another on my license.

On leaving my camp to go down country, I ran into a herd of elephants in kyaing grass on the edge of heavy jungle with thick cane undergrowth.

Hurrying forward, I climbed into a small tree between the elephants and the jungle they were making for; the man with me, a pensioned Gurkha Jemadar, getting up only four feet off the ground. My object was to have a good look over the herd. More than fifty elephants passed within five or six paces of the tree I was in. One elephant only showed signs of unease and let out a minor squeal. Lastly a party of eight elephants passed us, but I think must have been suspicious as they turned round and stood round the tree with all heads inwards; four of them were within one foot of the Gurkha Jemadar, looking directly at him. He was waving the barrel of my small rifle within six inches of the eyes of one elephant, whilst I took aim at the head of another at one foot-range in case of trouble.

The elephants stayed for perhaps five minutes before slowly going off into thick jungle. There was a slight cross breeze at the time.

I wonder why the elephant did not spot us as neither of us kept still, and one elephant looked straight at me at six feet without a sign of recognition of my presence. Any of the elephants could have pulled us off the tree. Perhaps when an elephant is very close with its trunk on the ground, it is unable to get the wind of a man three or four feet up. It is obvious that these elephants made no use of sight or hearing."

5.7 Smell

W.S. Thoms (18) speaks of the elephants sense of smell, and the inordinate care it takes of its trunk.

"Elephants have a very keen sense of smell. The power of an elephant's trunk is enormous and with it the animal can lift a ton with ease. Though immensely strong, such a trunk has its own peculiar dangers and its care is a matter of constant vigilance and anxiety to its owner. If threatened by a tiger it is curled up over the forehead. Still more dreaded is the poisonous snake. The common mouse, whose holing instinct may lead him to take refuge in one or other of the large nostrils, is likewise a danger.

On what basis he makes these statements is not known."

Krishnan (20) also notes the care bestowed on the trunk by the elephant. He states:

"When the animal is at peace with the world, the trunk swings freely and the ears flap from time to time; when the head is held high and movements are brisk, it is in high spirits. When undecided or perplexed, the tip of the trunk is sometimes inserted into the mouth or, in a tusker, the trunk is draped over the tusks and hangs from them. It is curious that both these ways of disposing of the trunk are repeated in sleep. K. Krishnamurthy once observed a proscribed rogue (which he shot later) asleep on its side, with the tip of its curled–up trunk reposing safely in the mouth, and in a big tusker observed by me standing asleep, the trunk was draped over the tusks. Instinctively, elephants take good care of their trunks (a vitally important organ to them) both in repose and in action.

Krishnan (20) notes that:

"The sense of smell, of course, is paramount. Even apprehension of fodder specially fancied seems to be by smell – a nearblind riding elephant was still able to know that a tree, the foliage of which she liked, was some 15 feet to one side of the path she was following, and to alter her course to eat the foliage. The presence of men nearby is often revealed to an elephant by smell, when it instantly pinpoints the smell with the tip of its trunk – it also looks hard in that direction. On two occasions, when I provoked a tusker to charge me, the animals instantly charged the moment I gave them my location definitely by walking into the wind. Even the reverse of seeking visual confirmation of the proximity of men perceived initially through smell was observed, that is, olfactory confirmation sought by the trunk being pointed in the direction of the men seen, when the animal could not possibly smell them, the wind blowing from it to the men. When an airborne scent is above the level of the elephant's head, the trunk is raised high to investigate it.

Elephants are well able to follow groundscents, like bloodhounds. A cow followed me entirely by groundscent, with a strong wind blowing from her to me and on two occasions wild tuskers followed the tracks of the tame elephant I was riding by groundscent: another wild tusker was observed sedulously following a groundscent, probably the track of a wild elephant."

The ability of elephants to follow ground scent had often been noticed by BNHS scientists, who have had bulls trailing them by smelling their footprints.

5.8 Sleep

W.S. Thom (18) opines that a solitary tusker usually sleeps on his side, flat on the ground like a horse with all four legs stretched out straight, and remembers once coming across a solitary bull elephant a sleep on the ground, which was making use of an ant heap as a pillow.

When and how elephants sleep has been noted by C.W.A. Bruce (19) who says:

"I have carefully noted the habits of tame elephants, and find that healthy animals sleep twice in the night, from about twelve o'clock to two o'clock and again about four o'clock till dawn; some, however, only sleep once, i.e. from four o'clock till dawn. If an animal sleeps oftener it is not well. They lie down full length on their sides to sleep. This early morning time for sleeping explains why it is so injurious to the health of elephants to march for days before dawn, as is frequently done in the hot weather by officers wishing to spare these animals the torture of marching in the sun. My experience is that, if a tame elephant lies down during the day, the animal is going to die."

5.9 Play

M. Krishnan (20) believes that "elephants are among the few animals that play even as adults. When bathing in company in a forest pool, it is not only the juveniles that revel in play: even the adults bump into, push down, and roll over one another with abandon — perhaps they find the sudden lifting of their ponderous weight off their feet by the water exhilarating. On land too, adult bulls may indulge in a long bout of play with their trunks, not in a tug–of–war so much as a pushing match, or in chasing each other."

R.C. Morris (36) also gives an example:

"Late in the afternoon of a day last January, I witnessed a wonderful sight from my observation machan over the Dod Sampagi tank in the jungle here. At 5 p.m. twenty–eight elephants came into the tank and for nearly two hours enjoyed themselves thoroughly in the water. The biggest of the herd – an old cow — went through the most extraordinary antics, at times she would sit up like a dog and from this position she would frequently go through a motion of half standing on her head as if she was considering turning a somersault. Most of them were at one time or another completely immersed in the water except for their trunks. Two half–grown tuskers sparred with each other for a while. There were two young ones in the herd, one not more than three feet high and I should say about two or three weeks old and the other was about four feet high. Both of them ran in and out between their mother's legs, and the smaller one seemed to spend its time stumbling into holes made by its elders' ponderous feet, and making frantic efforts to scramble out of them again. One of the herd, a small cow, had a dislocated hind leg, its hip–joint being out. This caused it to walk like a ship pitching and tossing. The poor brute's leg was as a result of the dislocation much longer than the other three and to drag it out of the mud the elephant had to lean right

73

forward. The leg seemed to be very swollen. An elephant Khedda was held on these hills last December and I think it is likely that this elephant was one of those caught, and that it pulled its leg out of joint in its efforts to release itself from its leg–ropes and was consequently released. This is, of course, only surmise. On reaching one end of the tank the herd smelled us, bunched together, and then hurried away into the surrounding jungle on hearing a low whistle from me.

There is nothing more fascinating than observing Game in this tank on a moon–light night. My observation machan is large enough to allow four or five people to lie on it at full length. I recently watched a fine stag Sambhar and two does romp and wallow in the water for about three hours."

5.10 Food

Krishnan (20) gives detailed notes on his observations on the food and feeding methods of elephants. He writes:

"In feeding, while the trunk is used to detach and convey food to the mouth, the forefeet are also used as aids to crush and break up large fruits and small branches or bamboo culms, and to dust grass against. Watching elephants feed, one is impressed by the care with which they select and prepare each mouthful for ingestion; they are choosy feeders.

Fodder naturally varies with locality and season, and what follows is merely indicative of the many kinds of plant food they eat. They are entirely vegetarian, and while hard stems and twigs are also eaten, the bulk of their food consists of foliage and soft plant parts, or succulent herbs.

Many kinds of tall grasses (all those appropriately and loosely termed 'elephant grass') are eaten, also some short grasses and purely herbaceous plants. Among the grasses commonly eaten are: *Saccharam spontaneum, Ischaemum pilosum, species of Panicum, Sorghum and Themeda, Apluda mutica, Arundinella holocoides, Eragrostis gangetica, Hackelochloa granularis, and Paspalum scrobiculatum.*

Some sedges, and some plants of the Zingiberaceae such as *Costus speciosus* and *Alpinia,* are also commonly eaten.

All these grasses and succulents are torn out in a sheaf or bunch with the trunk, dusted vigorously, and placed crosswise in the mouth. This is a highly skilled operation, to which we find no parallel in the feeding habits of other herbivores.

The sheaf is neatly packed before it is pulled out (the grasses usually by their roots): it is then dusted on the bent and raised wrist by being slapped sharply against it with a twirl of the trunk, or, especially when the bunch of fodder consists of short grasses with stolons or sedges, the trunk is formed into a double twist near its end and then violently untwisted in the air: this move generates considerable centrifugal force and the adherent mud and debris is sent flying away from the plant. When feeding in thick cover, when what is held in the trunk cannot be easily dusted against the foreleg, the trunk is raised high and the fodder swiftly twirled aloft to clean it. No doubt, in addition to clinging mud and dust and debris, the sheaf is also freed from insects, snails and the like by these manoeuvers.

The sheaf of grass is placed crosswise in the mouth, with the basal root part projecting from the lips on one side and the tips of the blades on the other, then, at a bite, the projecting parts of the sheaf are bitten through and allowed to fall to the ground, and the rest is masticated and swallowed. When the grass is tender, the blades are consumed, and it will be found that the rejected parts of sheaves (which mark the passage of the animal in the course of its grazing) consist largely of the basal stalks and roots; when the blades are mature and hard, but basal culms are succulent, the apical part of the sheaf is rejected and the culms (with only the roots bitten off) consumed. The placing of the sheaf in the mouth, and the consumption of a part of it, is a selective action and not purely mechanical.

Bamboo (both of the genera *Bambusa* and *Dendrocalamus*) *Ochlandra*, sugarcane and standing crops in fields are among the other grasses much fancied as food. In feeding on the giant bamboo, the entire clump is not pushed down: individual culms are selected, and these are either pushed down or pulled down, and then another culm is brought down. It is not only the foliage that is eaten, but also the culm. Elephants will, on occasion, eat even dry bamboo fallen on the forest floor. Ratan cane is much fancied and eaten, thorns and all' Banana plants are pulled down, the stem split open with the forefoot, and the 'pith' eaten – a noticeable preponderance of banana fibre in the dung betrays overnight raids on plantations.

When the water hyacinth (*Eicchornia crassipes*) first invaded the bheels of Kaziranga, the elephants and other wild animals would not touch it, but in 1968 I found buffaloes and rhinos eating the exotic weed occasionally, and elephants rarely. It is known that this plant has a considerable iodine content; in fact, it was utilised in emergency for the commercial manufacture of iodine. How far and in what ways the sustained intake (even in small quantities) of this iodine–rich plant will influence elephants (and other animals) is a matter which needs investigation.

Among the succulents eaten should be mentioned *Pandanus* spp. and *Ardisia solanacea,* both growing in brakes along forest streams: these provide a source of water even when streams are dry in summer.

An exotic that seems to be more freely eaten now than some 25–30 years ago is lantana.

The bark of certain trees, such as *Kydia calycina, Grewia tiliaefolia* and teak, is skillfully stripped and eaten; it is not the dry bark that is eaten, but bark that is sappy, especially the bark of saplings. To strip the bark from the tree, the elephant applies the ventral aspect of the base of the trunk to the tree with a firm pressure and then jerks its head laterally; this causes the bark to split and get detached from the wood at that point, in a strip some 4" to 6" wide; the lower broken edge of the strip is then gently lifted up with the trunk till the bark is stripped as high as the trunk can go and hangs from the bole. Then this strip of bark is held lax in the trunk, given two or three preliminary oscillations, and one quick upward flick that detaches it for another 2 or 3 feet up the trunk. After eating this, another strip of bark next to the peeled strip is similarly peeled and consumed. It was noticed that, in a *Kydia calycina* almost completely stripped of bark in 1963, by summer new bark had covered the wood.

Many shrubs and small trees are eaten, foliage and twigs together; among these may be mentioned *Helicteres isora, Grewia aspera* and other species, *Hibiscus lampas, Acacia concinna, A. intsia, A. ferruginea, A. catechu, Cordia myxa,* and *Zizyphus xylopyrus. Phoenix humilis* is much liked, both the foliage and the fruits being avidly consumed.

In the South, it is not rare to come across *Buchanania latifolia* saplings in the forests that look as if they had been pollarded. Wild elephants eat the crown of this tree when it is in new leaf, thus giving it this appearance. *Emblica* sp. and *Ficus mysorensis* and other species, *Premna tomentosa, Elacodendron glaucum, Albizia odoratissima* and other species, *Diospyros* spp. and *Bauhinia racemosa* are among the trees whose foliage is regularly eaten.

The aerial roots of the banyan are much fancied, and regularly broken off at the level of the elephant's reach, as they re-grow.

I have seen elephants laboriously gathering and consuming the flower heads of *Mimosa pudica*. Flowers do not form any significant part of their diet, but they painstakingly collect tiny morsels that they especially fancy.

A variety of forest fruits are eaten, among them *Aegle marmelos, Artocarpus integrafolia* and *A. hirsuta, Careya arborea, Cordia myxa, Emblic* spp., *Feronia elephantum, figs,*

Pandanus sp., and *Randia uliginosa*. The grain of seeding bamboos, and the seeds of Cycas are eaten.

The substantial part of the food of elephants consists of grasses, sedges, other herbaceous plants, and bamboo.

Young calves subsist on their mother's milk up to the age of about 6 months, when they begin to feed on grasses and herbs. They may be suckled occasionally till they are 3 years old. A young calf is singularly clumsy with its small, undeveloped trunk, which it places against the axilla of its mother while sucking milk. It is only as it grows up that the trunk develops and it acquires skill in the use of the organ. The breasts of a cow elephant have a slight outward lean, towards the flank, and this facilitates suckling the calf.

Elephants and gaur are usually found in the same forests, and it has been said that they feed amicably together. This has not been my experience. No doubt gaur benefit by following in the wake of elephants, and consuming the bamboo and other tree foliage pulled down by the latter, but elephants do not allow gaur to feed with them. In their feeding, they keep in a group or feed by themselves, and are quite unsociable. They do not like the company of other animals even at forest pools and drive them away or, where the water is tainted by other animals having drunk at the same pool, scrape fresh water–holes for themselves with their feet."

Sivaganesan (107) who did a detailed study on the feeding ecology and habitat utilization by elephants in the Mudumalai Sanctuary of Tamil Nadu records observation generally similar to Krishnan's notes on feeding behaviour. According to Sivaganesan grass formed 90% of the diet in all seasons. In the wet season the grass, *Themada triandra,* formed the main food resource from its availability and the larger percentage of young leaves. The species is an equally important food plant in Africa, too. Young leaves are a rich source of protein and soluble carbohydrates. This species fell off in favour in the dry season as it became fibrous. Sivaganesan (op. cit.) concludes that "elephants show a preference for a specific grass at certain seasons which is influenced not only by phenology but also by the distribution pattern of the grass. The heavy utilization of a larger portion of the entire upper parts of grass was coincident with the increase in the crude protein during the wet seasons. The lower fibre content and the soft texture are also factors

78

responsible for the heavy utilization of the entire sprouting grasses by the elephants. In the dry season Sivaganesan found that elephants show a strong preference for several species of short grasses, such as *Apulda mutica* which have a higher quantity of crude protein in the leafy upper portion as well as succulent soluble carbohydrates. Sivaganesan estimated that elephants removed not more than 16% of the total available biomass, and concluded that grass is not a limiting factor on elephants in his study area.

The intake of browse and its importance in elephant ecology in somewhat less clearly defined. The importance of browse or grass in the dietary of elephant is still being debated. In Sivaganesan's study area "browse constituted a minor proportion of the total diet of elephants except in the thorn forest. Browse was consumed mainly in the form of bark". This he attributes to the availability of calcium and magnesium in the bark. Bark also provided fibre. Though browse was equally abundant elephants consumed large quantities of grass in the moist mixed deciduous forests. The bamboos were, however, a favoured species wherever they occurred. From his study Sivaganesan concluded "that despite considerable variation among habitats and seasons, elephants have the ability to select a balanced diet of browse and grass from different habitats". He believes "that maintenance of diversity in various prime habitats is of foremost importance in the long term preservation of the elephant population". Browse was taken largely by adult males, females and it is suggested that adult tusker took more browse to maintain their fitness for breeding. Sukumar (111) considered browse to be of primary importance and that elephants are essentially browsers. From a study of stable carbon isotope ratios in the bone collagen, Sukumar (111) provides data to show that browse contributes on average 70% of the organic carbon for protein synthesis though browse may be less than 50% of food intake and concludes that browse is more important than grass in the elephants food intake. The effect of browsing on the habitat is a selective removal of favoured species. In Sivaganesan's study "The most favoured species was bamboo (98%)". The leaves and terminal branches of *Terminalia* sp., Teak and *Helicteres isora,* sprouting leaves of *Acacia instia* and *Zizyphus xlopyrus* were eaten in substantial quantities. The leafy branches of *Grewia tiliaefolia* and *Kydia calcina* were occasionally browsed upon. Bark was an important part of the diet and important timber species as teak and *Terminalia* were often debarked.

5.11 Salt lick
T.H. Hubback (45) suggests that the elephants use salt licks to purge themselves. Hubback writes:

"I obtained the answer to a phenomenon that has puzzled me for years when photographing elephants, and incidentally am able to record something to the credit of the salt–licks. I have often noticed that, at salt–lick frequented by elephants, there are enormous accumulations of droppings more or less in the same place and all looking as if they had been placed there at the same time. But as, in some cases there was so much, even what appeared to me to be far beyond the capacity of an elephant, I often wondered how they managed to do it. I know now. Here is the solution. When I went into the lick I carefully examined the edge of the lick with my glasses and saw that although the elephants or an elephant had been there about two days before, the rim of the pool was practically free from droppings. The big elephant came in about a quarter to five and after I had exhausted all my available film I left him to it. The following morning I went to the lick but the elephants had moved off. But, along the edge of the lick there was an accumulation of droppings which would have been a credit to an entire herd of elephants. No doubt the smaller one had been there too but he evidently did not go to exactly the same place as the big bull. I did not make any examination then because I expected to be there for some days and did not want to disturb the lick. But at the end of my last day there – the elephants never came in again – I made a thorough examination of the place and found that this enormous accumulation of dung – about half a bullock cart load – had obviously been made by the big elephant, partly on account of its size and partly on account of its coarseness. The dung of the smaller one was much smoother. I had a good look round the game tracks leading into the lick and I have no hesitation in saying that the night those two elephants had been in the vicinity they must, or at any rate the big one must, have gone in and out of the lick very many times. I therefore deduce that the sulphur, which from the length of time the elephant sucks up the water must amount to a considerable quantity, acts as a pretty quick aperient and the 'walk round' is done between times to get it to work properly! Finally I suppose when he feels he wants a little more of the lick, 'that salt–lick feeling' he goes down again and has a good drink. While there his tummy works and he adds to the mound. Of course there is a good deal of speculation about these deductions of mine, but I think it is more or less a fair conclusion to arrive at. The salt–lick is their chemist's shop, and in the case of a sulphur–lick it works very quickly."

P.D. Stracey (56) also believes that elephants eat earth at salt licks when they need a purge. He writes:

"On one occasion I took two 'koonkie' elephants to a saltlick at the foot of the Aka–Dafla Hills on the north bank of the Brahmaputra River, and they at once started to eat greedily of the grey earth, kicking great lumps out of the hillside with their feet and putting them into their mouths. It was with the greatest difficulty that we could tear the elephants away from the spot. On another occasion my Government elephant refused to touch any of the earth at another lick at the foot of the Bhutan Hills. Why? It seems that elephants eat the earth only when they are so inclined or are in need of a purge.

There are two kinds of licks in Assam, one known as 'pungs' and the other as 'mati–kolars'. The former are found at the foot of hills, invariably where a land–slip has occurred and the weathered soil extends as a talus or cone–like, grey sloe up to 100 feet or more. Water oozes out from the base and the place if obviously visited by all manner of animals, preference being shown for the freshly exposed surfaces higher up. 'Mati–kolais' are found on the plains, generally on the south bank, and resemble large white–ant hills, the sides and bases of which have been scraped away until a large shallow pit or hollow is formed in which water collects. Here the soil is much more clayey and yellow in colour, as compared to the grey, sandy earth of the 'pungs'. Some licks are more attractive to animals than others in the same neighbourhood, and the location of stockades for catching elephants depends on this fact."

In another instance R.C. Morris (55) describes the unusual love for ashes of a solitary elephant. He writes:

"A solitary elephant on the Cardamom Hills in Travancore seems to have a great predilection for ashes and frequently visits the vicinity of coolies' lines and ash pits for a feed of ashes. On one occasion it broke open the boarded wall of the local Sub–Assistant Surgeon's kitchen to get at the ashes in the fireplace, accomplishing this by putting its trunk through the vent, and one night the elephant not only visited each of the three ash pits behind the bungalow of the manager of the cardamom estate there, but actually got his forelegs in, having to kneel to do so, as we saw from the tracks the next morning.

Elephants on the Cardamom Hills appear to feed off the bark of the *Kydia calycina* tree but little, in contrast to the elephants on the Billigirirangans where nearly every tree of this species in the jungle has a portion of its bark removed by elephants at one time or another.

Morris also reports (102) --

"It is curious how elephants seem to go in for eating earth more in some localities than others. Recently, while on a visit to the Cardamom HIlls in Travancore, I was struck by the fact that throughout the jungles one came across numerous marks of elephant tusks in banks (mostly red clay) which are rarely to be seen on the Billigirirangans (North Coimbatore).

I sent down 2 samples of earth from the Cardamom Hills to Lt. Col. C. Newcomb, I.M.S., the Chemical Examiner to the Government of Madras, for analysis, and he writes as follows:

The results so far are :

	Red	Black
Loss on ignition	12.5	7.7
Alumina	21.4	7.5
Iron as Fe2O3	14.1	4.5
Silica	9.3	6.5
Sand and other silicous matter	43.1	74.5
Total	100.4	100.7

I believe the general idea is that elephants eat earth to remove 'bots, but I am also informed by the Director of Veterinary Services, Madras, that elephants often suffer from a condition known as 'pica', .a depraved appetite probably due to over-acidity, and desire an alkaline substance to correct this."

5.12 Home Range

The home range is the area within which an animal spends its life and finds its sustenance. Home range in the case of elephants relates to the area where a clan of related females, sub-adults and juveniles life. A clan may have a strength of 65+ elephants (B. Bhaskaran et al. in Daniel & Datye, 1993). In elephants, adult males have separate home ranges from the clans, but their home range may overlap a clan is.

The home range size has had various estimates in the studies undertaken in the range of the Asian elephant, and estimates vary from 30 sq.km. of clan operation in a low density area bordered by human settlements, to nearly 800 km^2 in the Nilgiri Biosphere Reserve as determined by telemetry studies. The mean home range size was 651 km^2 in the Nilgiri Biosphere Reserve for clans. Adult males appear to have two ranges - a home range of a limited area in the non-musth season, and an enlarged home range during the season of musth. Exact figures are not available as data on the home range in the musth season is not yet available.

Seasonal changes in the home range occur where populations are under severe stress as, for instance, in the Dalma Sanctuary. The summer range was restricted by climatic conditions and availability of water and was contained within an area of 35 sq.km. in the rainy season and thereafter however, when a large part of the population migrated into the plains of Bihar and south Bengal the ranges vary from 258 km^2 to over 4000 km^2 in the case of bulls.

Bhaskaran *et al.* (1993) conclude "that clans in large tracts of deciduous forests have large home ranges (600+ sq.km) and populations in smaller areas are likely to represent compressed populations with constricted home ranges. This does not mean that the populations living in smaller areas cannot be suitable for long term conservation. It would depend upon the density of elephants and the habitat quality, in the long run the densities are likely to increase and habitat quality will also decline (due to biotic pressure from human populations and possibly the impact of high elephant densities) resulting in the areas becoming less suitable for elephants. It would lead to a general decline in the quality of the elephant population and an increase in the level of man-elephant conflict, as poor habitat quality and increasing competition will force greater numbers of elephants into human areas. Elephant conservation areas that are of smaller size require both population and habitat management if they are to be viable.

Chapter 6

BEHAVIOUR

6.1 Social Organisation

Elephant society is a matriachal one, so the opinions and conclusions of Krishnan and others which follow are only partially true. What Prater calls a family unit is a clan, the basic unit of elephant society. Several inter-related clans may loosely join together depending on environmental conditions to form a herd and in the interaction behaviour of such herds, Krishnan is correct. In the relationship between bulls and the female herds, however, there has been from the early writings on elephants a tendency to speak of a 'herd' bull, and to confuse elephant social organisation with that seen in other animal communities where a male forms a harem. This is not true of an elephant herd. Here the association of the bulls with the female clans and herds is casual and for sexual purposes only and no other responsibilities are involved for the male, which from its adolescence leads a solitary existence or in the company of one or more bulls. The dominance hierarchy among the males is a different aspect where combat plays an important part and musth has a key role. The lone bull theory has no substance as all mature bulls are solitary or at the most may have a younger bull associated with them. Morris (62) has correctly appreciated the status of bulls in his area and also draws attention to a bull he had known in a particular patch of forest for many years. Ajai Desai had shown me an old single tusker which was always found in a particular patch of Mudumalai forest when not in musth. Bulls, in fact, have two ranges: a circumscribed non-musth home range, and a much larger range while under musth (see under Home Range).

M. Krishnan (20) has elaborated on his concept of social organisation of the elephant. He believes that:

"When Prater ("The Book of Indian Animals", Bombay Natural History Society) says that the herd is, in the main, a family unit it is to be construed liberally. A herd may consist of one or more families with an intermingling of unrelated individuals, and on occasions (while moving to fresh ground) two or more herds may unite into one large composite herd, marked by the presence of a number of big bulls, in their prime. In the course of daily foraging the herd (whether single or composite) usually splits into several parties which may feed at a distance from one another. Normally however, there is no intermingling of two herds, or two parties belonging to different herds, even if they are close to each other or passing each other along the same path. I have observed this in many different areas, in the Periyar, Mudumalai, Bandipur and Kaziranga sanctuaries and in Corbett National Park. As already said, normally, exclusiveness is a feature of elephantine herd associations. Very old animals as well as very young calves, and elephants of all intermediate ages, may be found in a herd. Where there are more than one adult bull in a single (not composite) herd, one may be very old and the other in his prime, or the lesser bull's acceptance of the dominance of the big bull may be evident; it is only rarely, however, that two big bulls are found in a single herd; all records showing several bulls probably pertain to composite herds. The following extract from a description of a large herd (evidently composite) seen by Sir Victor Brooke in July 1863 in the Biligirirangan hills of Mysore is vivid, and except for its conjecture of the probable descent of many members of the herd from the patriarch, no doubt factually true: 'There were about eighty elephants in the herd. Towards the head of the procession was a noble bull, with a pair of tusks such as are rarely seen nowadays in India. Following him in direct line came a medley of elephants of lower degree – bulls, cows, and calves of every size, some of the latter frolicking with comic glee, and bundling in amongst the legs of their elders with the utmost confidence. It was truly a splendid sight, and I really believe that while it lasted neither Colonel Hamilton nor I entertained any feeling but that of intense admiration and wonder. At length the great stream was, we believed, over, and we were commencing to arrange our mode of attack, when there hove in sight that which called forth an ejaculation of astonishment from each one of us. Striding thoughtfully along in the rear of the herd, many of the members of which were, doubtless, his children, and his children's children, came a mighty bull, the like of which neither my companion, after many years of jungle experience, nor the two natives who were with us, had ever seen before'. Nowadays it is seldom that one can see such a composite herd. That there were such huge herds even only 30 years ago is borne out by the testimony of those who have seen them when the elephant forests of the South were more extensive, and primeval."

Social Behaviour
6.1.1 Lone Bulls
Krishnan continues:

"Sanderson records seeing a young male calf all by itself. A 5 year–old bull calf was also seen by me, contentedly feeding by himself throughout the day – there were no other elephants around. Such solitary animals are most exceptional, and one never sees an adult cow by herself, though a cow and her grown calf were often seen grazing by themselves on a hillside, not joining the other elephants on that hill. Only adult bulls are normally seen by themselves.

These, as Sanderson points out, are seldom 'lone bulls', but the big bulls of some herd which may be, for the time being, staying away from the herd. He doubts if there is any such thing as a true 'lone bull' and dismisses the theory of an adult bull being driven away from the herd by a stronger bull as fancy. He is largely correct in much that he says, but while it is true that few bulls, if any, are truly solitary, there are records of bulls having been seen for years on end staying by themselves, or sometimes in close association with another bull; since such animals do not wander far as elephants in herds do in their seasonal quest of food, their movements are well known to the forest living people of the area. The question is really not one so much of fact as of terminology. If, by the term 'lone bull' is meant an animal that never, under any circumstances whatever, associates with others of its kind, Sanderson is correct and there are no 'lone bulls'. The loneliest of them will, on occasion, seek the company of a cow in season or even associate with another bull for a brief while. If the term 'lone bull' is applied, much more properly, however, to an adult male that is solitary as a rule and does not join a herd except in a transient association, there are lone bulls among elephants. The tusker that killed the camp elephant Shibji in the Jaldapara Sanctuary was known to have been solitary for years; similarly, the bull proscribed in the Mudumalai Sanctuary as a rogue was long known as a solitary elephant in the sanctuary, though on occasion he was accompanied by a small mukna. A big tusker with magnificent tusks and peculiarities of build that proclaimed his identity was well known as a true lone bull in the Periyar Sanctuary for over a decade, and was never seen in the company of other elephants, though elephants are seasonally common in the area. Other instances of a bull living by itself for years are known. Forest–living tribals and elephant men know the distinction between such truly solitary bulls and the bulls of herds that occasionally leave the herd to be alone for some time – they call the former 'lone bull' and the latter 'the lone bull of the herd', a contradiction in terms rendered necessary by the confusing social habits of elephants! In the field notes the term 'lone bull' has been used loosely to mean both kinds of solitary bulls, but the context will make it clear which kind was meant. True lone bulls may, on occasion, drink with a herd or stay close by a herd, or even mate with a female in a herd or elephant camp. Such a lone bull was seen near a herd (which included three adult tuskers) at a river, but when the animals left after drinking, the herd and the lone bull went their separate ways.

G.P. Sanderson's argument that a true lone bull is never an animal driven out of a herd but one that has chosen a solitary life of its own accord, while generally true, is not invariably so. K Krishnamoorthy once saw, first the big tusker of a herd and later the entire herd chasing a lone bull that had attempted to enter a herd over a long distance. A solitary bull cannot just walk into a herd and be accepted, even if he is prepared to accord priority to a larger bull already in the herd, as a matter of course. Elephants are exclusive in their gregariousness, and may not accept a newcomer; the truth is we do not at present know what prompts them to react differently on different occasions in this regard. Even among animals moving in a herd, there may be sharp antagonism between adult bulls. There was only one herd of elephants in the Palamau National Park in February 1969, in which there were two muknas, both in musth; the older and larger of the two muknas actively resented the presence of the smaller, and chased him away.

All solitary male elephants, whether or not true lone bulls, are usually considered dangerous and miscalled 'rogues'. Some of them are belligerent towards men; some are not.

It is not unusual to find two, or sometimes three, 'lone bulls' going about in close company – no doubt these are bulls from a herd staying, for the time being (which may be for 3 or 4 weeks, or a lesser period) away from the herd. In such associations the younger or smaller bull often displays a noticeably subordinate position to the big bull, and is termed his 'chela'. The most expressively overt act of such subordination is the offering of a choice twig or a sheaf of foliage by the chela to the big bull".

The status of solitary or 'lone' bulls has been further clarified by R.C. Morris (62) (67) who writes:

"Sanderson in his 'Thirteen Years Among Wild Beasts of India', excellent book though it is, makes several mistakes. In regard to elephants he commits two errors which are remarkable in view of the fact that Mr. Sanderson's knowledge about elephants, and his experience in the capture and shikar of Indian elephants has, I suppose been unequalled. He states in his book that 'a really solitary elephant is rarely to be met with. I am certain this is not the case. My experience is that solitary elephants seldom rejoin herds. A solitary tusker will certainly graze with any herd that may happen to be in the same jungle for the time being; but will generally stay behind when the herd moves on to new grazing grounds. I believe that when it becomes 'musth', a solitary elephant will seek a herd, but directly this sexual state in the elephant has passed off, it will return to its solitary life. The elephants on the Baragurs in North Coimbatore are certainly nearly all solitaries, and I do not suppose that there are ever more than three small herds for the whole length and breadth of that range. A single tusker (rogue) which I shot in March 1928 on the Billigirirangans had been known to be in the same jungle for at least 20 years, leading a solitary existence. I saw him there myself in 1913 or 1914 and, when I shot him in 1928, he was in approximately the same place! Solitary elephants are in my opinion not the leaders of nearby herds as supposed by Sanderson. I agree with Sanderson that it is highly improbable that any male elephant is driven from its herd, and I have always expressed this view in regard to both Bison and Elephant. I feel sure that in both cases the bull arrives at an age when it prefers to live a solitary life."

6.2 Combat between Bulls

Fights between bulls are related to dominance and most often a trial of strength leads to the loser fleeing the scene with sometimes the victor chasing and biting off a portion of the losers' tail. There are several instances on record however of a fight continued on and off for several days leading to the death of one of the combatants. The victor may not escape unscathed, and the wounds may cause him to become a 'rogue' and to be proscribed.

M. Krishnan (20) examines the causes which could lead to fights between bulls. He writes:

"Fights between adult bulls may be to the death, though much more commonly they are only skirmishes. Usually such major fights are between solitary bulls (whether or not one or both of them are true lone bulls) and may be sustained over a period of days, with breaks for feeding and drinking. Obviously sexual rivalry is not the cause of action (to borrow a convenient legal term) and the fight is not for the favours of a cow – such fights, too, are known, as already reported. It is not always that two bulls in the same area engage in such combats; even where a measure of hostility is apparent between the two, one may avoid the fight. Considering the fact that elephants are much given to wandering over a wide area (though solitary bulls are less given the habit), and the further fact that several parties, herds and individuals usually feed in the same area without disputing the territory, such fights do not appear to be motivated by territorial rights – at times, though, they appear to be so motivated. Probably they are fights in assertion of dominance, when the paths of two big bulls happen to cross—human analogies are not far to seek".

W.S. Thom (18) writes of an unusual find in the Arakan jungles, the reconstruction he made of what had happened in one instance, and the confirmation he had from a Chin tribal couple who had witnessed the gigantic combat. Thom writes:

"Some years ago, under rather peculiar circumstances, I found the remains of two wild tusker elephants both of which had met their deaths in fights with other tuskers. In the first case, I was fishing for mahseer in the Lemro river of Arakan in the unadministered territory of the Arakan Hill Tracts, Burma. Noticing a stale odour emanating from a neighbouring thicket some 300 yards or so away, I asked one of the two Chin boatmen who were with me to go and see what had died, as he might perhaps find that a sambar or a bison had been killed by a tiger, in which case there would surely be the head and horns. The boatman, however, declined to go, saying he was afraid of meeting a leopard or a tiger so, putting my rod down and picking up a magazine .355 Manlicher Schoenaur rifle that I always carried on these occasions in case of meeting barking deer and pig, I walked off towards the thicket, nosing up the smell as I moved along, the wind being right. After travelling about 600 yards or so I found the remains of a tusker elephant in an open glade with thick jungle all round. A tusk was still sticking in its socket in the skull whilst the other tusk was lying on the ground beside it. The ribs and bones of the animal were lying scattered about in the vicinity in all directions and the tree trunks close by were marked with the claw marks of tigers and leopards that had cleaned their claws there after regaling themselves night after night on the flesh. The skull and all the bones were bare of flesh of course, for the animal had been dead at least six or eight months. It seemed marvellous to me that the tusks of the dead animal had not been taken by some of the wild Chin tribesmen, but I learned that they were afraid to go into the clearing where the remains of the dead animal lay, as a really bad type of 'Nat' or spirit of the woods resided there. I tried to picture to myself how the animal had come by its end, and was told finally on my return to camp that evening that the Chins from a neighbouring village had heard two elephants trumpeting and roaring in the jungle about a mile or so above the spot where I had found the remains. The animal to whom the remains belonged had probably been vanquished in the fight by being gored to death by the other tusker, then, mortally wounded, had come into the thicket to die, as it was a quiet locality and near water. In the second case, I was out after bison (gaur) and rhinoceros along the banks of a certain stream in Arakan, when my attention was attracted by a strong odour of decaying meat, more pronounced than in the case of the last dead animal found by me. It took me about ten minutes to reach the spot from whence the stench emanated and, then I turned a bend in the stream, I was thunderstruck at seeing a magnificent dead tusker elephant in a kneeling position in the gravel bed of the river, with its head up clear of the ground, and a magnificent pair of tusks protruding straight out of its mouth. A number of jungle fowl, cocks principally, some eight or ten birds in all, were running about backwards and forwards over the body eating the maggots that crawled about on it. The smell was pretty overpowering, but being accustomed to that sort of thing from a long sojourn in the jungle, my stomach did not fail me. I went up and examined the animal thoroughly and noticed that it must have been killed by another tusker in a fight, as there were several deep stab wounds on either side of its neck and body, which had evidently been inflicted by the tusks of another elephant. Unfortunately my camera was in camp some miles off, and it was not till my men had extracted the tusks of the dead animal, which weighed 84 lbs. the pair, that it turned up, and I was able to get two or three photographs of the dead elephant. It was while I was superintending the extraction of the tusks that I found, purely by accident, the remains of another broken off tusk, 27 inches in length, weighing 18 lbs., deeply embedded in the skull of the carcass and sticking out from under the palate. The broken-off tusk had passed through the skull into the brain. Judging from the faint black circle round the tusk near the spot where it had snapped off short, it was apparent that it had broken off at the lips of the animal which won the fight. It was a unique discovery for I do not suppose such a find has ever been recorded before. The bushes and gravel in the vicinity, I then noticed, had been trampled upon, torn and scattered about in all directions. A portion of the hind quarters of the dead elephant had been eaten by a bear whose foot impressions showed up clearly in the soft wet sand by the side of the stream. Quite recently, I heard the story of the fight which had taken place between the two animals, and recorded it in detail. It seems that a Chin from a neighbouring village some four or five miles away had come down with his wife to the stream to fish, and had caught sight of the elephant which was subsequently killed, drinking at the stream at about 5 p.m. He and his wife, on seeing this, immediately ascended a tree for safety, being in a mortal funk, as the elephants in that locality were given to chasing and killing people. Some five or ten minutes after this another tusker elephant with shorter and straighter tusks came out of the jungle some sixty yards or so to the rear of the animal which was drinking. The latter immediately spun round and with lowered head faced his opponent, who, uttering a shrill trumpet, rushed forward in full charge, the two meeting head on with a terrific crash. Both animals then engaged each other with their trunks holding up their heads, and maneouvering for position. The younger animal then disengaged himself and backed for a distance of about twenty yards. The elephant that was vanquished subsequently then also started to wheel round as if to clear out, for he was at least fifty years older than his opponent, when the other elephant put on a spurt and, rushing forward, delivered a succession of deadly stabs into both sides of the neck of the older animal. Just at this time, some five or six female elephants accompanied by one or two calves appeared on the scene from

Family party - Nagarhole National Park

Cow and calf scenting us.   M Krishnan

M Krishnan

Tusker covered with mud, near Yerekatte.

Herd at Nagarhole National Park

AJT Johnsingh

M Krishnan

The Koomeriah in Kollakumalikatte. Note outwardly directed spout from the trunk and the ridge of water thrown up by the downward slap with the tusks.

Tusker demonstrating by goring a bamboo clump.

M Krishnan

Tusker in Bandipur National Park

Vivek R Sinha

the jungle, but kept at a respectable distance, squeaking occasionally as if in fear. The older elephant, whose tusks were blunter and more curved and in consequence not at all suitable for stabbing purposes was placed at a considerable disadvantage. The younger tusker, whose tusks must have weighed about 50 or 60 lbs. the pair, but were straighter and more pointed, simply made circles round his less active and older opponent.

It appears that the younger animal then met its opponent head–on in a final charge from in front and embedded (up to the lip), its right tusk in the skull of the older animal. When they parted company it was seen that the younger animal was minus his right tusk. The old tusker, standing stock–still for a few seconds, suddenly threw up its trunk in the air and gradually subsided on to its knees, in the same position as a tame elephant about to take up his mahout on its back. What would I not have given to have been there with a cine camera to witness this battle of the giants? I have been told by the Burmans that so long as the broken–off tusk, the 'Manswe', remains in my possession no harm can ever befall me, and that I shall always have the best of luck. I have had numerous requests from Burmans and Shans to sell them the 'Manswe' outright, if I will not give them a chip of it but, as I have always pointed out to those making the requests that, according to their own beliefs, it would be wrong of me to do so as it would bring me bad luck. So there it lies, still intact, in the hall of my house beside the tusks of the victim whose spirit doubtless roams the Elysian fields or the forests of Valhalla.

The literal translation of 'Manswe' in Burmese is, I suppose, 'Man' which means temper and 'swe' which means the tusk, or in other words 'The tusk that in a temper did the damage'."

C.R. Stonor (68) writes of witnessing preliminary skirmishes between two tuskers. He writes:

"Going out late in the afternoon after wild pig, I heard much crashing and rampaging in the undergrowth, not far from the forest track. I approached with my shikari as near as I dared; almost at once a big tusker reared up on his hind legs above the bamboo, and lunged forwards – followed by a crash as another bull, at which it was evidently aiming, lumbered off out of sight. The first bull did not follow it, but remained still, and the incident seemed over.

An hour later I was returning along the same path, and came on him moving about in much the same area as before; I sat down to watch, and suddenly this bull, up to now comparatively quiet, broke cover, and came past at full gallop, back arched and all his 'hackles' up – a gigantic and terrifying spectacle – to hurl himself into the thicket where the second animal had disappeared some time before. Nothing further transpired, as the other had evidently moved further on.

It was getting late, and I was unable to stop longer; but some way further down the path, I came on the second beast who had slipped away well to one side, and was standing motionless amongst the undergrowth.

The Kadar tribesmen of these hills and the forest guards inform me that running fights between bull elephants are quite frequent; they maintain that it is the general rule for a tusker sooner or later to develop a feud against another. These feuds are said to be kept up intermittently over months or even years, and with ever–growing intensity, until the climax is reached in a battle royal, lasting several days, and invariably ending in the death of one or even both combatants. The final stages are said to be extremely noisy, and the tribesmen follow at a safe distance to wait for the ivory of the vanquished.

I was told that such fights are particularly common during the two or three months immediately preceding the rains."

A.P. Mathew (69) gives the reconstruction of a fight between two wild bull elephants. He writes :

"While camping at Karupanthode (Reserve forests, Central Travancore) news was brought to us by the hill–men (Kuravas) that some ten miles away, in the interior of the reserve, there had been a furious fight between two tuskers, where one was killed. In an instant we were ready and ran to the spot. As we approached within a mile of the place where the dead elephant lay, signs of the death struggle between these monsters of the forest were evident. The shrubs and the bamboo clusters were all trodden down flat on the ground and splintered. A little further on there was evidence of a severe struggle. The ground was still moist and the earth was powdered to clay and mire. As we proceeded we came across three or four more of such arenas that bore the marks of a severe struggle. It would seem that in the affray, one was losing and was attempting to escape, but the other was following closely; hard struggles ensued, and these places marked the scenes of such engagements.

The last arena was really dreadful. There was evidence to show that the vanquished had been brought low to the ground and had been actually dragged a considerable distance along the mud. The victor does not seem to have relented; it is quite likely that it was at this time that he pierced the body of his antagonist with his tusks in a number of places – scattered all over the body. This was on a slight precipice and below a little brook, went merrily babbling along amongst the stones and pebbles, one of the tributaries of the river Achankovil. Into this stream the disabled body of the vanquished monster was hurled probably by his bitter antagonist. There he lay, as we saw him, an awful spectacle, his body partly washed by the swift–flowing current, partly resting on the banks of the stream. The body was covered by no less than 50 tusk thrusts – all huge gaping wounds that made one think of an old torn–up pin–cushion! One of these cruel thrusts piercing a side of the abdomen, brought out a few coils of the small intestine safely held together in its mesenteric fold.

Examining the wounds, we were struck to find that there were a few marks that were evidently quite recent. The hill–men as-sured us that these fresh wounds were made by the original antagonist and victor, who, his bitterness not in the least appeased by the death of his enemy, was still paying visits every night to the dead body, and venting his malice by piercing the corpse again and again. Their version probably has a bit of coloring, for they also told us that these nightly visits would continue till the body is all decomposed, and the skeleton alone lies bleached in the sun and wind, when the victor would scatter the bones about and trample on them – the last act of triumph, the closing scene in the story of a long–cherished hatred and bitterness, a vengeance that ceases not till the last trace of the foe is wiped off the face of the earth!"

The final episode in duels between bull elephants is related by H.F. Mooney (76):

"The following incident which resulted in the death of two wild elephants took place in the Feudal State of Athmallik, which borders on the Mahanadi River in Orissa. The story was related to me by a local official, and I visited the scene of the struggle about four months after its occurrence. The State contains some extensive tracts of forest watered by perennial streams which afford a sanctuary to wild elephants throughout the year.

During the month of February 1924 news reached the head-quarters of the State that two bull elephants had been fighting, and that one had been killed. This news was received four days after the actual combat took place, and on further investigation the body of one elephant was found while the second was discovered in the jungle close by, badly wounded. The survivor was successfully captured by means of trained elephants and was kept tied up in the vicinity for a few days, but when an attempt was made to take him out of the forest he succumbed to his injuries.

Unfortunately, four months elapsed between the above occurrence and my visit to the scene so that, although I saw what remained, it was impossible to detect any of the injuries from which the elephants died. Both were single tusker bulls, the tusks weighting 45 1/4 and 44.5 lbs. respectively.

I relate the above episode as I should imagine that it rarely that one of these combats ends in a double fatality, although many must be severely injured during such encounters".

6.3 Rogue elephants

Rogue elephants are more or less invariably the creation of man. Normally a bull's deadly reaction to man is caused by man's action against him when, as pointed out by R.C. Morris in the editorial note to (66) and L.L. Reade (64). There could be other reasons also, as pointed out by S.K. Ghosh (66) and K. Rajagopal (103).

S.K. Ghosh (66) offers the opinion that diseased tusk sockets are a cause for elephants turning into rogues. He writes:

"I wonder if any of your members has any information as to the real reason for elephants turning 'rogue'. The usual theory is that some old and cantankerous elephant is turned out of the herd specially during the 'musth' or rutting period, by a more powerful male, and this old and ill-tempered fellow gradually becomes a confirmed 'solitary', and in time becomes dangerous to human life and property. My experience in the Chittagong Hill Tracts (on the borders of Bengal, Bihar and Assam) leads me to question this for, on at least three occasions, I was attacked by well-known 'rogues' which after being shot turned out, in spite of their commanding size, to be quite young fellows, with no sign of wounds or injuries likely to cause them pain or discomfort, which might sour them in temper. One fellow who very nearly got me, was quite small, standing barely seven feet at the shoulder, and must have been only a young lad, yet he had been by himself for months in the plains during the rains, when all herds were away among the higher ranges. Every rogue I shot myself, and every other which was shot by others, and which I had the chance to examine, had undoubted need of a dentist for, at the root of the tusks of each one of these animals, I found pounds and pounds of live maggots, which must have caused them excruciating agony. I am inclined to think that it is the tusk disease which makes them, young and old, so bad-tempered, and forces the others to kick them out of the herd. Whenever tracking a 'rogue' or 'solitary' (undeclared rogue). I have noticed that the animal frequently thrusts his tusks through anthills, or soft saplings, and as I have never seen the marks of tusks thrust through in this manner when a herd has passed, nor have I seen our tame elephants doing this, I feel that I am not far wrong in holding that they do this in order to relieve the agony caused by the maggots far inside their jaws. During my stay in that area, I tracked and followed up herds and solitaries – literally by the hundred, so my observations were not quite casual, and were spread over a period of nearly four years. I hope this may bring some light on the matter."

Mr. R.C. Morris comments on Mr. Ghosh's letter as follows :-

'While agreeing with Mr. Ghosh that in many cases tusk disease is the cause of elephants turning into rogues, this is by no means the cause in all cases. Most of the elephants I have shot or helped to shoot in fact had no apparent disease in the tusks. Marginal gum disease of elephants is very common, occurring in the case of both wild and tame elephants, probably due to food packing under the gum, but this would not account for elephants turning into rogues. Frequently inflammation from old and fly–blown wounds may be the cause (the last rogue I shot had had its tail bitten off and the stump was diseased). Again, in some cases there is no apparent reason for the elephant having become a rogue. In two cases this was undoubtedly due to the elephants' tusks being crossed, resulting in difficulty in feeding. In only two cases was I sure that the elephants' ill temper was due to tusk disease. That elephants with tusk disease do thrust the diseased tusk into ant–hills and young trees is correct. A broken end of a tusk, about a foot long, was brought to me some years ago, the Sholaga had found it wedged firmly into a tree, and Sir Frank Colyer, to whom I sent the tusk, expressed the opinion that the elephant had been suffering from toothache.

Seven or eight rogue elephants have been shot in the Madeswaranmalai Reserve in this district in the past ten years. One of these was definitely handicapped, having tusks crossed too close to its jaw so that the elephant must have experienced considerable difficulty in feeding itself, but the others were healthy animals, and I put their ill–temper down to the fact that their favourite grazing grounds bordered a much–frequented pilgrim path up to the famous Madeswaranmalai temple. Nearly every day, devotees journeying up and down this path created a good deal of noise, especially once a week, and I think that this continual row used to irritate solitary elephants frequenting the bamboo jungle there. In every case the elephant was proscribed owing to its adopting an aggressive attitude towards pilgrims on this path. I am convinced that one of the chief causes of elephants turning into rogues nowadays is ryots firing at elephants raiding their fields. The herds are nearly always led by a bull. The ryots, who now nearly all have guns, cannot be blamed for their action in this respect, and it is up to the Government to create a Game Department, which will take measures to prevent the continuous raids that are now carried on in fields during harvest time by the increasing number of elephants'."

K.K. Rajagopal (103) reports on a strange find in an elephant's tusk socket, and suggests that this may have been the result of losing a tusk in a fight with another bull. The consequent continuous pain turned it into a rogue. He writes :

"On 8.8.65 in the Bolampatti Reserve Forest of Coimbatore district, I shot a declared rogue elephant which had trampled seven people to death and had established a reign of terror in the locality.

It had only the right tusk, the left tusk being completely missing. In the process of removing the right tusk, we also opened the socket of the left tusk. Stuck in the socket we found three arrowhead shaped bamboo pieces of about 3 inches each. From about 9 inches from the open end of the socket, we extracted a slightly curved piece of wood, about a foot long and 2 inches in girth. Further inside, reaching almost to the root of the socket, were pieces of wood decayed into a soft pulp and dark in colour.

There was a large quantity of pus in the socket. There was no trace of the missing tusk, except for a thin layer of ivory attached to the skull bones.

Obviously the animal was suffering from acute pain and irritation. A probable explanation for the presence of the wood debris in the socket is that to relieve the pain the animal rubbed its head against tree and bamboo stumps or trunks. Probably the pain and irritation eventually turned him into a rogue.

I also give the story told by the local forest staff and hill tribes. According to them, about two years ago they heard a terrific noise, and found two tuskers engaged in combat. The fight raged for three days and nights, followed by silence on the fourth day. When the hill tribes explored the trampled forest and teak plantation they came upon a dead tusker, obviously killed by the other elephant. They claim that this rogue elephant was the victor. Interesting as the tale is, apart from the missing tusk, there was no wound or scar to confirm the story.

We found a number of old gunshot wounds in various stages of healing and one or two in a putrefied condition.

Among other identification marks was a deformed left rear leg. All we could find was that this leg was longer than the other. The bones, however, showed no defect when the legs were removed for mounting."

Writing on rogue elephants in the Khasi Hills, L.L. Reade (64) states:

"In the Khasi and Jaintia Hills, there are always one or two solitary 'rogue' elephants, and not long ago in the Jirang State there were several of them. The local cultivators suffered heavily from the unwelcome and repeated visits of these animals. About the close of last year two such dangerous 'rogues' were proclaimed, and one of them was shot by me. This animal had lost its tail with the exception of a short stump left to indicate its position. On its left side alone, as it lay dead, I counted some seventeen partially healed–up wounds, which swelled out about 1.5" to 2" from the body. On opening out a few of them a thick and sticky matter came out. These were no doubt marks left on him of shots dealt by the cultivators during his visits to their cultivations. On the inner side of its right foreleg, there was a big abscess about a foot in diameter with plenty of maggots in it. It is not understood as to how it was wounded, though undoubtedly that was the one which nettled its temper most.

The animal, during some months previous to its death, had become a perfect terror to the neighbourhood, chasing people, robbing paddy from the fields and barns in the Umsaw and other adjacent villages and, on the evening previous to its death, went close to the village of Mawlein where it attacked a 'Khutiwalla's' shed, drove out buffaloes and their keepers, and killed one calf by goring it with its tusk. The rogue had a good drink of the whey in a wooden barrel, and upset the barrel when it no longer wanted it. Then it went to have a taste of the ghee in kerosene oil tins but, finding it not to its liking, knocked down the tins and their contents and, before leaving the place, pulled down the shed and trampled on it.

On the following day, I tracked this animal from the last scene of his depredations, and within a mile of the forest suddenly heard the shrill alarm raised by it. By the time I knew whence the sound proceeded, the big rogue was advancing towards me with the speed of a locomotive engine. Knowing that elephants, though they have a very keen sense of hearing and smell, have poor eyesight, I stood still (my guides had already deserted me) until the animal was only about 30 yards or so from me, then I moved towards its right side, about ten yards from its direct line of advance. The animal stopped for a moment when it reached the spot where he scented or knew that I was, and during that short interval I put in one temple shot which brought him right down, and there ended the career of one of the troublesome rogues in that locality."

6.4 Mother, Calf and Aunty

In a species noted for its matriachal system of social organisation, the care and devotion given to its young is exemplary. Apart from the mother, another member of the clan, the "aunty", assists the mother in looking after the calf. As Morris (97) reports :

"The Malayan idea that the 'pengasoh' (foster–mother) is the more aggressive when both female elephants are with the calf may not be far wrong. Some years ago I was out in the Minchiguli Valley of North Coimbatore with a friend, and we came up on a herd of elephants – separated from which were 2 cow elephants and a small calf. While we were watching the calf's antics with its mother, the wind suddenly changed, betraying our presence. The mother elephant shuffled off with the calf between its legs, while the other cow swung round and made a determined charge at us. We had to run for it!"

M. Krishnan (20) gives details of the relationship within the clan. He says :

"In a gregarious animal that is unusually exclusive in its associations the relationship between adults in a herd, and the infants and juveniles, assumes special importance. G.P. Sanderson provides a succinct and excellent account of the extraordinary consideration for the young animals in a herd shown by the adults, but on one point he seems mistaken. He concludes that cow elephants display no special solicitude or attachment to their calves, permitting men to handle their new-born young, and that from what he has noticed during the capture of elephants in stockades, the young calves of a cow are often violently repulsed by the other cows in the herd. Tamed elephants, used to having their needs, and directions, provided by men, might not show any apprehension at their infants being touched by men; my experience is that the most dangerous and aggressive of all elephants is the mother elephant (or even the 'aunt') apprehensive for the welfare of her calf; a remarkable instance of this was provided by two small cows, with a calf about a year or two old (the calf of one of them) between them, which came baldheaded for the riding elephant (a tusker much bigger than each of them) on which I was seated along with another companion and the mahout, because the tusker had moved inadvertantly close to the calf. While it is true that cows in a herd do repulse the calves of other cows on occasion, it is patently incorrect to assume that the behaviour of any animal when it is confused and panic–stricken and cannot escape is its normal behaviour; as several observers have pointed out (especially Williams, to whom we owe the word 'aunt') not only are cow elephants very patient with their own calves, but quite often they develop an attachment and a protective feeling towards the calves of other cows to whom they are specially attached. The camp elephant, Rati, at the Mudumalai Sanctuary, is known for her attachment to all young calves born in the camp. Occasionally both the mother of a calf or another cow may kick or push the youngster when it is being recalcitrant, but this is always intentional, and in few animals are the young in a gregarious association treated so gently and solicitously as in elephants.

It is well–known that in a herd certain adult cows develop a deep attachment (which can only be termed 'friendship') to certain other cows. Bulls, too, keep together when foraging apart from the herd, and it is a common sight to observe two or three 'lone bulls' together. This attachment of one cow for another has been observed both in the wild and among tame elephants. Indeed, so well is this recognised that in elephant camps they are not separated from each other even when put to work (as when used for timber logging), not out of any sentimental motives but because otherwise the work suffers. The camp elephant, Rati, (a fine upstanding cow in her prime) could not be used as a riding elephant at the Mudumalai Sanctuary, unless the aged Sundari was taken along with her. Among wild elephants, the tendency of certain members of the herd to group together when the herd splits into parties for foraging may be noticed."

6.4.1 Protection of the calf

Protective behaviour of members of the clan has been independently recorded twice at Periyar Wildlife Sanctuary, K.V. Laxminarayan (52) writes:

"Our party proceeded to Periyar headwater works. On the way, we noticed 23 wild elephants (all cows) feeding on the grass on an isolated hillock. One of us started taking a movie from our boat, when we were still some distance from the shore. Probably disturbed by the sound of the motor boat and of the movie camera, one of the elephants gave a loud trumpet call. Immediately, another batch of 14 elephants, which included one old tusker, two smaller tuskers, and five calves, came running. This new batch obviously belonged to the same herd, since they mingled freely with the old batch. Three of them, including the one which trumpeted, stood facing the boat. Four cows formed a square behind them, each animal pointing in a different direction, and two calves were driven into the square. A similar square was formed for the other three calves. Both the squares were closely packed. This phenomenon is obviously a curious protective device for the young."

In the second report K.K. Neelakantan (53) states:

"Our boat approached a small herd of elephants which was on a wooded slope close to the water. It consisted of five adults and four young ones. The calves were nicely graded in size, the smallest being a hairy creature not much larger than a buffalo calf. A slightly larger calf also had plenty of hair on its body.

When first seen the animals were feeding on the grass and occasionally flinging earth over their backs. As they formed a nice group and were very close to us. I tried to take a photograph. Within the short time spent in borrowing the camera and examining its 'settings' the elephants deliberately arranged themselves in such a fashion that I could see nothing but the hindquarters of two adults. All the adult elephants had turned away from us and grouped themselves in such a way, that the four calves were hedged in among them so thoroughly, that we could see nothing at all of the calves!

When the boat started again and moved on, the elephants quietly broke up their 'formation, and began moving away from the water.

Though it was quite clear that the larger animals had bunched up in order to encircle the calves, no animal trumpeted or showed any signs of excitement or fear.

It should also be stated that we came across larger herds with a good sprinkling of very young calves, but these herds did not react perceptibly to the sound or the proximity of the boats."

6.4.2 Seeking assistance

The following incident related by Frank Nicholls (60) poignantly brings out the value of the assistance given by the members of a clan to the mother and calf. Nicholls states:

"In April last, coming down the bed of the Bargang river one evening on my male elephant, we crossed a very recent track of a single elephant with her small calf followed by a large tiger. The tracks were so fresh (water was still discoloured in the footprints) that we expected to hear of some domestic trouble very soon. We had not long to wait, for all of a sudden there was tremendous loud trumpeting, with intermittent screams coming from the forest and about 200 yards in. We immediately made for that direction, but as we got nearer to where the sound was coming from, we came into terribly thick cane, with the usual 3 inch thorns, so we had to cut our way through, foot by foot, which delayed us considerably.

All of a sudden a mother elephant appeared holding up her front foot, which was bleeding, and placed her trunk on my elephant's trunk, as much as to say, 'Do come and see what awful trouble I am in!' She turned and led the way, we followed, and approximately 10 yards off, we came on to her calf which was about 3'6" high, standing with its head completely scalped, and holding up its front foot, which was turning round on a piece of skin – its foot, all but severed. With its little trunk about a foot or so long, it kept feeling its terrible head wounds.

We kept moving around slowly, trying to obtain a view of the tiger for fully half an hour, but due to the necessity of continual cutting, we never saw it, although we could see its footprints and smell it.

Whilst we were hunting for the tiger she stood by her calf, never leaving it, after having led us to it. We also stayed alongside the calf for full 5 minutes, while she herself was holding up her bleeding foot.

It was getting dark, and we had very reluctantly to leave that sad scene, and I with a lump in my throat. I have been asked by people why I did not shoot the baby, and put it out of its misery. To me, and to all people who have been associated with elephants, it would have been sheer murder, and mother elephant would never have forgiven me. The baby must have died shortly afterwards".

6.5 Demonstration and Charge

The reaction of elephants to disturbance by man and his close approach has been described by M. Krishnan (20). He writes :

"Once, when I was following a herd along with some trackers, we were halted by a singularly burly and powerful tusker which stayed behind, while the rest of the herd moved into thick tree cover, and staged a most impressive demonstration, pushing over a stout sapling and then kicking it between his legs, later, when we halted, he moved off in the wake of the herd. Frequently such demonstrations, to intimidate and halt men, take the form of pushing over trees or goring small clumps of bamboo or bushes. A cow may demonstrate displeasure to a man following her, by turning round and rushing towards the intruder in a short formal charge. Sometimes an elephant, resenting the presence of a man, may graze gradually towards him at a tangent, and then turn in sharply for a charge when near enough".

6.6 Tame and wild elephants

The reaction of tame elephants to their wild brethren depends on their training, and on the purpose for which they are being used. F.W. Champion (8) writes: that the wild elephants he had photographed in the U.P. forests were all photographed with a reflex camera from the back of a staunch tame female Forest Department elephant which did not exhibit the fear of wild elephants usual among tame elephants. Indeed, many tame elephants cannot be induced or driven to approach anywhere near one of their wild cousins, and the mahawats are often even more afraid. It is somewhat difficult to understand why tame elephants and mahawats should be so afraid of wild elephants, which are normally not dangerous, and which have allowed me to approach within a few yards on numerous occasions without any damage resulting therefrom. True, we were once charged viciously by a 'masth' bull in a herd, and on this occasion we were saved from a bad accident only by firing two barrels from a shotgun over his head, thereby causing him to swerve and rush past us at two or three yards' range. This was an exception as the 'masth' discharge was clearly visible at some distance, and we were simply asking for trouble in attempting to photograph this particular beast. The usual semi–solitary bull will either bolt the moment one attempts to approach him on a tame elephant, or else he will stand and watch one's approach with deep interest. Indeed, he will sometimes advance towards one as one is taking photographs, and such was the case with the old tusker who approached so close that his whole body could not come within the field of my camera. It is somewhat nervous work taking photographs of a wild elephant – who after all is never fully to be trusted – approaching one in this way, but if one's mahawat fires a shotgun over his head whenever he comes uncomfortably close, in most cases he will retreat, or, at least, not advance any further, so that such photography provides one with a good deal of excitement without being unduly dangerous.:

6.7 Intelligence

C.W.A. Bruce (19) giving his views on the intelligence of elephants writes:

"During ten years' residence in Burma I had many opportunities of closely observing elephants; both in a tame and wild state. During that period I had from two to ten elephants under my immediate charge. For six years I was in charge of the forests in one district, where there were over 500 tame elephants belonging to a single timber trading firm, besides numerous herds of wild animals, which I made it my business to observe whenever I could spare the time. I was then transferred to a district where the same firm (the Bombay–Burma Timber Trading Corporation Ltd.) had over 600 animals at work in the forests under my charge, there being also two small herds of wild ones, the whereabouts of which (the district being a fairly well populated one) were always known. It can be seen that I have had exceptional chances of learning a little of their habits, both in a state of semi domestication as well as in a feral state. My observations, if not of value, may be at least of interest. I put them forward with some diffidence, as I have come to conclusions directly opposed to those formed by such famous authorities as the late Mr. G.P. Sanderson and Mr. W.T. Blanford, F.R.S.

Now both these gentlemen make little of the intelligence of the elephant. I have kept a great number of pets, ranging from porcupines up to hooluks (*Hylobates hoolock*), and, with the exception of the latter, I do not think I have ever been so struck with the intelligence of any animal as I have with that of the elephant. I give examples, which any forest officer in Burma could, I have no doubt, confirm.

It is common to see an elephant break off a branch with its trunk, and use the bit broken to scratch some portion of the body ungetable by any other means. Again, in a long march I have often ridden on one of the baggage animals passing the time by reading a book, no portion of my body even touching the animal and, there being no mahout on the neck, the animal has steadily marched along the narrow forest track, carefully guiding itself in and out of the trees, so that no tree shall strike the baggage, and at the same time carefully pulling down and breaking low branches which might scrape me off the heaped–up pile of miscellaneous kit. Once I saw a female elephant run away. She had attached to her front leg a long tethering chain. On being called on to stop by her attendant, who ran after her and tried to grab the end of the chain trailing behind, she picked the end up with her trunk, so that she should not be hampered by stepping on it, and so that the man could not seize it, and made off into the jungle.

These few cases out of many which I could record certainly seem to me to denote great reasoning power."

The opinion of Sanderson and Blanlford is also held by others. Though an animal which has to remember several command words and act in accordance is certainly intelligent. Contrary views however, are held, and the one quoted here is by Kadambi (61) who states:

"Having been almost continuously associated with the Indian elephant (*Elephas maximus indicus*) for nearly a quarter of a century, and also having assisted in the capture and taming of a few hundred elephants in several khedda operations held at Kakankote and Budipadaga, names which are famous in this connection in India. I have to state from my experience that a high degree of intelligence cannot be claimed for the Indian elephant, at least not to the animal found in the extensive forests of the Deccan tableland. It is true that a tame Indian elephant can be taught to do some extraordinary feats requiring a high degree of skill; for example, balancing its huge body on a rolling cylinder, converging its four legs on the top of an inverted wooden tub too small to accommodate them all, picking up a minute object and handing it carefully to the trainer, and so on or a working elephant deftly directing huge logs of floating timber in between the piers of bridges spanning flooded rivers, to avoid damage to the bridges and piers, etc., but in these instances it is the intelligence of man which comes into play and makes use of the learning capacity of the animal; in other words, man utilises the animal's brawn for producing the desired results.

During each khedda drive, scores of elephants are driven into the khedda enclosure en masse, and this is done time after time in the same place and almost under identical conditions. I must say that it is the almost complete absence of reasoning power, or to put it in a crude way the stupidity displayed by most of these mighty animals, which enables man to impound them almost like sheep in the khedda stockade and subsequently noose them with ropes one by one. True, there are rare instances in which an elephant has shown a certain amount of reasoning power which we may term intelligence in the widest sense of the term, but such instances are very few and far between. They are rare exceptions, not the rule. The roping operation involves the slipping of a loose rope noose up the trunk of the elephant and on to its neck. For doing this, a score or so of elephants are first impounded in the roping–ring stockade, and they are then roped one by one, in full view of the other animals awaiting their turn to be roped. But, the animals which are looking on all the time while their companions are being noosed, learn nothing from what they see, nor do they help in freeing their distressed friend who, after the ropes are on him, is forcibly dragged out of the roping ring, bewailing his loss of freedom by heart–rending cries, and pour forth a constant stream of tears from his tiny, winking eyes. In fact, a captive which is in the act of being roped rarely, if ever, lifts its head, or attempts to push down the man roping it who remains perched, often precariously, on the back of a kumki elephant. It would have been nearly impossible for the roping squad of mahouts to enter the roping ring and carry out their dangerous task, had the wild elephants displayed the little intelligence required to use their trunk for pushing down the mahouts systematically from the backs of their kumkies. This never seems to occur to them, in ninety–nine cases out of a hundred the animals keep their heads bent and submit to the 'machinations' of the humans without any show of their enormous strength or the slightest streak of intelligence. True, they often make clumsy and ineffectual efforts to prevent the noose from being pulled up their long trunks, but this is done more out of animal instinct than from the consciousness that the rope is axing their freedom.

The fact that in their wild state no two elephant behave exactly alike when they see a hunter shows the meagreness of their reasoning power; one may bolt on seeing the hunter, the next may charge him. The first animal runs away from danger while the second turns to bay; this is a universal action common to all animals and not confined only to the elephant.

The elephant recognises its mahout by smell, since the animal's winding (smelling) power is better developed than its sense of hearing or sight. This is true not only of the elephant but also of most domesticated animals.

The sense of comradeship is generally well developed in the case of all those animals which associate in herds. A distressed comrade is not normally abandoned to its fate by such animals. For example, on several occasions I have seen a bull bison (gaur) in a herd shot and brought down to the ground, when some of his companions have stood around their fallen comrade and attempted to lift him to his feet. They have had to be scared away by shots.

Animals are generally unable to assess the gravity of personal danger; it is more on account of this than through any sense of personal heroism that they return to free a comrade in distress. It is the human being that assesses the degree of danger to which the animals have been exposed, and attributes a sense of heroism to them in his own measure. A sneaking hunter who worms his way through the forest undergrowth is never noticed by an elephant unless he is caught up–wind, when his smell gives him away, or unless he appears in full view of the animal at close range, in which case the animal either runs away from him or charges him outright.

As for the ability of the elephant to fashion steps against obstructing mud banks with the help of their fore feet and tusks, this is more the outcome of accumulated experience resulting from repeated efforts to climb an obstacle rather than from a reasoned–out plan. The accumulated experience of generations of elephants has now probably crystallized into an instinct. Its size and strength enable an elephant to cut the steps; for the other smaller animals this would be impossible. It is known, however, that while descending steep paths the elephant always keeps to the beaten track and never diverts from it even if there be an easier one within a stone's throw; this displays absolute want of reasoning power. I know of many an attempted 'river drive' at Kakankote (Mysore state) having failed on account of this simple fact, namely, the elephant's refusal to budge from its accustomed route, even if there be another in its neighbourhood which is a much easier and shorter one.

Most quadrupeds are excellent swimmers and the elephant can swim too. A new–born elephant, like most other new–born quadrupeds, cannot swim and has to be carried across deep water by the mother.

A full–grown elephant generally avoids falling into game pits not because of the reasoning power of intelligence, but more on account of the fact that it has the habit of constantly feeling with its trunk the ground on which it is about to tread. The trunk of the elephant can be compared to the stick of a blind person. At night, especially, the elephant with its weak power of sight has to depend more on feel and smell. The sense of touch, therefore, has been well developed. It is the calves that usually drop into the pits, but not infrequently half–grown animals, and occasionally even full–grown tuskers, drop in and are roped. Instances of attempts to rescue a fallen animal are by no means uncommon, but it is mostly the mothers or the foster mothers of the entrapped calves that return to rescue their young ones and even these are often easily scared away by firing a couple of blank shots. The mother returns to the rescue of her young one out of maternal instinct, rather than through any feeling of comradeship.

I must say that Indian elephants are mostly untrained engineers; elephant paths frequently go up and down hill ridges, often missing the saddles in the neighbourhood. Quite often they make gradients of 45 degrees which could have been easily avoided by skirting a small neighbouring hillock; but the animals always follow a beaten path – a path, whether good or bad, which has been worn smooth from use, but laid out for them from the accumulated experience and wisdom of generations of their roving forefathers. An elephant hitched to a timber log generally seeks the easiest gradient possible, but in this it is guided by the resistance offered by the log and not by the reasoning power of the animal. If, for example, the log is held up by any obstruction along the drag path, the elephant merely uses its brute force to overcome it, often snapping its drag–chain in the effort. It is never known to use its reasoning power for overcoming such obstacles, in spite of the fact that it may have done this sort of work all its life."

6.8 Reaction to Earthquake

The behaviour of elephants during earthquakes has been noted. In one instance it was running towards high ground perhaps to avoid boulders rolling down as reported by V.A. Jackson (57) who states :

"A severe shock of earthquake took place at 4–15, and lasted 3 minutes on 9th July. The Government elephants were feeding in front of the Courthouse at Tura. There was a very large mukna, a large female and a butcha tusker. As soon as the first and most severe shock took place, the elephants ran up the hill, towards the D.C's house, which is on a ridge overlooking a very deep valley. The distance from the Courthouse to the gate of the D.C's house is about 500 yards. The large mukna was first, reached the gate and tore it from its hinges, then came straight up the road with the small elephant holding on to his tail. The mahout had no control over him, and the other two elephants had no one on their backs. (My husband and I were standing outside watching the plaster coming down in the bungalow and the stone walls in the garden giving way). As soon as the elephant broke the gate, the Garos advised us to go in, as the "hatis" would pass us, and might attack us in their fright. Just as we got the verandah, the big mukna reached the front of the house. He never stopped but rushed along breaking down the 2nd gate – still with the butcha holding his tail. The female stopped in front of the porch, and proceeded to knock large lumps of turf from my lawn, making queer noises and striking her trunk, also trembling violently. The mahout clung to the trunk and quietened her down gradually. The other animals rushed up a very steep hill into the jungle and were only turned back by men with spears and sticks. If the little hati had not clung to the tail, the 'mate' on the back would have been thrown off, as the mukna is a most surly animal. Their instinct was to run up a hill into the jungle, and not along the big flat cart road. As I mentioned, the D.C's house is on a ridge with two roads leading to it. One, with the gate, is more or less a carriage road, the other skirts the garden below and is used as a public road, the elephants always use this lower road on their way to grass and water it runs along the side of the hill, and it received part of the stone wall from the garden, or large boulders, shaken down by the shock. The "hatis' seemed to realize that it might have given way and kept on the top of the hill, breaking down the gates guarding the top road, in preference to going on the open khud road.

The Garos say butchas always catch the tails of larger elephants when in a panic. These hills are full of elephants; they do much damage, and Garos are more frightened of them than tigers or bears.;

Frank Nicholls (58) reports that:

"Last March, there was quite a severe shock one morning about 6 a.m., when I was camping right inside elephant country on the bank of a river. My own elephant, a tusker, was just approaching for me to mount, when he started to trumpet. I could then hear wild elephants trumpeting all round, some at a considerable distance, then came the actual 'bump'. Just prior to this, there was a distinct roar as the earthquake was approaching, it was during that period that the wild elephants and my own, were trumpeting.

I had the same experience some ten years ago in the heart of the forest, so it would appear this trumpeting is natural at the time of approach of an earthquake, or anyhow at a time of quite a severe one".

Chapter 7

BREEDING

7.1 Sexual Maturity

The age at which elephants attain sexual maturity bears a remarkable resemblance to the human age of sexual maturity. Robertson (43) gives the age of maturity of a tusker:

"In Coorg, a Forest Department tusker named Krishna came into musth when his age was believed to be only 15 years. A Madras Forest Department cow elephant, Meenakshi herself born in captivity, calved when she was only 13 years old. Meenakshi was the daughter, by a wild bull of Chik Lakshmi, who was the daughter of Lakshmi. Tradition has it that Lakshmi was a Burmese elephant transferred from the Commissariat Department. Meenakshi's son referred to above Dosti Jehan·was a muckna, and being also precocious like his mother, was a father at 20, his ·son Abdul Ali being a tusker. The last–named is now 11 years old, so before many years the Forest Department may expect the arrival of the sixth generation of this family."

A.E. Foot (44) draws attention to the breeding of a very young pair of elephants in the Munich Zoo which, unless there is some error in age calculation, seems to be abnormal.

"With reference to the time of sexual maturity of the elephant, it may be of interest to record the details of the elephant 'Wastl' born in captivity at the Muchener Tier Park on 8th May, 1932. The father, 'Boy', was nine years old and the mother 'Cora' eight years old. The elephant was conceived at the end of August 1930 and the period of pregnancy was only 20 months and 7 days; the accepted time of pregnancy of elephant is between 22 and 24 months. There is reason to suppose that the birth in this case was premature as the baby could not reach its mother's teats when it was first born, and even when he was fed from the mother in a lying position the milk was unsatisfactory, and for the first twelve days he was fed by bottle. The milk from the mother was a thin and watery fluid containing only 4 per cent of fat instead of the normal 22 per cent. The baby at birth weighed only one hundredweight instead of the usual two hundredweight. These particulars are taken from the June 1932 number of the magazine `Das Tier und Wir,' published monthly by the Munich Zoo which contains a series of extremely attractive photographs of the baby and its parents."

7.2 Calving interval

E.P. Gee (38) estimates the calving interval of a wild cow caught with its calves:

"On the night of 17th–18th February 1953 a small herd of five wild elephants was captured in the Garampani stockade, in the forest not far from Jamguri in the Sibsagar District of Assam. It consisted of an older cow elephant and four smaller female elephants of varying sizes, all of which milled around together in a family fashion. The experienced elephant catchers who were there with me all agreed that this was almost certainly a family party of a mother and her four calves, possibly successive calves. This appears to be unique in the annals of elephant catching, and the Senior Conservator of Forests, P.D. Stracey, I.F.S., confirmed later after a study of the photographs that it was almost certainly a cow and her four calves. He had himself seen a cow captured with three calves, but never with four as in this case, and his experience in this field is considerable.

Several of the spectators at the stockade were villagers from nearby villages; they recognised the herd, mainly by the deformed animal, as the very herd of five elephants which had been raiding their rice fields on the fringe of the forest.

The three youngest calves were roped in the stockade and removed to the elephant training depot. As the Director of the Regent's Park Zoo of London had just written to me asking me to obtain a baby female elephant, I immediately purchased the youngest calf, Lakshmi, which measured exactly 4'1"; this was sent by air about a month later to the London Zoo where she still is. The next calf measured 5', and the bigger one 6'2". The eldest calf was badly deformed, and was therefore released with the mother.

Now from the measurements of the calver, it was seen that Lakshmi (4'1") must have been approximately one year old when captured. The next calf at 5' must have been either three years old or even slightly less, as Parbati was 5'1" when three years old. It can safely be deduced therefore that in their wild state cow elephants can produce a second calf within two years, or even slightly less, of the first calf. In this particular case the cow must have mated again when her young calf at heel was only about three months old, presuming the gestation period was 21 months.

The largest of the three calves extracted from the stockade was 6'2", and probably seven (or eight) years old. So in this case the spacing was either four (or five) years, or else a calf may have died in the meantime

With regard to the eldest and deformed calf, it was difficult to assess her age owing to her bad condition, and estimates varied between ten and fifteen years. It is possible that she had been trampled" ......

C.R. Stoner (68) relates an amusing story of his sighting a cow with calves of different ages and speculates on the calving interval. His story is:

"March 7: I had come unexpectedly on a solitary bull, and beat a rapid retreat to a safe distance. He turned off the forest track and, after browsing a little, vanished into the forest. I was on the point of continuing, when another elephant appeared round a bend in the path this time a calf. It is naturally unheard of for a calf to be on its own, or to lead the way at any time. But very close behind it, there came into view the head and shoulders of a big cow; the two of them advanced down the path, the calf leading all the while, and both moving with extreme, exaggerated slowness. From my cover, eighty yards distant I could only wonder what so strange a reversal of normal habit might mean, until, as the line of the track brought them into side view, the mystery explained itself; for, hidden, almost invisible beneath the body of the mother was a second and minute calf, perhaps born only few hours previously. As far as I could see it suckled continuously.

The pitiable reluctance of the larger calf – a picture of sulky bewilderment – to lead the way instead of trotting safely at its mother's side was comical to watch. It tried again and again to turn back, only to be countered every time by a swing forward of its mother's head and trunk. She kept up a ceaseless rumbling–grumbling, which I took to be a warning to her larger offspring to keep its place in front. Her skill and patience in controlling simultaneously each of her two offspring was quite remarkable. She moved at a shuffling walk, infinitely slow, stopping at frequent intervals, adjusting her every movement to keep step with the faltering pace of her newly–born calf. She as successfully kept the older one at 'trunk's length' in front, goading it forwards away from its normal position, so preventing any risk of interference with its diminutive brother or sister.

After some minutes she guided the party off the track, and into a stretch of light jungle, where I did not care to follow her.

Size is notoriously difficult to estimate in the field, but the larger calf appeared to be about four and a half feet at the shoulder or rather less; local opinion put its age at about two years. I do not know at what intervals elephants are known to breed, but in this instance, allowing for the recognised gestation period of 641 days, and assuming the age of the larger calf as correctly estimated, it seems that the two calves must have followed each other in immediate succession, the mother being possibly in breeding condition very soon after the first calf was born. It is curious that the customary female helper or 'nursemaid' which is known always to assist with a calf, should have been absent, but I think it likely, especially in view of the very slow movements of the small calf, and the obvious bewilderment of the larger, that the smaller one was not more than a few hours old, and the 'helper' had not yet started on her duties.

I questioned the Kadar tribesmen and the forest guards concerning the breeding season; they stated quite definitely that they see small calves in each month of the year, and did not believe the 'Ana' to have any fixed breeding season.

The brief glimpse of courtship, the pugnacity of the bulls, and the additional fact that there were large bulls with every herd I saw, indicate February and March – the two months preceding the rains – as a time of breeding activity. On the other hand, the newly–born calf I saw must have started existence about June 1942, at the height of the rainy season."

The age of sexual maturity of the female, the number of calves born to a female, and the calving interval have been excellently described by V. Krishnamurthy (110) based on data on the birth of 210 elephant calves over a period of 104 years in the captive elephant establishment of the erstwhile Madras Presidency. According to Krishnamurthy, female elephants in captivity normally attain sexual maturity at the age of 15 ±2 years. He records reports of earlier maturity, for instance 'Nisha' an elephant of the Kerala Forest Department which delivered a calf at the age of 11 years. Another elephant which provided precise data was Meenakshi of the Madras (Tamil Nadu) establishment, born in captivity on 9th March 1889, she gave birth to her first calf when she was 13 years and 4 months old on 17.7.1902 suggesting that she was sexually mature when she was about 11 years of age. She had a reproductive life of 41 years, dropping 11 calves (5M 6F) at a mean calving interval of 4.11 years. She died at the age of 68 years in 1957. The intercalving period showed a mean of 5.07 under captive conditions, and the interval could be reduced to 2.35 years by weaning calves when they are 12 to 15 months.

The age at sexual maturity varies widely, particularly under captive conditions where nutrition seems to play a major part. It has been given as varying from 5 to 16 years by Flower (112). Schmidt and Khyni U Mar (113), on the basis of the data available on 278 calvings in the period 1991-94 in Myanmar, note that the first calving was at the age of 12 years 5 months; the age of puberty being about 10.75 years. The oldest cow to calve was 55 years of age. The prime reproductive age group was 21 to 35 years. Twin calving was one in 140 births, and the calving interval could be as low as 2 years.

7.3 Breeding in captivity and gestation

Contrary to the opinion expressed by Sanderson the elephant if given the opportunity, breeds freely in captivity, C.W.A. Bruce (19) states:

"The trouble experienced, in common with other Government forest officers and forest managers of timber firms in Burma, is to prevent the female domestic elephants from having calves. It is very inconvenient for a forest officer to find that one, or sometimes both, the baggage animals allowed him by Government are heavy with calf, and have to be put out of work for a time, whereas the loss to a timber firm of keeping a good dragging female idle for a considerable period is a serious one.

For some time I had five females and a tuskless male attached to my division as transport animals. Four of the females in one year gave birth to young; three of the calves were born at various times during one rainy season, while one was born in the middle of the following hot weather, the morning after the mother had made a long march with a heavy load of baggage. Two of the calves were males and both tuskless, corroborating the assertion of the mahouts that the tuskless male was the father. I felt quite convinced that this tame male was the father, as the females were always under my personal supervision, and I know that no wild elephant had any access to them; moreover, my experience is that tame females, as well as males, show great terror for even the propinquity of wild elephants. Of course there are exceptions to this. All these calves when I left Burma in 1900 were still alive, and on the books of the Forest Department, being then rising five years old, strong and healthy. The elephants of the Forest Department in Burma have calves continually being born, and numerous ones are on its books; some, indeed, are now at work as baggage animals. One particularly fine little tusker, twelve years old, was a special favourite of the Conservator of the Southern Circle, Upper Burma. My experience is that elephants are affectionate and careful mothers, though male full grown animals seem to object to youngsters near them. In the Salween district of Tenasserin almost every Karen village has a few female elephants, which are kept for breeding purposes. There are no wild elephants about, and elephant breeding from tame males is a well–known and lucrative source of income for the villagers, elephants being used as pack animals, and often in the rains for ploughing the paddy fields. Mr. Roberts, Manager of the Bombay–Burma Trading Company Limited, Pyinmana, kindly collected statistics of births among elephants under his charge (some 600, male and female). I regret to say that I have mislaid his most interesting statement, but it may be summarised as follows:– It is so common an occurrence as to give rise to no comment, beyond a little strong language. The calves are invariably strong and healthy, and only 3 per cent die. The cause of death can always be traced to the mother being put on to heavy work too soon after the calf is born, which tends to stop the flow of milk.

The Bombay–Burma Timber Company have many elephants now in work which were born from dragging or transport females, and their mahouts all assert the fathers are nearly always domestic elephants too. The mother cannot be worked while the calf is small, as she is frightened of damaging her child, the latter's favourite position for walking being just underneath the mother, almost between the front legs. Elephants in Burma are not kept in stables but are hobbled (either the two front legs or the two hind legs being tied together), and are then turned out to graze. Hence it is not a matter for surprise that they do breed. I regret I have no absolutely reliable data of my own to quote as to the period of gestation, but I give the following extract from an interesting letter on the subject which appeared in the *Indian Forester*, April, 1899."

"In June, 1897, one of the mahouts reported that his elephant had been covered by the tusker attached to the division whilst the animals were turned out to feed. The act was observed every evening for about a week from about May 18 to May 25,

1897. Neither of the animals had shown signs of sexual excitement previously, though the male paid assiduous court to the female for a few days before coition was permitted. They were both at work at this period, dragging logs, and gave no trouble to their attendants. The report was noted but, I am sorry to say, forgotten till Nov. 3, 1898 when, in the evening, the elephant gave birth to a female calf.

Fortunately that day she had only carried a light load for a short march. The baby, though so weak that it had to keep itself upright by holding on to a bamboo with its mouth, was perfectly healthy and well formed, and after a day could stand and suckle. The period of gestation, therefore, had been a little over seventeen calendar months, or almost exactly eighteen lunar months. – C.B.S.""

J.C.A. Wilson (105) states:

"I have kept a record extending over a number of years and put the period of gestation at 22 months. An elephant may calve after 20 months, but if she does it is due to overwork or over-marching, and the calf, if born living, will at first be weaker than a calf carried for the full period. More usually it is born dead.

My records comprise cases when I have seen the act myself and also cases when I know that a cow elephant has been covered by a bull within a period of a very few days."

7.4 Musth

It would best to start with what Evans has to say about in in his classic "Elephants and their Diseases" as given in the editorial footnote to Gordon Hundely's (37) note. Evans in his book says:

"Male elephants, and very rarely females, on attaining maturity are subject to peculiar periodical paroxysims of excitement, which seem to have some connection with the sexual functions to which the name musth' is applied by the natives of India, and `mon–kyathi' by the Burmans. It is probably analogous to the rut in deer.

Causes – It occurs both in wild and tame animals, and in the latter is more often met with in highly fed pampered beasts that receive insufficient exercise. It occurs most frequently in the cold season and may perhaps be due to ungratified sexual desire in some cases, but not always so, since the society of a female by no means always quells or even pacifies animals in musth. At other times an animal in musth undoubtedly seeks a mate of the opposite sex.

Symptoms – Musth occurs frequently in some beasts, seldom in others, so that the intervals are variable in different animals and in the same manner so are the symptoms. More or less excitement is usual, but on the other hand some elephants become dull and morose. The behaviour changes, shown by disobedience to commands, trying to break away, or showing violence to man, destructive tendencies, and being altogether out of sorts. The temples become puffy, due to the swelling of the temporal glands which lie beneath the skin, and at this stage is called by many mahouts `kherr musth'; later an oily discharge exudes from the hole or duct over the gland which is then called `musth' by the natives. When musth is established there is often a partial retention of urine, the water dribbling away. As soon, however, as the urine is passed freely the natives consider the dangerous stage over, irrespective of the amount of discharge from the glands.

The attack may last a few days, weeks or months. In some cases cowardly mahouts are said, at a certain stage of the attack, to administer some species of pumpkin which has the effect of abating the excitement. The effect of such treatment, however, is said to be very prejudicial to the health of the animal. Mr. Petley informs me that once musth is established it ought to come on every year although in no particular month, and he has known elephants in which, owing to overwork or ill–health, the usual occurrence of musth has failed, to become useless for work. The only remedy is to set them free for months until musth again comes on, after which care should be taken to see such animals are treated with extra care."

J.C.C. Wilson (105) comments:

"I differ from Mr. Hundley when he states that "musth" has little to do with the sexual instinct. Bull elephants on "musth" always become queer tempered at that time and many very dangerous both to men and to other elephants and have to be tied up and starved until "musth" abates.

If a cow in season can be provided for the bull it will tend to reduce his "musth", but he will drive away and even gore a cow which is not in season and will, therefore, not allow him to cover her.

We had a case only last April in our elephant rest camps, when a tusker, a dangerous man–killing beast even when sane – went musth and got loose without his hobbles. My two travelling elephants were fortunately close at hand and were fortunately still both in season. He covered them both repeatedly, which so reduced his "musth" that our men were able to recapture him. He was then tied up and in spite of starvation, his "musth" increased for some days, but he would have nothing to do with another cow introduced to him.

A bull going "musth" usually gives fair warning of his approaching condition, by the glands in the temples swelling some days before the discharge commences.

In the wild state, judging from cases I have known of wild tusker coming down to worry our tame herds and occasionally inducing a tame cow to elope with them, "Musth" usually comes on at the end of December or in January when vegetation is at its best, but in tame herds, which are generally worked till the end of February, "musth" does not come on until later, after the elephants have had time to pick up strength and get into good condition.

There is something medically wrong with any mature bull which does not come on "musth" at least once annually and, if looked into, the cause will be found to be ill–health, or more usually overwork which may have taken place one or even two years before. To my mind the only cure in either case is complete rest in a good grazing area for six months, a year, or even longer, though tonics may assist matters a bit.

A cow elephant in season will very often have a slight discharge from the glands between the eye and ear, similar to the discharge from a "musth" bull, but of course to a lesser extent, in fact merely a slight dampness visible when the skin of the elephant is dry".

M. Krishnan (20) comments extensively on the nature of musth, and his experiences with elephants on musth. He writes:

"The periodic occurrence of musth in adult elephants, marked by a dark, oily exudation from the temporal gland with a pore on either side (roughly midway between eye and ear) and a tender swelling of the temples and forehead, is something peculiar to elephants, and its full significance is not yet known. Little that is original in addition to what G.P. Sanderson wrote about musth a century ago is available in literature on *Elephas maximus*. Musth afflicts old elephants as well, and some animals on musth are in very poor condition – in what follows, the manifestation and consequences of musth in tame elephants have been left out of the reckoning, as so many artificially–imposed conditions supervene then that it is not safe to draw any conclusions from the behaviour of tame elephants when in that condition. Almost invariably, it is an adult bull that gets into musth, but in rare cases a cow may do so. G.P.Sanderson records two instances of cows in musth, 'in newly–caught females in the prime of life, and in very full condition'. During the long period of pregnancy (one of the longest among all mammals) before a cow is far gone in calf, she does often give the impression of being, not obviously pregnant, but in very full condition. All the cow elephants I have seen in musth were probably pregnant, of the 2 observed within the survey period, one was heavily and patently pregnant, and the other was very probably pregnant, appearing to be well–fleshed and in full condition. It could be that the rare incidence of musth in cow elephants is in some way related to pregnancy.

Bulls in musth often exhibit a marked lethargy, as remarked by Sanderson; this lethargy does not manifest itself in immobility or slowness of movements, but in a marked indifference to the surroundings –– a bull in musth often appears to be in a state of somnambulance, though its stride is not shortened. This, however, is not an invariable feature of musth. Some bulls observed in musth were wide–awake and even aggressive, for example a tusker in West Bengal, a makhna in Assam and a tusker in Mysore, when first seen, were in a highly excited state. Other elephants in musth have exhibited that somnambulistic indifference to their surroundings that made it possible to approach them closely for a picture. In a party of elephants it was noticed that the cows were attentive and considerate to the tusker in musth. Bulls in musth frequently squirt water over their swollen musth glands and forehead, and apparently the lavage serves to unclog the musth pores. A tusker in musth invaded the elephant camp Kargudi and mated with a cow that was in season – his aggressiveness towards men was not caused by his condition, but due to his resentment of being closely watched by crowds, and shouted at.

A peculiarity noticed in tuskers in musth is that they often carry tight–packed clay on their tusks, so closely adherent that even a swim in fast–flowing water does not wash it away. This adherent clay is acquired when the tusker gores earth banks and even the clayey bottoms of forest pools while in musth: this goring is not something done in a frenzy, but evidently indulged in to cause by the pressure imposed on the swollen glands the free outflow of musth from the temporal glands. The duration, frequency and heaviness of the musth affliction all vary with individuals, and even from one bout to another in the same individual. At times the exudation is thin, and at times so profuse that it stains the entire cheek and runs down the face.

Musth in females has been known to occur occasionally as pointed out by Krishnan and Wilson. N.L. Bor (108) describes instances of musth in female elephants, and a female with tusks which regularly came into musth. Bor writes:

"Col. G.H. Evans in his well–known book `Elephants and their Diseases' opens his paragraph on musth with the words `Male elephants, and very rarely females, on attaining maturity, are subject to peculiar periodical paroxysms of excitement ... to which the name of musth is applied" ....

In view of the above statement by such a well–known authority, it may be of interest to note that during the Departmental Keddah Operations conducted by the Forest Department in the Goalpara–Bhutan Mahal, Assam, 1925–26–27, two female elephants exhibiting unmistakable signs of musth had been caught. The cases are as follows:–

"No.1. A very large female elephant of the Kumeraband type was caught in November 1925. This elephant had very large tushes and, at first from her size and build, might have been taken for a makhna. Although full grown she had never had a calf, and there is no doubt that she was barren. While in the stockade she gave a good deal of trouble, attacked her fellows and the koonkies, and eventually broke both of her tushes on a tree inside the stockade.

This paroxysm of fury while in the stockade was succeeded at the depot by an impassivity and 'don't care' attitude which was just as remarkable. The temporal glands were greatly swollen and gave forth a profuse oily discharge. Her training proceeded with remarkable rapidity, and she was able to go out without koonkies ten days after her capture. Shortly afterwards, however, symptoms of blood poisoning were observed, due to the severe wounds the broken off ends of the tushes had caused in the mouth, and the animal was released in an effort to save her life.

No.2. A very large female elephant of the Kumeraband type caught in November 1926. This elephant was not of such fine build as the former, and in addition had had calf. Her temporal glands were swollen and gave forth a copious discharge. She seemed very drowsy while at the depot but her training proceeded without incident and she left for her owner's home about a month after capture.

The question, what causes the condition of musth in elephants, is one that has not been satisfactorily answered. It is true that some bulls when in this condition court the society of females, but it is by no means an invariable rule, and it cannot be dogmatically asserted that this condition is due to· a lack of sexual gratification.

As regards both the cases cited above, they did not show any perceptible desire for male company at the time, nor did tuskers or makhnas at the depot exhibit any interest in them.

One cannot lay down conclusions from two cases only, but it seems clear that the symptoms of the condition in the male and female are exactly the same. First the violent stage in which all animals are attacked, and pain does not seem to be felt. This is succeeded by a drowsy stage in which the animal takes its fodder as usual but seems oblivious of its surroundings, and the attack then appears to wear off gradually. In both stages the temporal glands are swollen, and give out a characteristic discharge.

The first case was apparently captured in the earliest stages, and the second in the latter stages.

Both these animals were caught in the month of November in the stockades which are a few miles from one another. All the other members of the respective herds were normal.

Some years ago an Assamese gentleman, Rai Sahib Rajant Kanta Chowdhury of Sorbhog, owned a female elephant which was locally known by a term which was the equivalent of 'female tusker'. This was a North Cachar elephant and owed its sobriquet to the fact that it had longish tusks and went musth regularly each year until its recent death.

Elephant attendants have told me that male elephants go musth up to an advanced age, in fact none of them could recall an elephant that had not gone musth even in its old age.

We shall probably not get an explanation of why female elephants sometimes exhibit these secondary sexual characteristics of the male until some anatomical light is shed upon the question".

7.5 Mating
Some curious beliefs have been held in the past about the mating of elephants as shown by Paul de Launey's (46) note:

"The manner in which elephants mate has long been a moot point. Owing perhaps to the position of the generative opening in the cow it has been suggested that during congress she lies on her back – some have held that she digs a hole. The question, if there yet remains any doubt as to the manner of fecundation, may definitely be set at rest now.

The female was purchased on 13th February, 1936 being wild and just caught in a Khedda. Her age is about 30 years and height 7'6". The tusker is aged 35–36 having been in captivity for about 30 years, his height is 8'5" in. At the time the female had been partly broken in – she could carry a pad, but did not know all the words of command. The pair had been brought in from the hills where they are let loose, fettered, and lead a seminatural life often mixing with wild herds. The tusker mounted about eight times, but the female did not respond as she kept crossing her hind legs. Subsequently the tusker mounted on several occasions, either in the compound or in the hills. The female is now in calf. The tusker has been getting musth for the last 5 years, the attack generally lasting from 10 days to a fortnight, when he is unapproachable. The attack comes on usually in April or May. When in musth he always seeks the company of a female, and mounts whether she is willing or not. A point to be emphasised is that he was not musth in this instance".

The note had been accompanied by a photograph and the editors wrote in an editorial footnote:

"We have not published the photograph submitted by the writer. There are a number of photos in existence which prove that elephants copulate in the position usual to quadrupeds. In the female elephant, the peculiar position of the female external generative opening, which hangs down in much the same position as the penis in the male, led to widespread doubts as to whether that was possible. On plaques and in ancient Indian sculpture, in which elephants are sometimes represented in coitu, the female is shown literally standing on her head. The weight and vigour of the male may force the female to go down on her fore–knees and rest her forehead on the ground. Under sexual excitement the generative opening in the female is raised from its pendant position and assumes a situation more or less normal in quadrupeds. The alteration in position has been observed by ancient anatomists. Aristotle refers to it in his `Historia Animalium'. An interesting note in the `Oriental Sporting Magazine' indicates that the animals may at times take advantage of irregularities in the configuration of the ground and so ease the burden of weight. In the referred note, the writer saw pair of elephants mating; the female was standing in a dry nullah which was not more than five feet wide. The male rested his forefeet on either bank and so relieved the cow of the weight of his body. EDS".

M. Krishnan (20) gives a more elaborate discussion on the mating of elephants. He states :-

"As among most herbivores, the sexual act occupies only a very short time, less than a minute but the love–play preceding it is elaborate; coition is usually repeated many times during the three or four days the bull and cow are together – even when in a herd, the pair are seen by themselves when the cow is in season and has accepted a bull. The belief, held by many professional elephant men, that the cow decides with which bull she will mate seems to be factually sound, although it is also true that rivalry among adult bulls may become acute when a cow is in season. In elephant camps it is not unusual for a wild bull to arrive at the camp when a tame cow gets into season, and frequently the first act of the intruding bull, even before he seeks the cow, is to attack other adult tame bulls in the camp. In the Kargudi elephant camp of the Mudumalai Sanctuary two adult tuskers personally known to me (Caesar and Addi) were grievously wounded by wild bulls attracted to the camp by a cow coming into season. As in most other mammals, the condition of the cow is advertised by scent, but the elephant is unique in that a cow in season actively advertises her condition. Visually flagrant signs of her being in season are not manifested (even the mahouts know that their charges have come into season mainly by circumstantial evidence, such as the interest manifested in the cow by the bulls), but the cow bends her tail between her hind legs sharply so as to slap the abdomen with its tip, and then draws the brush at the tip firmly up, rubbing it against the vagina; the tail is then held aloft in the air and waved about in a scent–flag.

While it is true that in most animals the male cannot mate unless the female is co–operative, the peculiar anatomy of the elephant and its courtship habits makes it absolutely necessary for the bull to have the co–operation of the cow for successful coition. Because the pre–copulatory play is gentle in the elephant, the bull cannot, by aggression or force, compel the co-operation of the cow – a situation that may arise in some other animals where there is little courtship prior to the sexual act. During this phase of courtship, the bull caresses the cow with his trunk and there are repeated gentle bodily contacts. While the bull elephant is not peculiar in his genital anatomy, except that the testes are not discrete in a scrotum but located within the body (a feature shared by some other animals, such as the whales and dolphins, shrews and sloths), the cow elephant has the widest perineum known among the mammals. Her vagina situated low down, a vertical slit at the end of the abdomen; this renders it necessary for the cow and the bull to be precisely aligned before copulation can be effected; the bull lays his trunk along the cow's back from behind and manoeuvres her into position before attempting to mount her, a move dependent entirely on the willingness of the cow. During the brief period of copulation the animals move around in a quarter circle – this was noticed in two matings between wild elephants observed from a distance and also in the mating between the camp elephant Suguna and a wild tusker observed and photographed from nearby".

J. Gonzalez (47) recounts the actual mating of wild elephants he witnessed in Pegu Burma. He writes;

"While out shooting wild elephants in 1919 on the west of Payagale, about 20 miles north–west Pegu, Burma, I chanced to witness a unique sight, and was sorry to be without a camera at the time. It was the mating of a wild bull–elephant and cow-elephant. I was searching for a tusker that morning and came upon a herd of wild elephants which were scattered, grazing. Entering stealthily in their midst, followed by two Burman guides, after an hour's stalking, I saw from a hill streamlet, two wild elephants – a bull tusker and a cow – far away from the herd, just at the foot of a hillock. The bull had its trunk round the left hind leg of the cow–elephant, and at the same time pressing his right tusk on her left rump, using this as a lever to inflict pain so that the cow would be obliged to submit to his wishes. No resistance was shown, apparently because the bull had a thorough hold on her.

From my place of vantage, say within 50 feet away, I saw the bull forcing the cow, held in the above manner, to walk up the rising ground for about the space of 20 or 30 yards; they turned and the bull, loosening his hold, rose on the cow in the act of service. They gradually descended in this manner to the foot of the hill. On reaching level ground the bull got off, laid hold of the cow again as described above and made her repeat the ascent. This movement was carried out three or four times in succession apparently until the service apparently came to an end.

The wild bull then released the cow, which ran away to join the herd once more. The bull stood for some time before he moved away.

The scene was so impressive and unique that I was loath to shoot the tusker, and allowed him to go his way. I don't think such a sight has been witnessed by many shikaries, and I, therefore, record this note".

A wild tusker mating with a domestic cow elephant, and coming out of the forest for the purpose, has been recorded by A. Aiyappan (39) who writes:

"An interesting elephantine romance was brought to my notice by Mr. A.S.M. Nair, Commissioner, Hindu Religious Endowments Board, Madras. According to reliable reports he had obtained, a female elephant, belonging to the Sri Emuri Bhagavati Temple, at Kallekulangara, near Palghat, in the Malabar District, was covered by a wild tusker, on or about 19th November, 1938. The tusker probably came from the outskirts of the Olavakkot forest to the place where the cow elephant was tethered. The tusker remained with the cow elephant for three days, so the courtship and mating were watched by the inhabitants of the locality. The report that the tusker did not eat a morsel of food during the three days has not been verified by me. Efforts made to capture it by doping seem to have failed because of the tusker's extreme wariness. The tame female elephant calved on Friday 6th September 1940 – this date was noted by the Manager of the temple, Mr. E. Chathu Achan, of Akathethara village – and the baby tusker, now about five months old, is said to be thriving and sucking its mother's milk.

The period of gestation in this case was about 21 months and 18 days. In the case of a male calf reported by Corse (Tr. Roy. Soc. 1799) it was 20 months and 18 days.

I was informed by the Manager of the temple that in August 1945, the same wild tusker came again to the old spot to meet the female elephant, and this time was driven away with the greatest difficulty. The people of Malabar are so elephant–minded that reliance can be placed on their identification of the tusker as the one they knew in 1938".

7.6 Redirected sexual activities
There is also on record one instance of redirected sexual activity by a tusker unsuccessful in mating with a female. According to K.K. Ramachandran (50):

During our field studies at the Periyar Tiger Reserve two instances of unusual sexual behaviour were observed in wild elephants.

On 25th July 1979 a herd of elephants were grazing near the Periyar Lake shore at Manakkavala. There were two sub–adult tuskers in that herd. One tusker attempted to mount a female with a two years old calf. The cow did not allow the subadult tusker to mount her. The cow and the calf went towards the forest, followed by the tusker. The tusker attempted to mount the cow again. The penis of the tusker was everted from its sheath throughout the period the tusker continued to follow the same cow, with its trunk holding the tail of the cow and pulling it. The cow freed itself by moving forwards, and hurriedly returned to the herd with her calf. The tusker went to the other smaller tusker which was in knee–deep water, and smelled its penis with the trunk tip. The tusker then mounted the other tusker with its everted penis. The second tusker moved away and then they began pushing each other. The bigger tusker again mounted on the other tusker and after some time they left the water.

This kind of unusual sexual behaviour shown towards smaller individuals after several unsuccessful attempts to mount has been described earlier in Asiatic elephants. This behaviour has been termed as "redirected sexual activity".

In Periyar the sub–adult tuskers seem to get comparatively more opportunities for mating, due to the fewer number of adult tuskers in the elephant population".

7.7 Birth in the wild

The birth of a calf in the wild is usually the cause of considerable excitement to the herd which makes a tremendous amount of noise heard over quite some distance. It is not clear whether the reason for this mass Euphoria is to intimidate others, or just a celebration! Vincent (40) reported on such an event in south India:

"On Christmas Day 1903, in the Anamalai Hills, near Coimbatore, about 9 in the morning, the late Mr. G.A. Marsh and I went to visit a small plantation of bananas, on the Peralai Estate, which had been damaged by elephants. Hearing a herd of elephants a considerable distance away in the jungle making a tremendous amount of noise, much more than usual – trumpeting, squealing, and breaking branches,— we decided to investigate and, proceeding towards the herd, which could not be seen owing to the extremely dense jungle, we soon found a wild fig tree, very easy to climb, on one of the branches of which, about 25 feet above the ground, we perched ourselves. Shortly after this, three female elephants came up to our tree, and one of them entered a cane brake, right under the branch on which we were sitting. The other two remained outside the clump of Eeta, apparently keeping guard for, on the approach of other members of the herd, (it was a fair sized herd of about 30 animals we thought) they were definitely warded off. After a time – about half an hour – the two guards went away, but we could not descend from our tree because we knew the third elephant was still in the cane below us. We were very mystified, as we could not even guess what was happening. We waited there.for a full hour, at the end of which the third elephant emerged, went a few steps, put its trunk to the ground, and made that peculiar drumming noise one so frequently hears an elephant make. At once a very small calf came out from the cane, and went with slow steps towards its mother. It was wet and shiny, but not very dark skinned. It was suckled for a short while, then the mother moved on towards the direction of the herd which was a quarter to half a mile away, still making much more noise than usual.

When the mother and calf had disappeared and we considered it safe to do so, we descended from the tree and inspected the cane brake. We found the placenta there – a very pale pink, and weighing, we judged, about 10 lbs. This placenta looked rather like pale raw liver. There were two or three very much thickened portions roundish in shape, about 3 inches in diameter, which we judged might have been the attachment of the placenta to the body of the mother. These thicker portions were between 1/2 to 3/4 of an inch thick, but the rest of the placenta was much thinner – not more than 1/16th to 1/8th of an inch.

By this time it was noon, and we went home. We had no weapons with us. Unfortunately the cane brake was so thick that we could not see the actual birth of the calf, and so are unable to state whether it was delivered by the mother standing, or lying down but, judging from the marks we saw, we thought the mother must have been kneeling. So far as we could guess, the calf when it came out of the cane was about the size of a half–grown wild pig.

I am afraid these notes do not add much if anything to our knowledge of the subject, but they may be interesting"

Tutein-Nollkenins (41) writes of a somewhat similar incidence in Sri Lanka, and draws attention to the value placed on the placenta by the local people as a valuable indigenous medicine. He writes:

"During a shooting trip at the end of last year, at Christmas, my friend Mr. N.H. Dendy of Tillieoultry Estate, Lindula, came across something so unusual and interesting that I think it should be recorded in the Journal.

Mr. Dendy was camped near the Menik Ganga, the river, one of the natural boundaries of the Yala Wild Life Sanctuary, soon to be declared the first Strict Natural Reserve in Southern Province, Ceylon. One morning quite early Mr. Dendy and his men, walking along the high river bank, disturbed and watched a cow elephant and her calf.

After about half an hour the mother and calf moved away slowly into the dense forest along the river. The men remarked that the calf could not possibly be much older than a day or two. They had never seen such a small calf.

Going further, something red on the sands drew their attention and, going down to look, they found the perfectly fresh placenta of the elephant. Knowing the elephant's habits, this must be an extremely rare experience, and it would be of interest to know if this has ever been recorded before. It was early in the morning, so the sun was not yet high enough up to shine and dry it. A certain proof the elephant had calved that night or even, and I think more likely, only a few hours before the party reached the place. It is known that an elephant calf is able to get up and follow the mother about two hours after birth, while various authorities state that the elephant eats the placenta.

At any rate it must be extremely rare to find it, as the sun would soon dry it up, if jackals or crocodiles, had not made away with it. The very exceptional drought this poor country has suffered from so severely no doubt made the elephant choose this unusual place for the calving, knowing that the pools left in the river were the only water she could get within miles. As a rule the elephant mother chooses the most dense cover she can find, which is all the more reason few, if any, have ever come across such a remarkable find in the jungles and wildernesses.

In the sand, Mr. Dendy and his men could see clearly the place she had lain down to give birth.

Mr. Dendy estimates the total weight of the placenta at about 5 to 6 lbs. The far side, darkly coloured, consisted of more or less solid flesh, the lighter coloured and a small patch on the right, was like frothy blood. Much to the surprise of Mr. Dendy, after some hesitation, the excited men asked if they might take it; they explained that when washed and dried, the solid part would make very valuable and excellent medicine. It is said that a small bit of the dried substance, dissolved in a little lime juice and water, will at once relieve a woman's labour pains, or will help to advance an overdue confinement. All folklore is of great interest, but considering the great rarity of ever finding a wild elephant placenta, this bit of jungle lore is all the more stranger.

Both men, as well as others who have spent their lifetime as watchers in the sanctuary and the neighbouring reserve, had never seen a placenta, and knew of no one who ever had. The two men with Mr. Dendy had never previously come across the calving place of an elephant, a very rare thing to find. And yet, they one and all knew the story handed down for generations, of this most valuable medicine.

It was not quite clear, from the impressions in the sand, the position the cow elephant had occupied, but in all probability she must have been lying on her right side, her back turned towards the place where the men were standing".

C.W. Allan (42) relates a similar story to Vincent's, and the finding of the placenta which was considered a delicacy by his Burmese assistants.

"On Christmas Day, 1910, my camp was at Kyoukpazat on the Phatashin stream in the Henzada District. Mr. E.V. Ellis, Deputy Conservator of Forests, had come over to spend the Christmas holidays with us and to do a little shooting. During the early hours of the morning we heard wild elephants trumpeting and making a great noise up the Phatashin stream, not more than a mile or so from camp, and when we started the first beat of the morning the elephants were in a little valley just below the spur on which the guns were posted. The beat proved a blank, for nothing came out, and although the beaters made a fiendish noise the elephants did not make off. The next beat was on the next spur and again the elephants were just behind us. That beat was also a blank. Whilst the beat was coming along I noticed that the beaters seemed very excited and kept on saying to one another "let's catch it after the beat." So when they got up to us, I asked what the excitement was about. They then told me that an elephant had given birth to a calf in the stream and they wanted to catch the calf, presumably to kill and eat. But as a young calf had been caught and brought to me the year before from a place not four miles away presumably of this very herd, and I had a deal of bother over it, not being able to get sufficient milk to feed it on, although I had bought two cows to supply it with milk, I did not feel like being saddled with another calf, so told the men that they were not to catch it. I then told them to take us to where the birth had taken place. This was in the bed of the Phatashin stream close by, and we soon got to the spot. The elephant had selected a soft spot in the bed of the stream close to the water, and dropped her calf there. The ground was a bit cut up and the Burmans went poking about and soon unearthed a small bag full of water. After this, they crossed the stream which was only a couple of yards wide (the watery part) and dug about in another place where the ground was turned up, soon producing another bag, the "after–birth" (achin), which was buried about a foot deep in the sand and pebbles. The Burmans were highly delighted at the find, so I naturally asked them what they were going to do with it, to which they replied "why, eat it of course". They soon had the "after–birth" washed and tied up in their sheets.

Talking of the parturition of elephants, Lieut.–Colonel G.H. Evans, Superintendent of the Civil Veterinary Department of Burma, in his Treatise on Elephants, "Elephants and their Diseases", notes on page 96 that an elephant gave birth to a calf at Pazundaung near Rangoon and that the Burman attendant stated that the dam ate the "after–birth". I wonder if this happens only in the domesticated state or whether wild elephants eat it, too. In the case noted by me the dam certainly did not eat the "afterbirth", for we found it intact. I have often noticed that domesticated goats, cows, buffaloes and sheep eat the "after–birth". I would be glad if some one would explain the reason for this to me. Does the dam eat it to clear herself?"

In an editorial note it is said that G.H. Evans in his work on Elephants and their Diseases describes the birth of an elephant calf on information obtained from an experienced Burman – "When about to give birth the female seeks soft ground. The calf may present head and fore–feet, or the hinder parts may appear first. If the membranes are not ruptured by an attendant, the female does it with her foot. The young one lies from one to two hours after birth, occasionally moving ears, trunks, limbs, after which it gets upon its legs and can walk. Elephants even in the wild state may die in labour – the author records an instance. A newly born calf can walk well enough after a few days to follow the mother on a short march and, in the wild state, when a calf has been dropped, the herd remains in the vicinity until the baby is able to follow the mother, which is generally in about 48 hours. The author is of the opinion that the 'afterbirth' is usually eaten. It comes away 15 or 20 minutes after the birth of the calf."

In the same context of the birth of an elephant calf, R.C. Morris (97) under the heading of 'The Birth of an Elephant Calf' states:-

"In the Journal of August 15, in Vol. xxxvii, No.3, I referred to the death of a wild elephant while calving. This elephant was found dead lying on its left side with only the hind–quarters of the calf only exposed.

On another occasion I happened on a spot where a cow elephant had calved on a sandy path in open scrub jungle; there was no sign of the placenta".

7.8 Twins and Triplets

The birth of twins and even triplets has been recorded (48). Gordon Hundley (73) mentions twins born in the elephant camps of Steel Brothers of Burma in 1920. The twins were born in June 1920 and measured 2'10" at the shoulder. Writing in 1927 he stated: "They are now in harness aged about 6.5 years the male twin with a height of 5'9" while the female twin measure 5'8" at the shoulder".

Priya Davidar (74) gives the details of the birth of another pair of twins, and refers to earlier records. She writes:

"The elephant camp at Teppakadu, situated in the middle of Mudumalai Wildlife Sanctuary in Tamil Nadu, enjoys the reputation of having produced the largest number of elephant calves in captivity. But this record would have been incomplete had not Devaki, the 40 year old cow, given birth to twins recently. Twin births and even triplets are not unknown. But they are distinctly rare. The chances of both calves surviving are rarer still.

Sanderson, the well–known authority on the Indian elephant and the father of the Mysore Khedda, did not come across a single case of twin births in his thirteen years in India. He, however, acknowledges that this is possible and writes 'I have heard of what appears to be a well authenticated case of a female, elephant having two calves at birth'. The birth of triplets in Siam and two pairs of twins in Burma are recorded in this journal.

The fact that Devaki was pregnant was known at the camp. She was given progressively lighter tasks and special rations, like all expectant mothers. She looked normal and none suspected that she was carrying twins. On 20th May 1971 at 6.45 p.m. after all the camp elephants were assembled and fed, it was noticed that she was in distress. She bit her trunk, sat on her haunches and showed other signs of discomfort. This first spell of pains lasted 5 minutes. At this stage, Forester Selvaraj who is in charge of the elephants took charge. Instead of letting Devaki go out into the jungle at night as usual, he had her secured on the outskirts of the camp.

The second bout of pains set in at 8.40 p.m. and, at 8.45 p.m., the first calf arrived – a normal birth, head first.

Devaki set to work cleaning the calf of the amniotic fluid with earth gathered from the area, and in 10 minutes the calf was able to get up.

At 9.00 p.m. the 2nd calf was born, also a normal birth. To Devaki, who had given birth to four calves before, this was something new and she kicked the calf aside, perhaps mistaking it for the placenta. The calf fell into a depression, and Forester Selvaraj and his assistants dragged it aside and cleaned it of the birth fluid. This calf took half an hour to stand up. It took Devaki considerable time to get reconciled to the fact that the second calf was hers too.

The calves were not weighed, but their weight, according to the Forester, was normal. They stood 2'11" and 3' at the shoulder –– the average height at birth being 3'.

Tara, another cow elephant at the camp, gave birth to twins some five years previously. Only one of the calves survived and the other was presumed to be a stillbirth. These calves were born in the jungle, as in the majority of cases.

But for Forester Selvaraj's initiative, and the care and attention he and his staff bestowed on Devaki, the 2nd calf would have surely been trampled and written off as a stillbirth, if it had been discovered at all in the jungle. This may, perhaps, be the reason why twins are thought to be so rare among elephants."

D.F. Macfie (49) reports on the birth of triplets:

"On 27th October 1913, one of our working female elephants gave birth to triplet calves, all males.

We have no note of the date of impregnation, but the mother was heavy in calf, in October 1912, and was said to be due in one to two months. Of the calves, one was stillborn, one was normal and one was very small; the two latter survived only until 8th and 9th November.

Everything was done to bring them up, but the mother would not look after them and kicked them away when they came to suckle, or if let loose would run away from them.

The mother's height is 7'4", she is probably about 25 years old and has never to our knowledge had calves before."

It appears that births of twins and triplets as far as elephants are concerned is abnormal, and is not accepted by the mother who expects to have only one calf. Unless the birth occurs in camp, the additional calves are likely to be rejected.

Chapter 8

GROWTH/MATURITY

Gordon Hundley (51) gives a statistical record of growth based on calves born in captivity and also information on maturity, etc. "The data have been compiled from a Register of Working Indian Elephants (1,507) and Calves (365) born in the service of a firm extracting teak in Burma. He writes

1. No one has any reliable information regarding 'milk tusks' and none of our employees has seen them.

2. Percentage and Sex –– (a) A tusker calf shows its tusks from the age of 2 years to 5 years. (b) Cases of calves with double tusks shedding one and so becoming 'tehs' are now authenticated. (c) Tuskless male calves (Haings) are known to have tuskers as fathers. Tuskless males, as fathers, have reproduced double tusker calves.

Musth – Reports by eyewitnesses prove that 'musth' in males was not present in the majority of cases of coition, and that the female has a periodical time of heat, which cannot usually be detected by a human being. A few cases have been recorded of females discharging from the musth gland, when apparently not on heat.

A tusker calf came on musth in his 15th year.

Reproduction – A female calf, 15 years old, has produced her first calf. She must have been covered when just over 13 years old.

Height Increments – Calves measured within three days of birth averaged 3'9" in height. 109 males and 111 female calves measured produced the following results in heights:–

In 1st year	6 males averaged	3'0"	8 females averaged		3'0"
2nd	8	4'2	5	5	3'11"
3rd	7	4'5"	–		–
4th	4	4'10"	3		4'6"
5th	4	5'6"	3		5'1"
6th	9	5'8"	10		5'5"
7th	11	5'10"	12		5'7"
8th	8	5'11"	13		5'9"
9th	9	6'1"	4		5'11"
10th	7	6'5"	4		5'10"
11th	6	6'9"	6		6'0"
12th	6	6'10"	8		6'4"
13th	7	6'11"	5		6'6"
14th	6	7'2"	4		6'5"
15th	4	6'11"	5		6'7"
16th	2	6'11"	–		–
17th	1	7'5"	3		6'6"
18th	1	7'6"	3		6'7"
19th	1	7'8"	4		6'8"
20th	1	7'5"	1		7'6"
21st	1	7'4"	1		6'8"
22nd	1	7'3"	–		–
23rd	2	7'5"	1		6'7"
24th	1	7'10"	1		7'0"
25th	1	7'10"	1		6'8"
26th	1	7'10"	–		–

An exceptional tusker calf, not included in the above, measured 8'1" in his 19th year.

We do not consider these statistics accurate, for a margin of error during measurement has to be considered. Also, far greater numbers of calf measurements are needed. As statistics progress, however, this margin of error will decrease".

E.P. Gee (38) describes the growth of a calf from birth to the 5th year and also points out possible errors in Hundley's data (vide supra). Gee states:

"On February 5th, 1950 an adult cow elephant named Deokali, 7'6" in height and belonging to the Forest Department of Assam gave birth to a baby, subsequently named Parbati. As this event occurred only three miles from my tea estate, I was able to go immediately to photograph the baby on the day of its birth, and subsequently every year on its birthday – February 6.

Each year, from 1950 to 1955, I have carefully measured the circumference of the forefoot and the height to the shoulder, taking the average after repeating the process four times. Thus an accurate record of the rate of growth of an Indian baby female elephant has been obtained under near natural conditions, as the mother was laid off work and allowed to roam in her forest habitat every day. The heights and other information are as follows:

Date	Age	Forefoot	Height	Increase	Remarks
6–2–50	0	....	3'0"	...	Could not be accurately measured on day of birth. Estimated at 3'0"
6–2–51	1	...	4'1	1'1"	Forefoot could not be measured. Suckling well.
6–2–52	2	2'4.5"	4'8.5"	7.5"	Still suckling
6–2–53	3	2'6.5"	5'1"	4.5"	Still suckling two or three times a day.
6–2–54	4	2'9"	5'5.5"	4.5"	Was said to be occasionally suckling. Ridden by mahout occasionally.
6–2-55	5	2'11"	5'9"	3.5"	No longer suckling. Ridden regularly by mahout.

147

This is probably the only accurate and detailed record of the rate of growth of a baby Indian elephant under near natural conditions. I have studied the measurements given by Gordon Hundley of Messrs. Steel Brothers & Co., Ltd., (Jour. Bombay nat. Hist. Soc., 37: p.487), but these appear to be unreliable. For instance, no measurement is given for female calves of two years old, measurements were not taken on the dates of birth, and the height given at the ages of nine and thirteen years are less than those at eight and twelve years, which is not possible.

Male calves are slightly bigger than female ones at varying ages, and from the comparison of many figures I estimate that 7% or 8% added to the height of a female calf would give the approximate height of a male calf of the same age (this would apply only to calves between the ages of one and twelve years).

The manner in which the Deokali cow elephant came to be mated is interesting She ran away from her pilkhana at Jamguri in the Sibsagar district of Assam on 15–2–45, and spent some years in the nearby forest with wild elephants. Then she was captured with a herd of wild elephants in khedda operations on 15–3–49 in stockade in the same stretch of forest. She was quickly recognised to be a ban guarasia (escaped–tame–one–run–wild), and was claimed by the Forest Department and returned to her former pilkhana at Jamguri.

Recently both Deokali and her baby Parbati, now five years old, have been transferred to Kaziranga Wildlife Sanctuary, where both animals are being ridden by visitors coming to see rhino and other wildlife in the Sanctuary".

An excellent analysis of the growth gradient in elephants has been given by Bernard Rensch and K.W. Harde (16). According to them :

"Up to the present, only absolute measurements of Indian elephants have been published. Hence, in the course of investigating the behaviour of working elephants in Mysore in Spring 1953, we took the opportunity to study the growth–gradients of some proportions too. We took measurements of 15 elephants of different ages and different body–size, and tried to find out some postnatal growth–gradients of these largest land mammals. We could complete these statements by calculations based upon the absolute measurements of elephants in Ceylon published by P.E.P. Deraniyagala (1953).

Statements of the age of Indian elephants are not always reliable, because most animals are not born in captivity and their age has only been estimated after capture. Particularly in older publications this estimation often is too high. We now know that Indian elephants do not reach an age of 80–150 years, as W.T. Blanford (1891), G.H. Evans (1910) and other maintained, but that they normally reach an age of 60–70 years. The age of the two oldest animals investigated by us has been estimated as 62 (male) and 60 years (female), and in P.E.P. Deraniyagala's publications (1951, 1953) 22 the oldest specimens measured were 65 (male) and 55 years (male). In view of this factor of inaccuracy, we have to expect a relatively large variation of the values, if we relate body–size to growth. But in practice the range of variation can be lowered by averaging two neighbouring values and

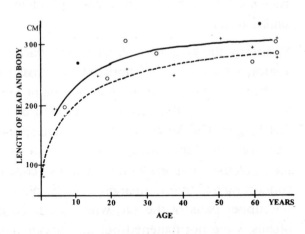

Fig. 1 : Absolute growth of the length of head and body. Each spot is the mean value of 2 specimens, in 5 extreme cases the value of 1 specimen. + females,• males from Mysore; x females, 0 males from Ceylon (ear-hole to root of tail, measured by Deraniyagala).

plotting such average data in a system of co–ordinates with the

149

increasing measurements of head and body on the abscissa and the increasing age on the ordinate.

Figure 1 shows our own measurements, and also those of Deraniyagala (1953). We measured the length of head+body from the frontal base of trunk to the hind part of pelvis region by plotting a corresponding distance on the ground beside the elephant. Deraniyagala measured from the ear–hole to the root of the tail, but apparently directly along the vaulted body. These measurements correspond with ours to a high degree. The distribution of the values follows the usual curve of growth (fig.1) showing a quick increase at the beginning and then a successive slackening of the growth. The curve shows that Indian elephants are not fully grown, before they have reached an age of 25 years, but that afterwards a little growing continues until a later age. On average therefore, the oldest specimens are the largest ones. On average, males are a little larger than females. By plotting the maximum height of the back into a system of co–ordinates in a corresponding manner we got a similar result.

Measuring the heights of shoulder and back was done by using a stick, which was held horizontally across the relevant points of the elephant's body so that a straight vertical line leading from the ends of the stick to the ground could be taken as the real height. The length of the ear corresponds with a vertical line from the upper margin of the ear to its lowest point. The width of the ear corresponds to a line crossing vertically, and connecting the anterior margin with the hindmost tip of the ear. The upper parts of the ear, which are tilted over in older ele-phants, were not flattened out for measurement. We measured the length of the forefoot up to the elbow, the length of the hindfoot up to the knee and the circumference of forefoot and hindfoot with a thread around the nails.

The oldest male (Elephant Stable, Mysore) was the largest specimen measured. Its length of head + body was 335 cm. and its height (of back) was 310 cm. According to the statement of

Mr. Eswarappa its weight was 6 tons and 224 English pounds – 6199 kg. But the average of the values of head + body of 6 adult females older than 24 years is only 269 cm; and the height at the shoulder averages only 242 cm.

The largest Ceylon elephant measured by Deraniyagala was a younger male of 32 years having a length of head + body (ear–hole to root of tail) of 315 cm.

An old rule is that, in elephants, the height at the shoulder is about twice the circumference of the forefoot – this holds good for our measurements, the error being less than 5 per cent.

If part of a body grows allometrically, i.e. if the growth ratio in relation to the body remains constant for a certain time) then the growth follows a rule stated by J. Huxley: $y = b.x^a$, meaning: size of the organ = b. body size. The exponent a is the coefficient of correlation between organ and body, whereas b is a constant of integration, which indicates the value of the organ when the body–size is 1. Now this allometry–formula may also be written log y=log b+a.log x. That means that allometrical increase of an organ or of a part of the body can also be shown by plotting the size of the organ on the ordinate, and the body-size on the abscissa of a system of co–ordinates progressing logarithmically in both directions. If the organ grows allometrically, the value will coincide with a straight line. The angle of inclination of the straight line is a measure of the degree of allometry.

It is also possible of course, to show the correlations between organs and body– size by plotting the body–size on the abscissa and the relative organ–size (in percent of the body-measurement) on the ordinate of a *normal* system of co–ordinates. But in most cases the variation of values will be fairly large and the allometry, i.e. the constancy of the relative growth ratio, will not be proved exactly.

If we examine the *height at shoulder* (fig.2) and the *height of back* (fig.3) by double logarithmical plotting of the absolute values, we see that in both cases the values exactly form a rising straight line. As the inclination angle is less than 45° the growth is negatively allometrical. Hence,

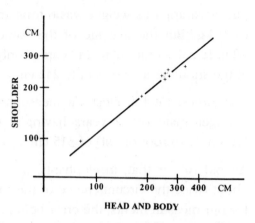

Fig. 2 : Allometrical growth of height of shoulder in females from Mysore. Abscissa : length of head and body, ordinate : height at shoulder. Double logarithmic plotting.

the height of a young elephant is relatively greater in relation to body–length than in older animals. This proportion decreases constantly, parallel to increasing age. The same holds good for the *length of the foreleg* (fig.4). Here, the variation of the values is a little larger, especially the value of the young female of about 3 months which does not coincide with the straight line. This means that the negative allometry is more intense at the beginning. The same holds good for the *length of the hind leg of the baby.*

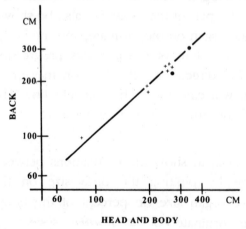

Fig. 3 : Allometrical growth of height of back (Ordinate). + females,• males from Mysore.

But afterwards the growth becomes isometrical. Apparently, the relative height of shoulder and back is chiefly determined by this successive alteration of the relative length of the legs. In this respect elephants have developed phylogenetically parallel with other hoofed animals, such as Perissodatyla and Artiodactyla, which also show a relatively greater length of leg in young animals. The phylogenetic development of such a growth–gradient

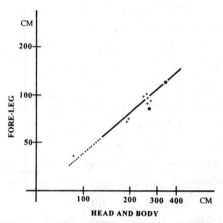

Fig. 4 : Allometrical growth of length of fore-leg (Ordinate). + females,• males from Mysore.

probably took place because it is an advantage, enabling a young animal to run quickly, if young animals had the same relative length of leg as adults, they would run *relatively* quicker than the adult animals, because the capability of function of the legs grows proportionately to the cross sections of the muscles in the second power, but to the value of the body in the 3rd power. The *absolute* speed of the young animals, which is important for selection (flight from enemies, long marches to watering places, etc.), would be less, but, by

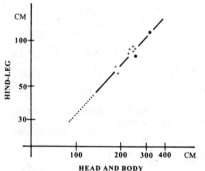

Fig. 5 : Allometrical growth of length of hind-leg (Ordinate) +females,• males from Mysore.

developing relatively longer legs than adults in the course of phylogeny, their absolute speed is increased. During individual growth the legs successively become shorter, showing a negative allometry. (Fig. 5)

The *Circumference of the forefoot* (fig. 6) shows slight negative allometry, and in this case, likewise, the value of the 3 month old calf is not on the straight line. Young elephants have relatively broad feet. The length of the hindfoot begins with negative allometry (baby), but afterwards shows slight positive allometry (nearly

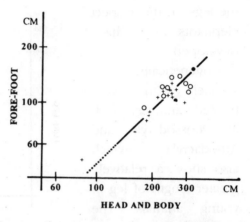

HEAD AND BODY

Fig. 6 : Allometrical growth of circumference of forefoot (Ordinate). Abscissa : length of head and body (specimens from Ceylon measured from ear-hole to root of tail). + females,• male from Mysore, x females, o males from Ceylon (after Deraniyagala).

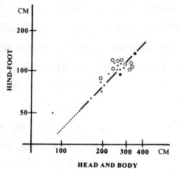

HEAD AND BODY

Fig. 7 : Allometrical growth of circumference of hindfoot (Ordinate). + females, • male from Mysore; x females, o males from Ceylon (after Deraniyagala).

isometry). In these cases we could add the values calculated from the tables by Deraniyagala as well. They fit into the range of variation of the animals measured by ourselves in

Mysore. Deraniyagala's data (unfortunately there were no values from young ones) also enabled us to calculate the gradients of (Fig. 6) (Fig. 7) the trunk (fig.8) and the tail (fig.9). The former grows with negative allometry, the latter

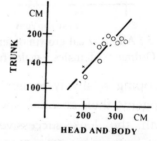

HEAD AND BODY

Fig. 8 : Allometrical growth of length of trunk (Ordinate) x females, o males from Ceylon (after Deraniyagala).

isometrically. But the variation (Fig. 8, Fig. 9) of the values is larger, apparently caused by the unavoidably inaccurate measuring here. Finally, the growth–gradients of length of ears (fig.10) show slight negative allometry. Once again in the young female, a higher degree of allometry shows up.

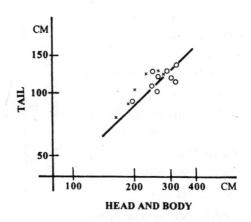

Fig. 9 : **Allometrical growth of length of** tail (Ordinate). x females, o males from Ceylon (after Deraniyagala).

The width of the ear (fig.11) at first grows with negative, afterwards with positive allometry.

There is a similar behaviour of all these growth– gradients in both sexes.

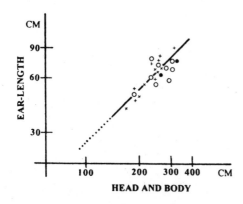

Fig. 10 : Allometrical growth of ear-length (Ordinate). + females, males from Mysore; x females, o males from Ceylon (after Deraniyagala).

In this connection, it is also of interest to consider the foetus 7.5 cm. long and figured by Deraniyagala. This specimen has relatively large head and eyes, that is to say, after birth, head and eyes grow with negative allometry as in other mammals. But the ears are relatively small. Apparently they grow with positive allometry until birth and with negative allometry, later on, as we have seen, but the width is still with positive allometry. The legs of the foetus are relatively long and the back is relatively high, even relatively higher than in the young female of 3 months. Probably the negatively allometrical growth of the height of the back already begins in the small embryonic stage." (Fig. 10, Fig. 11)

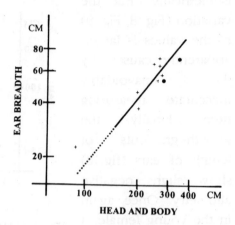

1. P.E.P. Deraniyagala (1951): `Elephas maximus', the elephant of Ceylon. Vol.I (Nat. Mus. Ceylon), Colombo.

Fig. 11 : Allometrical growth of ear-width (Ordinate). + females, males from Mysore.

2. (1953): Elephas maximus, the elephant of Ceylon. Part III. Spolia Zeylanica, 27: 111-124.

Chapter 9

AGE

The stories, on the age to which elephants live, give us an example of how fables are concocted. Guy Dollman (12) published a note on a report in `The Times', London, on a 170 year old elephant. He wrote:

"In connection with the longevity of animals, concerning which some correspondence appeared `The Times', a few weeks ago, my attention has been drawn by Dr P.E. Pieris, Trade Commissioner for Ceylon, to the record of a remarkably long–lived Asiatic elephant. In a translation of Joao Ribeiro's 'Ceilao' by Dr Pieris (third edition, 1925) mention is made of a famous elephant, Ortela by name, which was probably a fully adult animal prior to the siege of Colombo in 1656, since we are told that the animal at this time had 'offspring and descendants'. The same specimen is referred to by Emerson Tennent in his 'Natural History of Ceylon' (1861) as still being alive when the British flag was hoisted in Colombo in 1796. This elephant is reported by Tennent to have been found in the stables by the Dutch on the expulsion of the Portuguese in 1656, and served under them during the entire period of their occupation, more than 140 years. During the siege of Colombo, Ortela was the only elephant out of 15 animals which was not eaten by the defenders, and it is said that it did much useful work in bringing trees to repair the breaches in the city walls.

From the available, evidence it would appear that an elephant's age is determined by its teeth, and that as soon as the last molar tooth is in position on each side of the jaws a period is set to the animal's existence. Elephants' grinders succeed each other by horizontal, not vertical succession, moving forward in the arc of a circle and pushing the old teeth out in front. There are six cheek teeth developed on each side of both jaws, three being the so–called 'milk molars' and three the permanent molars. Not more than one, or parts of two or sometimes three teeth, are in use at one and the same time, the elephant being very economical regarding the use of its teeth. Each successive tooth, with the exception of the fourth, or first permanent, molar, is more complex than its predecessor, the number of ridges increasing according to the following formula: 4, 8, 12, 12, 16, 25. This formula applies only to the Asiatic elephant, the African beast having its teeth arranged on a more simple plan, the ridges not being so numerous (3, 6, 7, 7, 8, 10–12). Doubtless when the animal's diet is free of grit or sand the teeth will last longer than when these impurities are present, but under the most advantageous circumstances an elephant living for 170 years or so is a fact which is very astonishing".

A correction to this extraordinary claim was published by N.G. Pillai (13) :

"What age do elephants reach?

An answer to this question is contained in a recent article in the P.Z.S. Vol. 117, Pt. 4, pp. 680–88 (1948) by the late Major Stanley S. Flower, where he has come to the conclusion that 'there is not a single well authenticated record of either Indian or African elephants reaching the age of 70 years, in spite of the many popular and journalistic exaggerations about the longevity of these elephants'.

In this study, Major Flower has gone to the available evidence in regard to the ages of well-known elephants, such as 'Jumbo' and 'Alice' of the London Zoological Society, Napoleon's elephant 'Siam', 'Princess Alice' of Australia, all alleged to have lived for more than a hundred years. In every instance, the actual age as verified by him has been found to fall far short of the fantastic age quoted in the press, and approximates rather to the 'three score and ten' average for Man.

'Jumbo' and 'Alice' said to have carried generations of London children were found to be actually 22–24 years of age. Besides, the names 'Jumbo' and 'Alice' have been associated by popular journalism in the last fifty years with individual elephants in menageries in Europe, America, Africa, and Australia which have all been assumed to be identical with the original `Jumbo' and Alice' of the London Zoo. 'Princess Alice' the popular Sydney circus elephant, claimed to have been 150 years old, was only 23 at death, when the facts were checked by Major Flower. Similarly 'Siam', the male Asiatic elephant long believed to have been presented to Napoleon by a Turkish Pasha. and subsequently made over to the Budapest Zoological Gardens, is now established, on the evidence of Mr. F.A. Cerva, the well-known Hungarian ornithologist, Prof. O. Antonius, Director of the Schonbrunn Menagerie at Vienna and Dr Tilly Edinger of the Museum of Comparative Zoology, Harvard, U.S.A., to have come direct to Vienna from Siam on 11-11-1897 as 'at most' a five-year-old calf. Thus, the report, of its having belonged to Napoleon and attained an age of 150 years, is a further example of journalistic exaggeration.

The case of 'Ortela', the 170 year old elephant from Ceylon, published in `The Times', London of April 21, 1931 by Captain G. Dollman and reprinted in this journal, was also investigated by Major Flower and is recorded as 'age unknown' in his table of alleged and actual ages given at the end of his present paper. 'Ortela' was a fully adult animal in 1656, according to Joao Ribeiro, author of 'Ceilao' (translated by Dr. Peiris) and was stated by Sir J.E. Tennent in his 'Natural History of Ceylon' (1861) as alive 'when the British flag was hoisted in Colombo in 1796'. Commenting on a passage later on in the same work, that 'amongst the Singhalese the ancient fable of the elephant attaining the age of 2 or 300 years still prevails but Europeans and those in charge of tame ones entertain the opinion that a life of about 70 years is common to both man and the elephant', Major Flower remarks that "Tennent evidently regarded the great ages to have been reached by some elephants as rare exceptions from the general rule, for he (Tennent) adds "of 138 elephants belonging to the Ceylon Government which died in the years before 1856, whose duration of life was recorded, only one reached the age in captivity of between 19 and 20 years".

Again, Tennent is quoted as mentioning an elephant of prodigious age, having been in the service of the Dutch and English Governments in succession for upwards of a century, which died at Colombo in 1848. Her skeleton is now in the museum of the Natural History Society at Belfast. With the help of this clue, Major Flower was able to trace the skeleton, which was evidently Ortela's, and got Profs. A.J.E. Cave and Thomas Walmsley to examine it. The latter reported that the skeleton belonged to 'a female (from its general size and the size of the tusk holes; one tusk remains, but it is badly eroded)'. From the dentition and other skeletal details he concluded that she was not an aged beast.

Ortela's age of over 170 years does not seem therefore, to have any scientific basis, and cannot be taken as established.

R.D. Richmond (14), analysing the age data of 78 elephants in the possession of the Madras Forest Department, lists one as over 60 years of age, 7 as over 20. Among these only four with ages of 44, 43, 32 and 39 were born in captivity and therefore provide an accurate records; the others commence with an estimated age at capture. Richmond concludes that "the majority of the elephants being young ones, below thirty years of age, no useful estimate, regarding the average period of captivity nor the age to which an elephant lives in captivity, can be made. The oldest, 'Peri', aged 67, was captured in 1889, when she was 15 years old, and has a record of 42 years' service, whereas 'Eva' aged 56, of the South Coimbatore Division, purchased in 1885, when she was 9 years old, has a longer record of 47 years. Similarly 'Theebaw', aged 54, of the Nilambur Division, captured in 1886, when he was 8 years old, has a record of 46 years; while 'Akbar', born in 1888, of the South Coimbatore Division, has remained with the Department throughout the past 44 years.

According to the Inspector of Livestock, elephant 'Peri', mentioned above, is the oldest there has ever been in the Department. Elephants are reported to have lived for over ninety years in the Mysore Palace. This is attributed to the fact that they are maintained solely for ceremonial purposes. Mr. F.X. Mascarenhas, retired Inspector of Livestock, states, however, that an elephant named `Noor Jehan' lived to an age of ninety years in the Wynaad Division, and that another named `Parvathi' was given to the Madras Zoo when she was ninety years old. He mentions also that he had to deal with an elephant named `Dodda Laxmi' and that she was then nearing 120 years. But there is, unfortunately, no written record.

There recently appeared, but the source is forgotten, some fabulous story of elephants in Ceylon passing from the Portuguese to the Dutch and so to the British – some very great age was mentioned".

An interesting story about the old Travancore States' finest Tusker is narrated by N.G. Pillai (15) who states that:

He was a magnificent animal standing 10' at the shoulders. Captain S.S. Flower (later Major), Director, Egyptian Government, Zoological Service, who visited Travancore in 1913, described him in his Report on a Zoological Mission to India as the 'tallest male elephant' that he 'saw actually measured in India'.

The elephant `Chandrasekharan' died in 1940. The records about his age vary and are conflicting. From his appearance he must have been past 95 at the time of death. He was taken over to the Royal Stables in 1883 from the Travancore Forest Department. His tusks were symmetrical and graceful and swept up in a semicircular curve. The weight of them was 142.5 pounds.

Major Flower, writing on the age of `Chandrasekharan', says that he had an ascertained minimum age of twenty–five and a supposed approximate age of forty years in 1913. This would mean that the animal might have been between 52 and 67 years of age at the time of death. Major Flower's study on the duration of life in vertebrate animals which appeared in the

P.Z.S., 1931, based on actual observations for a number of years brings out 50 as the average life of elephants. It is interesting to note that the thirteenth century Jain Zoologist, Hamsadeva, has said in his 'Mrigapakshisastra' that the maximum age attained by elephants in captivity is 100.

The elephant was particularly remarkable for his sagacity, gentleness and almost human intelligence. He never harmed a living creature until his death. Various stories are current evidencing one or other of his qualities, an authentic one being his refusal to erect a pillar in one of the pits dug for the purpose in connection with one of the Murajapam festivals in Trivandrum. Usually the elephant was a very willing worker, and his refusal to hoist the pillar which he held still with his tusk and trunk surprised the mahout who, on looking in the pit found that a stray dog had fallen asleep in the pit. It was only after the dog was roused and driven away that `Chandrasekharan' lowered the pillar into the pit."

Evans (17) describes the signs of old age thus:

"With regard to age, the appearance of an old animal is as follows:– The head is lean, deep hollows are present over the eyes, there is frequently a certain amount of opacity around the margin of the cornea (Arcus senilis), and an abnormal flow of tears. The edges of the ears are torn and frayed, the skin of the trunk is rough, something like shark skin, the trunk itself seems to have lost a certain amount of suppleness, the skin over the body is much shrivelled, the tail is hard, and the end may be devoid of hair, the skin around the nails presents a rough or warty appearance, and the legs are thinner than they ought to be. Other indications of age are:– the general appearance and an awkward mode of progression. A rough guess at the age may be made by observing the condition of the ears, the upper edges of which lap over to the extent of an inch at the age of thirty, which increases to two inches between this age and sixty years. The teeth also afford some information as to probable age; it is, however, most difficult to determine with any degree of certainty the age of these animals."

M. Krishnan, (20) writing on age of elephants, concludes that -

"In the period of infancy and growth to adolescence and maturity, in its longevity, the elephant bears striking points of resemblance to the totally unrelated human being. A cow elephant may be said to be adult at 16 years of age, and is capable of breeding then, though still not full-grown, and a young bull at 20. Gain in height, and especially in substance, continues till the animal is 30. It is in its prime from 30 to 40, middle-aged from 45 to 55, and definitely aged at 60, though it may still be quite robust. Cow elephants continue to breed till about 55 years old, and seek the society of bulls even when past 60.

In recent years, doubts have been expressed by some foreign writers on the elephant being a really long-lived animal, and it has been said that it does not live to beyond 70 years. No doubt, it exceeds this classical span of three-score-and-ten on occasion, even as men do, when free and wild. Anyone who has some knowledge of wild elephants in India will appreciate how much better conditioned than tame elephants they are, and how much less subject to wear. G.P. Sanderson has argued this point ably".

Chapter 10

DISEASE

Information on diseases of elephants on the wild is uncommon. In a letter to the editors A. Laurie (92) draws attention to two extraordinary glands noted. He writes:

In answer to your letter of December 29, regarding the Bellagalla Rougue Elephant shot, whose snap I sent as I thought the two extraordinatry glands on the neck might be of interest to you, I will give brief further particulars.

This elephant used to frequent the forests between Coimbatore District and Mysore State, adjoining the Billigirirangan Hills. I shot it in the valley about half–way between Attikan and Kollegal.

During the past two years or more, it had become a great menace to the people living in the wilds round about, as it took to destroying their crops, and no one dared to go anywhere near to drive it away as it chased them. It made short work of a few unfortunates whom it got hold of, and from all accounts it simply trampled them flat. It was proscribed a rogue about two years previously and, though many set out after it, they did not have the fortune to meet it. Mr. Ralph Morris of Attikan, who I believe is well known to you, promised to send me a wire if any reliable khubber reached him about rogue elephants, of which there were many, making their appearance off and on round about Attikan, and as luck would have it he wired me on October 24, and I managed to get to him on October 26. We got in touch with the rogue on 29 and after much tracking we came upon him in an opening in the thick jungle, quite suddenly. I feel sure he had his eye on us. He stood quite still about 40 yards away giving us a broadside shot. Morris let me have the shot and I got in a well–placed shot between the eye and ear which stunned him, and Morris immediately followed up with another shot so he swung round falling on his side on the slope of the hill, and I placed another good shot at the base of the skull which ended his career. It was all over in a minute or so. On going up to him I noticed the two glands (I call them glands, but maybe I am wrong).

The one on the upper side (right) was about 3 to 4 inches long, whereas the one on the underside was 9 inches long. They were both very slimy in appearance and to feel. They were coated with a whitish fluid (slime) and seemed to be merely two bags or envelopes, which you could distend, being very elastic. They were black in colour.

I know Mr. Ralph Morris cut off the lower gland with the idea of sending it to you. I do not know if he actually did so for I had to leave hurriedly.

The people of the forests who accompanied us told us that they had never seen any elephant with this extraordinary formation under the neck. I have made enquiries of others who have had a lot to do with elephants, and they say the same. It will be interesting to learn, if possible, what function these glands could possibly perform.

The editorial note added that `regarding the above tusker and the extraordinary 'glands' Mr. Ralph C. Morris writes us as follows':-

"I was with Mr. Laurie at the time he shot the elephant, and we were both amazed to see, when we went up to the fallen tusker, that it carried a most extraordinary pair of appendages on its neck, one on either side behind the lower jawbone. The appendages were in the shape of sausages, the upper one being about 5 inches long, and the lower a good 9 or 10 inches. To the touch they were tender and appeared to be covered with a skin of unusual thinness, the skin being of a raw appearance, mottled greyish pink in colour and moist. Apart from the fact that the elephant was clearly in "Musth", there being a flow from the "Musth" gland orifices, I cannot think what was the cause of these extraordinary growths, nor can I assign any reason for them. I referred the question to Mr.

Saunders, Principal of the Veterinary College in Madras, but Mr. Saunders could advance no theory on the matter. He had seen nothing of the kind before, and although I have been in at the death of eleven or twelve proscribed elephants I have never seen a similar case before, nor have I seen growths of this kind mentioned in any work on elephants. I had the larger of the two appendages cut off and gave instructions for it to be pickled preparatory to sending it to the Madras Veterinary College for examination. Unfortunately my instructions were misunderstood by my skinner who, instead of preserving the whole appendages, skinned it, threw away the inside and pickled the skin! Can you ascribe any possible reason for these growths, and have you heard of a similar case before?"

Mr. A.J.W. Milroy, I.F.S., of Assam, who has had considerable experience of elephants, both tame and wild, writes to say that he has never come across any glands of this sort.

"A Pathological Report on the Condition by G. Carmichael Low (93) states that Mr. W.S. Millard, of Tunbridge Wells, to whom a portion of the extrodinary gland of the elephant was sent, kindly cut me a section of it. The piece of tissue sent measured 2 inches in length, by 1 inch in breadth, and had dried up into a hard, horny mass. So hard had this become that it was only possible to remove a portion of it by sawing it off. Dr. Newham, whom I consulted on the matter, suggested we might try softening it with caustic soda. This was done and, as the piece was then sufficiently pliable, it was carried through the ordinary alcohols, xylol, etc., and embedded in paraffin. Sections were then cut and stained with hamatoxylin and eosin and considering the condition of the tissue on arrival, were extraordinarily good.

They showed that the tissue was not glandular as supposed by Mr. Laurie, but consisted of ordinary fibrous tissue with very few cells present. The tumors are typical fibromata, very similar in structure to those seen in man and other animals.

E.P. Gee (94) reports on an epidemic of Anthrax which affected the wild population of elephants in Assam in the late forties of the present century. He writes "further to my letter of 7th December 1949 on the above subject, more information has now been received. An investigation tour was undertaken by the D.F.O. of the district, accompanied by an Hon. Forest Officer. I give herewith the substance of the latter's report.

`During a twelve–day tour a great many wild elephant skeletons were found and, taking these into account as well as the number of tusks and tushes actually produced, it now appears that the number of proven deaths is 74. Taking into consideration the area searched, and the areas left unsearched, as well as the numbers of skeletons found in the different localities, it would seem safe to infer that a similar number of deaths has gone undetected. The total number of wild elephants which died therefore may be in the neighbourhood of 150.

In addition, the skeletons of 3 bison were found, and it was reported by the Beat Officer that 3 bears (species not mentioned) had also died at the same time. There were reports from villagers, too, that some bison, bear and also sambar had died.

There were reports from villagers in three cases that they actually saw elephants dying, lying prostrate with severe purging and unable to move. One took a week to die, another less. Flatulence is mentioned, and dung mixed with blood.

I have discussed the foregoing report of the tour of investigation with an experienced veterinary officer, and his opinion is that the disease was probably the intestinal form of anthrax. He was not able to inform me definitely whether elephants are susceptible to rinderpest or not, but from the foregoing symptoms it appears to be anthrax. As far as I know, no examination of the remains of the dead animals has been done by any veterinary officer.

The Conservator of Forests has informed me that catching operations have been stopped in this area, and that steps are being taken to try and prevent further occurrences.

Anwarrudin Choudhury (96) also notes on the basis of information supplied to him that there were two outbursts of anthrax epidemic in the present century, the last one being in the mid-forties, which devastated the elephant populations of the N.C. Hills (Lahiri Choudhury, pers. comm.).

One unusual case of the death of an elephant from rabies is on record. J. Beckett (95) reports that:

"On 16th January this year, one of my cow elephants was bitten on the trunk and round the hindquarters by a dog. The wounds were immediately cauterized, and on 24–1–1932, though the dog had not been recovered and identified as mad, a course of anti–rabies treatment was commenced. Fourteen injections of vaccine at the rate of one per day were given, until 6–2–32. The wounds healed up properly, and until 26–2–32 the animal was in normal health, eating its rice and fodder as usual. On 27–3–32 the elephant went lame in the off hind leg. On 28–2–32 paresis set in, and the animal fell down on her stifle joints but, though in much pain, made attempts to get up again. She ate a little fodder and drank water. This condition continued on 29–2–32, but on 1–3–32 it became aggravated, and she was only able to recline on her elbow and stifle joint. Her appetite was poor, and a few wisps of green grass was all she could manage to eat. On 2 and 3–3–32, the paresis developed into paraplegia with absolute loss of the use of the hind quarters.

On 4–3–32, swelling of the tail and hind quarters was apparent, with a total loss of appetite and failing consciousness.

On 5–3–32 total paralysis set in, with loss of consciousness, rapid, irregular and feeble pulse, laboured breathing, cold and hidebound body, cyanosis of the mucous membranes and on 6–3–32 the animal died.

During the period of sickness the animal grew very thin.

Miscroscopical examination of the brain by the Pasteur Institute revealed positive rabies.

It is noteworthy that at no time was there the slightest sign of the disease taking a violent turn.

Chapter 11

DEATH, NATURAL AND UNNATURAL

As in the case of age, the death of elephants in nature has also been the subject of myths. W.S. Thom (18) writes:

"A wealthy American, who had done a great deal of shooting in Africa and other parts of the world, asked me whether I had ever found animals in the jungle at the point of death, or which had died from natural causes, or any animal cemeteries. My reply was that in the whole of my experience which extended over a matter of 45 years I had never done so, and I suppose I would almost be safe in saying that it would be possible to count on the fingers of one's hand the European sportsmen who have done so, although they may have roamed through all the forests of the world for years. I have come across the remains of serow, a species of goat–antelope, barking deer, and sambar, that have been killed by leopards or tigers, but never any animal that was at the point of death or had just died from natural causes. What becomes of all the animals that die from old age or disease is a conundrum that has been asked many times.

In the Rangoon Gazette, some years ago, I wrote an exhaustive article on the subject of 'Where do elephants die, and animal cemeteries'. It would take too long for me to go into this subject again here as fully as I did then. It must not be imagined that because an elephant is such a huge beast the carcase or skeleton will remain visible above ground for years, like the vulture– or crow–picked skeleton of a camel, mule or horse, that may have perished in an arid desert where the rainfall is practically nil and where the absence of jungle and undergrowth, not to speak of animal and insect life, preclude its disappearing for a very long period. It is a very different matter in tropical countries like India and Burma, where all organic matter tends to decay rapidly, and where the jungle is usually alive with insect and animal life. The carcase of any dead animal very soon disappears owing to torrential rains, swollen streams, white–ants and a host of other insects, dry rot, damp rot, the heat of jungle fires, and the ceaseless gnawing of the remains by a multitude of large and small animals. It should not be forgotten that the skull and bones of an elephant are full of oil, and will burn rapidly in a jungle fire. Is it to be wondered at then that the remains of even such large animals as elephant bison, rhinoceros and tsine are seldom encountered?"

A somewhat similar opinion is expressed by C.W.A. Bruce (19) who writes:

"Now for another matter – the finding of remains of wild animals in the forest. This subject has given rise to many pretty fables, and sportsmen, because they personally have not found dead animals themselves, believe all sorts of fairy tales. I would ask sportsmen to try and remember how many times they have found the remains of any of the larger species of mammalia, such as gaur, rhino, or tsaing, in the forests— very seldom I venture to think— tropical rains, birds, animal, and white ants will soon destroy all traces of any organic matter. The finding of dead wild elephants however, is not quite unknown. In 1893 I was camped some ten miles (in very thick forest) from an assistant, Mr. A. M. Burn–Murdoch, now Deputy Conservator of Forests; he wished to send me a note on business, and sent a peon with it. The peon, having been gone a few hours, returned to his camp saying he had found a dead wild tusker in the forest, quite fresh. Mr. Burn–Murdoch informed the head man of the nearest village, and ordered him to proceed to the carcase to take charge of the tusks as Government property. The villagers ate the flesh, and on my interviewing the head man he informed me that it was perfectly fresh, and had not a mark on its body to show how he came by his death. I notified the find all over the district. There was no Government animal missing, nor any belonging to the Bombay–Burma Trading

Company. I examined the tracks, and was convinced the animal belonged to a herd of about a dozen which had recently crossed towards the Chin Hills. The tusks were consequently sold as Government property, and the sum paid for them may be seen in the books of the Forest Department of the division to this day.

In the same division one of my hunters told me that a large male tuskless elephant died one rainy season on a sandbank in the river having lain there for two days. As I could not confirm this with any European evidence, owing to the animal being tuskless, it was not reported to the Government. I give this report for what it is worth, though I knew the hunter well for six years, and always found him truthful and not given to exaggeration.

Again, Mr. Hannyngton, of the Bombay–Burma Trading Company, once, when tracking wild elephants in the Teungchoingyi forests, came on to a dead wild female; she had been dead about two days. She was not a Government animal, nor one belonging to the Company, and Mr. Hannyngton told me that he was convinced she was a wild one.

I was for six years in charge of the frontier–revenue station, where all forest produce from the semi–independent country had to pay duty. Tusks, old and brown, were continually being brought down for the payment of the Government royalty, and on my questioning the Chins they declared they had found them in the forests. This, however, is little proof, for I believe the wild Chins use poisoned arrows, which, of course, would account for dead animals being found."

Death is often the result of combat between males. Leahy (77) reports such an instance:

"We had heard the elephants making an awful noise in the jungle a few days before this 'subject' was brought to my notice by some coolies. I gathered there had been a fight between two males, but it was confirmed when I arrived at the spot where the loser was awaiting death. His leg, which was badly swollen made him completely immobile. If the popular belief about elephants going to the accustomed burial ground be true, there is very good reason why this one couldn't do it as he couldn't walk. This is not the first elephant, however to die in the 'Civilisation' of this District. There was another only a few months ago, but, I have no information about that one. It is quite possible that he too, was wounded.

It is a common belief that elephants, and several other animals, anticipate death and accordingly retire to a common 'burial ground', but though certain circumstances suggest this belief, such as the discovery of the remains of several animals in one locality, there is yet no proof forthcoming and must be treated as a popular belief with no foundation. It seems possible however, that a wounded or otherwise weakened animal may retire to a secluded spot in the jungle, or as in the case of elephants, into a river or other marshy ground; they do so, not because they anticipate death, but as a means of self–protection. The wounds in the meantime perhaps become septic and the animal is impeded, or the ailment may increase beyond recovery and the animal succumbs to its fate. The point of seclusion may possibly be the only one in the neighbourhood and on this account many animals may consequently retire to the same spot to die. This would undoubtedly result in an accumulation of remains which would naturally give rise to the secular belief of a 'communal grave yard'. But that this is not so is supported by the fact that several animals have been recorded as found dead in the forests".

In the Tropics the agencies of destruction under natural conditions are so rapid and complete, that even the carcasses of large animals soon disappear without leaving any traces. It is on this account that dead animals are rarely met with in the jungles."

F.W. Champion (8) comments on the extraordinary paucity of information on natural deaths and writes:

"Perhaps the most remarkable feature connected with wild elephants – a feature which has puzzled all who are intimately acquainted with them – is the extraordinary paucity of records of elephants which have been found dead, having died a natural death in the forests. Indeed, this subject has been exploited by novelists to a considerable extent in the shape of romances dealing with the hidden stores of ivory, which are supposed to exist in Africa and elsewhere, as a result of the accumulations of centuries of remains of elephants which have all collected in the same place when they felt death approaching them. It is said that expeditions have actually been financed in Africa with the sole object of finding these supposed treasure troves of ivory, but none has ever been found, and the mystery still remains as to what happens to the bodies of wild elephants when they die. It is to be noted that even Mr. Marius Maxwell, whose recent splendid book Stalking Big Game with a Camera' is practically a monograph on the African elephant, never found a dead wild elephant during his expeditions, and in his writings seems rather studiously to avoid this subject, which is of extreme interest to all who are interested in these magnificent creatures.

I have, therefore, attempted to collect all records of wild elephants which have been found dead in the United Provinces forests during recent years, and have tried to ascertain the cause of death in each case. The particulars of each record are as follows:–

(1) A dead middle–aged bull elephant with biggish tusks was recorded in 1921 by my brother, Mr. H.G. Champion, I.F.S., from Harai, in Haldwani Division, where it was found on a fireline about two days after death. The distance from water was about half a mile and the cause of death was uncertain, there being no sign of external injury. Some arsenic had been used in the neighbourhood for killing the Rohini (*Mallotus philippinensis*) trees but, as elephants do

not eat either the leaves or bark of Rohini, it seemed unlikely that this was the cause of death.

(2) A second dead elephant, a small female, was found some four days after death at Goria Rau in Haldwani Division the same year. It was not inspected by any officer, but it was said to show a number of wounds on the throat and neck, and may possibly have been killed by a tiger, although such an occurrence is very rare in these forests, however frequent it may be in Burma.

(3) A third cause is recorded by Mr. E.A. Smythies, I.F.S., also from Haldwani Division – which, incidentally, appears to be a fatal place for wild elephants. This animal was a fine solitary tusker with six foot tusks, and was found in November 1925 by a marking gang. He had apparently died about the beginning of October in a patch of what would have been swampy ground – but not quicksand – at that time of the year. His legs were embedded in the ground about 2.5 to 3 feet deep, and he was half squatting, halflying, on his left side. It did not appear that he had been caught in quicksand – elephants are very clever in avoiding such danger–spots – as there was a solid bank with trees and shrubs about two yards in front of him, and he was not so deeply embedded that he could not have struggled out. He was not an old or feeble elephant, and it is possible that he may have been sick at the time, and thus temporarily lacked the strength to struggle out, or he may have been bitten by a hamadryad.

None of these elephants, however, was a particularly old beast, so that the finding of their carcasses does little to help towards a solution of what happens to old elephants when their time comes to depart from this world. The same remarks applies to the two dead elephants recorded by Lt.–Col. Faunthorpe in his articles entitled 'The Most Dangerous Sport', which were published in the Pioneer during 1926; but a dead elephant has now been found in this (Landsdowne) Division which appears to be a genuine case of a wild elephant dying of old age. The case is sufficiently interesting and remarkable to justify my giving a full description of it here.

At the beginning of November 1926, I received a report from one of my Range Officers to the effect that on October 28, 1926 a female wild elephant had died in the Zemindari Forests of the Bijnor District and that he had gone to see it on October 30, 1926. I instructed him to see that the corpse remained as intact as possible, so that I could come to inspect it personally as soon as opportunity offered. This occurred on November 5, 1926, so that I saw the corpse exactly a week after death. It was lying on its side in open grassforest containing a few scattered trees, and was only about 400 yards from the huts of some graziers, who had brought in the news of its death. Decomposition had already set in and the meat had been attacked by vultures, pigs and hyenas but, owing to the very thick skin, they had not been able to eat very much of it. It was a large female in a very emaciated condition, and the general appearance suggested advanced age. There was no hair on the skin, which was very light in colour, and the upper rims of the ears were very markedly turned over, although the lower fringes were not frayed. At the time of death there had not been any diarrhoea, which generally occurs with cattle disease, and there was no blood or any sign of an external wound. The graziers who found the corpse said that they had known this elephant for the last year and that she was so old and weak that she could not run away with the other wild elephants when driven from the crops of the neighbouring villagers. To prove their statement they pointed out the droppings, which contained whole leaves and pieces of grass quite undigested, this being one of the main signs of old age and failing teeth. I then had the jaws cut open with an axe, and found that, in the upper jaw, only one molar remained, the grinding surface of which was worn right down to a perfectly smooth surface, whereas the molars in the lower jaw were mere stumps. Under these circumstances, it is remarkable that the beast could have managed to remain alive as long as she did and, to my mind, this appears to be a clear case of a wild elephant dying of old age in the open tree forest, which it had frequented for a year or more before death. It is to be noted that, unless death overtook her suddenly, which seems unlikely under the circumstances, no attempt was made to seek seclusion in the very dense and mountainous Reserved Forests which border on the site of death.

A remarkable feature of this case is that the Ranger saw the corpse on October 30, 1926, and noted its position carefully, but when he came with me on November 5,1926, we found that it had been moved to a different position. A dead elephant weighs something in tons, and the spot is practically uninhabited except for a few graziers, so that I am certain that the corpse was not moved either by man or by scavenging animals such as pigs or hyenas. The graziers state that one or two other wild elephants visited the place while the corpse was lying there, and it appears that they almost certainly tried to move her away or lift her up. Wild elephants are very long–lived animals, so perhaps they do not understand what death is, and thus attempted to help one of their fellows in distress.

I would suggest that the tradition of wild elephants collecting in some secret place to die has little foundation in fact, and that the hidden treasuretroves of ivory exist only in imagination. Elephants live in very sparsely populated districts in tropical forests and their life–span is long. Deaths are, therefore, not common, and may occur anywhere within immense tracts of forest. In tropical countries corpses are attacked by innumerable scavenging creatures such as vultures, crows, hyenas, jackals, pigs and porcupines, whose work is soon supplemented by ants, termites and fungi. Following upon these agents comes the annual monsoon which produces, in a few months grass and other rank vegetative growth twenty or more feet high, so that a single season may easily remove the entire body and much of the skeleton of an animal even as large as an elephant. The tusks may easily be covered with vegetation and they are certainly largely gnawed by porcupines; they must also be very old, worn and broken by the time an elephant dies of old age, so that they also might easily disappear after a few years' exposure to a tropical climate and its attendant decomposing influences. Records of wild elephants which have died of old age are however, extremely scanty and one cannot argue from a particular case".

Champion's note on the death of elephants brought a response from R.C. Morris (78) who wrote:

"With regard to Mr. F.W. Champion's interesting article in which he quotes instances of elephants having been found dead, the case of the elephant found dead in the Lansdowne Division certainly seems to be one of death from old age. Is there not just a possibility, however, that it had been poisoned by villagers? Mr. Champion mentions that the graziers had known the elephant for a year, and that it was too old and weak to run away with the other wild elephants when driven from the crops of the neighbouring villagers. This may be so; but I have known of elephants frequently refusing to be driven off from villagers' crops, remaining in cover close to the fields when the rest of the herd had retreated back into the jungles. I once came upon the decomposed carcasses of three cow elephants at the foot of these hills. The local forest subordinate informed me that he thought the elephants had probably died of anthrax — though he could advance no evidence in support of his theory: no other elephants had been reported sick or dead: nor did I hear of any other deaths. The elephants were lying dead within a few yards of each other. I do not think that the anthrax theory was possible, nor do I consider it at all likely that the elephants had died of natural causes. I was assured later by my trackers, that the ryots in the fields these elephants had been in the habit of visiting and causing considerable damage to, had put out a number of poisoned pumpkins, which elephants had eaten. Here there was the possible cause of their death. Mr. Champion speaks of the elephant having been moved from its first position. This is quite possible. I have seen a wild elephant trying to move a tusker (a proscribed rogue) I had shot, and in the case of a herd tusker shot by the late Mr. R. H. Morris the carcass was actually shifted a few yards by other elephants of the herd which returned to the spot later when I was with him, Mr. A.L. Laurie of Coimbatore, shot a tusker in November 1927, on a slope above a stream which was moved a few yards down to the edge of the stream by elephants in a herd which visited the place a day or two later. This elephant was clearly in 'Musth' there being a discharge from the 'Musth', gland orifice between the eye and the ear on either side of the head. It is remarkable how quickly the skeleton of an elephant will disappear, and Mr. Champion in no way exaggerates when he says that 'a single season may easily remove the entire body and much of the skeleton of an animal even as large as an elephant.' A couple of years is sufficient to remove all traces of a dead elephant – except perhaps the skull which may be found hidden away in long grass and dense undergrowth for a year or two longer. Protection has undoubtedly contributed to the increase of elephants in South India. Probably the Khedas held by the Mysore Government do more than anything else to keep their number down in these parts, but even then I consider that elephants are rapidly increasing. When I was in camp last March there were at one time four separate and distinct herds of elephants near our camp besides three or four solitaries.

H.F. Mooney (10) makes some interesting comments on the deaths of elephants. He writes in the context of Orissa that -

"Much mystery has become attached to the death of elephants. They are reputed to seek out some remote and secluded spot, to which they retreat when they feel their powers failing and death approaching. This legend is very widespread, but has not yet been substantiated. It is a picturesque story, which seems in keeping with such a unique animal as the elephant. The actual facts appear to me to be very ordinary. When one takes into consideration the long life span of an elephant, deaths amongst them must be comparatively infrequent. One would not, therefore, expect to find many corpses even where elephants were numerous. Furthermore, the rapidity with which decomposition sets in and removes all traces of the animal must be seen to be believed. Two rainy seasons are sufficient for the complete destruction of everything except the largest bones.

In the area with which I am dealing, a few elephants are found dead annually and some tusks are brought in for the reward. Even though much of the tract is sparsely populated, I am of the opinion that most elephants that die are found by the villagers living on the outskirts of the forests, and are thus accounted for. Such deaths probably do not exceed three or four annually in the whole area, if as many. In addition, a few rogues are occasionally shot. Thus, the total decrease from death and capture would not exceed twenty to twenty–five yearly.

Of the deaths recorded, a large number seem to be the result of wounds inflicted in fights between tuskers. Two instances of this have come to my notice in the last four years in which both animals succumbed, and two other cases of tuskers being gored to death were reported. As to the cause of death in other cases, I am unable to give any details, but mortality from old age must be extremely rare.

A very curious incident which is worth recording took place in Keonjhar State in November last.

A villager was sitting in a machan watching his crops, when an elephant entered his field and commenced helping itself to his paddy. In the hopes of driving the animal away, the man fired an arrow at the elephant which was fifty feet from him. The elephant, which turned out to be a very ancient and decrepit cow, left the field and was found dead two hundred yards away next morning with the arrow in its forehead. The villager was arrested for killing the elephant and there was much discussion as to whether the arrow was poisoned or not. The man himself said that it was not, and this is probably the truth as the aboriginals of these parts do not normally use poisoned arrows. It is unfortunate that the skull was not examined to ascertain how far the arrow had penetrated. It must, one presumes, have reached the brain to have caused death, but it is difficult to believe that an arrow shot from an ordinary bow could do so in spite of the fact that it would have to pass only through soft tissues, and little or no bone. Again, even had the arrow been poisoned, death seems to have followed very rapidly upon the infliction of the wound. Whatever the exact cause of death, the fact remains that the elephant was struck by the arrow, and was found dead close by next morning.

The facts of this remarkable incident were related to me by the magistrate before whom the case was brought, and by the forest officer of the State within a month of the occurrence and their accuracy can be vouched for".

F.W. Champion (79) comments on R.C. Morris's response to his earlier note, and gives another example of death in the wild.

"I was very interested in Mr. Morris' comments on my article. I am glad to hear of other cases of wild elephants attempting to move the carcasses of their dead companions and it would be of absorbing interest to learn why they attempt to do this. A 'jungle funeral' by elephants would certainly form a very fine theme for those who write fantastic stories on life in the jungle!

In my own mind I have little doubt that the case I previously recorded was a genuine one of death from old age, but Mr. Morris' suggestion of poisoning by villagers is a very sound one, which had not occurred to me before and which might certainly account for the deaths of some wild elephants. In this connection we have recently had another death in the jungles in my charge, and it is possible that this case might be attributed to that cause. The elephant in question was a medium–sized tusker, with tusks 48 inches and 44 inches long, and total weight of 65 lbs. The tusks were in moderately good condition, and did not appear to be very old. The animal was found dead at the side of a small stoney stream on June 1, 1928 and had presumably died the night before. I was, unfortunately, unable to visit the spot, but I give below some notes on the case, based partly on my own knowledge and partly on a report from a local Range Officer.

History. This tusker had been living alone in the Rawasan forests for some years. He was quiet in temperament, and did not attempt to interfere with the local jungle workmen.

Appearance. The carcase was found lying on its side at the edge of the water. The body looked fairly healthy and was not emaciated. The skin was considerably wrinkled, and there were deep depressions above the eyes. The ears had lost their shape after death, but they were not ragged. Unfortunately no observations were made as to the amount of turnover of the upper rims of the ears.

Teeth. There was one small very worn molar at the back of each side of the lower jaw. The upper jaw was damaged in removing the tusks, so that an examination of the upper molars could not be made. The tusks were 48" and 44" long respectively, and together weighed 65 lbs. They were in moderately good condition.

Dropping. Old and fresh droppings and the contents of the open stomach, were examined. In all three cases the bark of Pula (*Kydia calycina*) had been eaten and was not properly masticated or digested, long fibres being present.

Cause of death. No wound of any sort was visible on the upper side of the carcase, which was too heavy to lift for an examination of the lower side. As far as a layman could tell, a contributory cause of death was impaired digestion owing to failing teeth; but, although the animal was considerably past his prime, he did not appear to have been sufficiently old to have died from this cause. There is extensive cultivation on the edge of the jungle less than a mile away from where the elephant was found dead, and I know that he and other local wild elephants occasionally raided the villagers' crops, particularly during the monsoon. The villagers indignantly deny having put out poison for the wild elephants, as they must do if they wish to avoid prosecution, but there is a distinct suspicion that this may have been done, and I much regret now that I did not have samples of the blood and stomach contents taken for microscopic examination.

In any case, whatever the cause of death may have been, it is to be noted that the carcase was found in a very open riverbed, at the edge of the water, and within half a mile of human habitation. It may be that, if the animal had been poisoned, death came so suddenly that it did not have the chance to seek seclusion in the dense neighbouring forests, which it should have done if we are to accept the usual theory on the subject.

Death can be from one of several natural causes, and R.C. Morris (80) describes the death of an elephant while calving.

"On the 30th of last month my wife and I came on a cow–elephant that had just died while giving birth to a calf, a case of breech presentation. The elephant had apparently been lying there in great pain and had actually been shifted a few yards by other members of the herd in their attempts to help her up. An examination of the elephant showed that the breech and hind legs of the calf were born. While we were there, another elephant came up within a few yards of us, very silently. A day or two later I shot a wild dog feeding on the dead elephant's trunk. Some days after I observed that 5 King. Vultures were in full possession of the carcase while hundreds of their common kindred were perched on the surrounding trees. The herd remained in the vicinity for 3 or 4 days and were, from the volume of trumpeting and other vocal efforts, apparently disturbed over the whole affair.

I understand that a cow–elephant died under very similar circumstances on the borders of Pampadampara Cardamom Estate on the Cardamom Hills in Travancore last month.

The half–born dead calf was removed from its dead mother and, under instructions from the local Forest subordinates, I was informed. This is interesting, in view of the prevailing Hindu custom in South India of extracting the dead body of a child from the corpse of a pregnant woman.

Death from natural causes could also be from eating poisonous food. R.C. Morris (81) describes such a case:

"I am indebted to Mr. A. Wimbush, the Chief Conservator of Forests, Madras, for the following information connected with the death of 14 elephants from eating Kodo millet, known locally as 'Varagu'.

On the morning of 17th December, 1933, the villagers in the fields adjoining the Vannathiparai Reserve Forest came upon 11 elephants lying in the patta fields, and 3 in the adjoining Reserve. By 3 p.m. in the afternoon the elephants in the fields were dead, while the 3 in the Reserved Forest were obviously in a very bad condition, and died later. The Veterinary Surgeon of Periyakulam conducted a post–mortem on two of the elephants, and the viscere were sent to the Chemical Examiner.

Ripe 'Varagu' occasionally gets into a poisonous condition though its appearance then is no indication of this, and the knowledge that the grain is fit for consumption is said to be gained by either cooking and tasting a very small quantity or observing the condition of the cattle during the threshing season. The antidote for the poison is said to be tamarind–water or buttermilk in large quantities.

Results of the chemical examination showed that the elephants had died from Kodo millet poisoning. It is reported that a similar case of elephants being poisoned by 'Varagu' occurred some years previously in a field in the same area. When this grain is in a poisonous condition it is apparently known as 'Kiruku Varagu' (= mad varagu).

In the case of the 3 elephants that were found in the Reserve Forest, the Range Forest Officer reported that water and tamarind fruit were supplied to them by the villagers, and by this means the life of one of them was saved, but this is not confirmed".

In a note the editors give an explanation of the poisonous nature of the millet.

"The poisonous millet referred to by Mr. Morris as 'Varagu' is undoubtedly the millet known as Kodra or scientifically as *Paspalum scrobiculatum* Linn. The species is well known for its occasional poisonous properties and effects on man and beast. Dr. Mann writes: 'The grain as well as the straw of Kodra frequently, if not always, contains a poisonous narcotic principle which causes vomiting and vertigo. For this reason care is taken at least in the Konkan to prevent cattle straying into Kodra fields. The poisonous principle is probably produced under unfavourable conditions of climate and season, and the grain and straw are only poisonous in particular seasons. It is said that the narcotic property is to some extent neutralized by steeping in cowdung and water, or by keeping the grain for a number of years. Though the poisonous and non–poisonous grain cannot usually be distinguished by ordinary people, yet cultivators in Gujarat claim that the diseased grain can be detected while threshing, as the effect of the poisonous dust is felt by both the threshing bullocks and their driver."

According to Dr. Lisboa the symptoms of poisoning resemble those caused by Datura, and are more severe in cattle than in man, due no doubt to the eating of the grain and husk, and to the absence of vomiting".

Another instance of death from possible poisoning by Koda millet is described by N.G. Pillai (84). He writes:

"During October and November last year there were several deaths among elephants in the Periyar Game Sanctuary area of the State Reserve Forests. Altogether eight elephants died, one on 13–10–1953, two on 10–11–1953, four on 16–11–1953 and one on 19–11–1953. Fearing the outbreak of an epidemic, the Disease Investigation Officer of the State Animal Husbandry Department was deputed to investigate the cause of this mortality. Upon arrival at the scene of death, he found that vultures and other carrior–feeders had already made short work of the carcasses and reduced them to bones and scraps of skin so that he could not secure any material for bacteriological or other examination. From the fact that there were no more deaths among elephants in that area however, after the last death was reported i.e. 19-11-1953 (there has been no further report up to the time of writing), and from the healthy condition of the five survivors of the herd that had sustained this mortality and which he found feeding in the neighbourhood, he ruled out the possibility of infectious diseases such as Anthrax, Rabies and Haemorrhagic Septicemia. The absence of casualties among domestic cattle grazing in and around the place where two of the elephants had died, as well as the fact that cuts and skin abrasions, sustained by the labourers who were assisting at the post mortem of one of the animals, healed up normally, leant further support to this view. The possibility of insecticides and fertilizers used in the neighbouring tea–gardens as a source of poisoning was also considered, but it was reported that they did not contain enough poison to kill any of the higher animals, much less an elephant. Even if, contrary to assurances, they did have any strongly poisonous substance, at least stray cases of death either then or previously, among cattle or elephants should have come to light, for insecticides and fertilizers have long been in use on these estates. With the above causes of mortality thus eliminated, there only remained the possibility of the elephants

185

feeding on some poisonous plants. During the course of the inquiry, it transpired that some of the estate labourers had raised one or two crops of Koda millet along the border of the reserve forests. Can it, then, be that the elephants had raided these crops and were poisoned in the process?

Paspalum scrobiculatum Linn., the Koda millet, is known occasionally to develop a narcotic principle which then becomes fatal to man and animals. Tamarind and buttermilk are believed to be antidotes for this poison. Gruel made out of green gram meal, the juice of the stem of the plantain and the astringent juice of the guava are also reported to counteract its poisonous properties.

In another unnatural death reported by R.C. Morris (82) the method used was probably how mammoths and mastodons were killed by man's forefathers. Morris writes:

"In March 1945 six elephants (4 cows and 2 calves) fell over a precipice on the Biligirirangan Hills, and died a lingering death. The circumstances surrounding the event are something of a mystery; but that the local aborigines, the Sholagas, were not unconnected with the tragedy is more than a rumour.

The small herd was in the neighbourhood for several weeks, and had made serious inroads into the Sholaga's plantain topes (= gardens): this much is acknowledged. The rest of the story has been related to me by a Sholaga; and though I cannot vouch for the truth of his statement, yet I feel it is probably not entirely divorced from the actual occurrence. The story goes that late one evening the aggrieved Sholagas spotted the elephants grazing on the hillside just above the precipice; and saw their chance to be delivered of the herd once and for all. Escape to the north was not possible, the precipice being the highest on that side. Up the hill eastwards, and along the slope southwards, were the only escape routes open. Quickly forming 2 parties, one lot climbed to the steep ridge above the precipice, while the second party worked round to the south-west of the precipice. On the top of the ridge were rocks in abundance. The lower party started a jungle fire which, fanned by a stiff breeze, swept up the hillside, effectively cutting off escape to the south, and menaced the elephants, which then commenced to climb the hill. It was then that the Sholagas on the ridge came into action. Elephants are petrified by rolling rocks. I have watched a large herd get into an absolute panic when a single rock rolled down a hillside on which they were grazing. A number of large boulders were rolled down on the unfortunate climbing elephants and in a few seconds they were beating a panic–stricken retreat down the hillside, trumpeting shrilly. On the edge of the precipice they bunched, but only for a few moments, then the rocks knocked the calves over. A game path runs down the southern end of the precipice; all right for deer, and possibly bison, but quite unfeasible for elephants in normal circumstances. It is thought that, in their terror, the wretched animals tried to negotiate this possibly slender avenue of escape and tumbled over the precipice one by one. There they lay with broken legs and internal injuries until death ended their agonies.

I was not able to visit the spot until November 1945 – when only the skulls, skeletons, and large pieces of skin remained; also, curiously enough, the soles of the feet of the 2 calves".

And finally A.C. Tutein Nolthenius (83) describes the process of natural death in a wild elephant. He writes:

"In July 1943 we were filming wildlife in the Yala Strict Natural Reserve on the south–east coast of Ceylon. We were camped on the banks of the Kumbukkan Oya, the large river which forms the eastern boundary of the Reserve. This river has several small islands which, in the dry season May–September, make splendid observation posts from where any kind of animal and bird can be seen and watched. As a rule a `hide' is not needed, which is a great advantage as it leaves one free in one's movements when wanting to follow up possible subjects with the heavy cameras.

The best time to start is 3 pm. and, for an hour or more, G. and I had been watching several herds of deer, buffalo and some elephants as they came down to the river to drink from the small pools and the streamlet left in the bed. Nearest to us were a cow elephant and two youngsters, one a fine little tusker.

At about 5 pm a lone bull came wandering out of the jungle just in front of us, from the direction of the small family group. There was nothing remarkable about this animal but some feet of colour film can always be useful, especially with the sun on him against the lovely green foliage background. When he came closer it was noticed that the organ was fully extended and that this remained so all the time we watched him.

On coming towards us, several times wandering about and moving, nothing out of the ordinary was noticed. The elephant appeared to be in good condition, age abut 20, height 8 feet 6 inch to 9 feet. We had ample time to study him, as had our men, both experienced trackers. It did strike us that he was somewhat restless which – rightly or wrongly – I put down to the vicinity of the cow. Time and again he seemed to look at her although she must have been some 100 yards away. Several times he sniffed at the water, but we did not see him drink.

The light was getting poor, anyhow it was no use wasting precious colour film on so simple a subject. We must have watched him for half an hour or more and took a few stills. Suddenly he started to move and came straight towards the tripod and cameras. We were smoking on the island's bank. When within a few feet of the cameras – we were just going to save – he turned and slowly walked past us to our left. Little did we then realise that we had been filming and watching till it got rather boring – a dying elephant.

Some 20 yards away, just near the bank of the river, he stopped and stood leaning against a tree and while we were watching he suddenly 'slid' down against the tree trunk to lie on his left side. This very unusual behaviour made me realise that all could not be well. It was exactly like a drunken man clasping a lampost, and then sitting down on the pavement!

After some ten minutes and, as we got near, too dark to photograph and heavy shade overhead – the elephant managed to struggle to its feet with considerably difficulty. For a while he stood looking very dazed and then very slowly wandered up the low river bank into heavy jungle.

It was time to pack up and return to camp when – a sound like a deep and heavy moan, followed by a terrific crash came from just inside the jungle where the elephant had been seen to enter. We had no torches and it was too dark to follow.

Next morning the elephant lay dead, only eight or nine yards within the jungle. A deep fresh gash across the left cheek had been caused by a sharp broken sapling. How valuable a post mortem would have been. The dung was normal and fresh. It was not old age, while it is practically certain that this elephant did not die of any injury or an old shot wound as he fell miles away from any habitation or shooting ground. Of course, this is no proof knowing how wounded elephants can and do travel for miles and even days, but if he had been wounded it is difficult to believe that none of us four, with a fair knowledge of the jungle and elephants, would not have noticed it. Under the tree he was lying on his left side, he fell dead on his right side. The extended and somewhat swollen organ made us wonder if death perhaps was due to some sexual reason or damage.

The true reason will never be known; the strip of film is a sad souvenir. I am writing without my diaries, but believe that this was the fourth or fifth wild elephant I have found dead where it was impossible to establish any kind of reason or proof unless an expert post mortem had been possible. I remember one small elephant – later on proved to have been shot at by field watchers a week or so before – lying dead in the centre of three jungle road junctions. As far as I could ascertain, it had travelled a good ten miles to get here and meet its end. The wound in the neck made by a muzzle–loader from above, was a mass of inflammation and matter some six inches in diameter.

Twice, I have come across dead elephants lying in a stream or river, where it was impossible to make any investigations of any value. In both instances the dying animals had, of course, come to the water as their last hope.

The 'burial ground' idea, although romantic, is a myth as are so many of such ideas about the wilds. The wilds hold little romance where death is concerned."

Chapter 12

ELEPHANT AND TIGER

The tiger has the distinction of being the only predator of elephants. As G.H. Evans (17) says:

"The elephant is no doubt "King of the Forest" as they are rarely interfered with by other wild beasts; now and again, however, a hungry tiger may attack a solitary animal. A year or two ago, in the Tharrawaddy district, a tiger attacked, on different occasions, one or more animals, the property of a Burman contractor, inflicting such severe injuries that, I believe, one or more succumbed. It is the calves that usually fall victims to tigers, and the manner in which they catch them is as follows:— A tiger having observed calves in a herd lies in ambush close by, awaiting an opportunity (which usually occurs while the herd is busily engaged feeding), and then springs out, seizes a calf by the leg, just above the pad, and bolts. The herd after his attack is on the qui vive, so he keeps out of the way, but while they are moving off to fresh ground the tiger follows; the little one, being lame, probably lags behind, thus giving the tiger another chance. If he does not get one, he waits till the herd settles down again to feed, and then when the opportunity offers he makes another dash at his victim, and invariably bites a second limb. The calf is now hors de combat, and the tiger knows that he has only to wait, since the herd, if large, cannot stay long in one place; twenty or thirty animals will soon clear all the "titbits" on the ground where they are feeding, or they may want water, so the young one has to be left behind. I believe, however, that they will not abandon a calf until they are forced. As soon as the herd is clear, the tiger finds a young beast easy prey, and no doubt a very excellent meal. In January last a tiger attacked a calf in a cane–brake. The little fellow was crying pitifully; his legs were so badly bitten that he was really unable to walk a few yards, so had to be shot. Two cows were on guard, and charged so furiously that they also had to be killed. All this occurred within fifty yards".

If Evans had left it to nature only one elephant would have died, but in interfering in what is a natural system, Evans had to kill two more elephants!

The possibility of tigers trailing elephant herds for reasons other than preying on a calf has been suggested by Anderson (35) who writes:

"When out shooting the other day, I came across the tracks of a small herd of elephants in the bed of a stream. By the tracks it was clear that there was a young calf with the herd, and when I saw the tracks of a tiger following those of the elephants, I suggested to my Burmese hunter, a very experienced old man, who has lived all his life in the jungles, and shot quite a lot himself, that the tiger was following the elephants in the hope of having the calf for dinner. He seemed amused at my crediting the tiger with so much audacity and told me that the tiger was merely following in order to eat the excrement of the calf. He explained that the diet of the calf was milk, and that tigers looked upon the excrement as a bonne bouche. The idea is a nasty one, but from the point of view of natural history, it is an interesting thing in connection with the habits of tigers. I have never read of this anywhere, and it would be interesting to know whether any one else has ever heard of it.

The tracks of the elephants were a day old, and there were droppings of the adult members along the tracks, but strangely enough, there were none of the calf's In the hope of finding some I followed the tracks for some miles, coming on places where the herd had stopped to feed for a considerable time, but no droppings were found. Personally, though no naturalist, I am inclined to believe the hunter's explanation. At any rate it seems reasonable enough.

I wonder if you could get the views of some of those who are qualified to give opinions on this matter?

All those the editors consulted opined that the reason given by the Burman was unacceptable.

"JBNHS 7:119 (1892) Mr. A.G. Corbett, writes of three casualties among elephants due to attacks from tigers – the first was that of a two-year old elephant calf which was attacked and killed. The mother had come to the rescue but, was unable to do anything except get badly mauled about the hindquarters, and was apparently driven off. The second case mentioned is that of a contractor's elephant which escaped after a severe mauling, and the third case that of a very big tusker which was similarly attacked and succumbed five days later. Most authorities agree that tigers do not find their prey by scent but depend rather on sight and hearing".

Tigers apart from preying on elephant calves, occasionally attack adults or are drawn into conflict with adults. E.A. Smythies (63) describes such an encounter:

"The account below of a jungle battle to the death was given to me by entirely reliable eye and earwitnesses, and in its main details very well authenticated.

One of the major rivers of the Himalayas, the Sarda river, where it debouches from the hills, spreads out into a mile–wide bed of boulders and sand, dotted with islands of Shisham trees and coarse grass. On the right high bank, sixty or seventy feet above the river, is the small townlet of Tanakpur, with a railway terminus, a bazaar, and several bungalows situated on the bluff, looking across the wide river bed to the wild forest–clad foothills of Nepal. In the cold weather Tanakpur is alive and populated with hill people. Forest contractors are busy exporting timber from the extensive forests, and there is a stream of cross traffic to and from Nepal. In the rains, it is almost deserted. Malaria then drives away the hill people, and the flooded river cuts off all communication with Nepal.

Late one evening in the last week of September, three men were fishing with nets in the waters of the Sarda, two or three furlongs from the bungalows on the bluff, when suddenly two tigers and a half–grown cub emerged from one of the grassy islands close by. The men shouted and yelled and the tigers moved off across the dry bare bed of the river towards the forest on the right bank, a quarter of a mile away up stream from the bluff. Simultaneously from this forest the men heard the trumpeting of a wild elephant. Shortly afterwards the fishermen, and the few dozen inhabitants of the bazaar, heard the nerve-shattering roar of a charging tiger, and the fishermen saw a big male tusker elephant come out into the open river bed, being attacked by the two tigers. For three hours the battle between the elephant and the tigers raged up and down the river bed, below the high moonlit, bluff, in full view, of the bungalows on the cliff. Would I had been there to see and hear! The bazaar inhabitants were so terrified at the appalling noise and infuriated roars of the tigers so close at hand, that they barricaded themselves in their houses and no one, except the petrified fishermen who were cut off, saw this awe-inspiring and unique spectacle. At about 11 pm. the noise died down, and next morning the tigers had departed, but the dead elephant was lying at the foot of the bluff, within a stone's throw of a bungalow.

The marks on the unfortunate elephant were most instructive. The trunk was quite untouched and so was the face for except deep scratches around the eyes, and both eyes had been clawed out. There were terrible bites and scratches on the top of the head and neck, back and rump, and finally the throat had been bitten and torn open – evidently the coup de grace.

These are the facts as told to me by the eye-witnesses, and by the tahsil officer who heard the battle, and who had the job of getting rid of the body of the elephant. From them we can deduce the probable –– course of events.

It is inconceivable that the tigers made a senseless and unprovoked attack on the full-grown tusker elephant, and equally unlikely that the elephant started the fight. (He was neither 'musth' nor a rogue). It is probable that the tiger cub was the cause of the trouble. He may have blundered into the elephant, or gone sniffing around in curiosity, and received a kick or a blow for his trouble, causing him to yelp. This would at once raise the maternal fury of the tigress, and the tiger would come to the help of his mate.

The wounds on the elephant give an indication of the tactics of the tigers. It is clear that no frontal attack was attempted, or the trunk and face of the elephant would have been mauled. Probably one tiger threatened or demonstrated in front, enabling the other tiger to leap on the back (an easy leap for a tiger) and start biting and scratching. It was probably shaken off several times, but again returned to the attack. At some stage in the fight, one of the tigers must have managed to jump or crawl on to the top of the head and from that position to have clawed out the eyes, perhaps deliberately, for it seems a natural instinct of the cat tribe to go for the eyes. One can imagine the poor blind elephant, tortured with the fiendish laceration of its back, stumbling along in agony over the boulders and rough ground, falling ultimately over some low bank, and exposing its throat to a hellish mauling from the other tiger, and dying from loss of blood or severance of its wind–pipe. Truly the tigers took a terrible revenge for any possible injury to their cub.

No measurements of the elephant were taken. The tusks were small but old and worn, about 32 inches long, excluding a foot or more embedded, and 14 inches girth at the base, and the two tusks together weighed 122 lbs.

Although I have heard of elephant calves being occasionally killed by tigers, I have never before heard or read of a fight to the finish between tigers and a full–grown bull elephant. That it should have taken place before eye–witnesses, and within ear–shot of many more, is a piece of remarkable luck.

Chapter 13

MAN AND ELEPHANT

Where and how the elephant was domesticated is undetermined but the method of capture was probably the pit trap, a method used by man for thousands of years to trap and kill animals beyond the capacity of the feeble weapons he had until the latter part of the current millennium. D.K. Choudhury (1988) suggests that, if one took rock paintings into consideration, the history of elephants in domesticity in India has been recorded from about 6000 B.C. He also believes that though the Harappan culture has evidence of elephants in captivity, it is not clear whether they were domesticated or trained. Evidence of the elephant as a part of human culture becomes clear from the time of the Aryans, who entered the country about 1500 B.C. The Rig Veda describes the elephant as hastin or 'the beast which has an arm', the root for the Hindi name hathi. Though the Aryans had a horse-orientated culture by about 400 B.C., elephants rather than chariots had become the Royal Mount (MoEF, 1993), a position they continued to hold till India gained independence in the mid-twentieth century. In earlier periods, and up to the invention of modern weapons such as the gun and the cannon, they were a formidable though somewhat unstable part of the armies of the Subcontinent. Kautiya's Arthasastra (300 B.C.) describes how war elephants were trained in rising, bending, crossing fences and pits, charging straight or zig-zagging and trampling underfoot horses, chariots, and infantry. The elephant excited the wonder and amazement of the Moghul Emperor Babur and his Tartar hordes as no other Indian animal did. It is possible that neither he nor his followers had ever beheld an animal of such gigantic proportions before, possessing such power yet tractable and docile and a faithful ally in battle. All of Babur's descendants shared his acceptance and special regard for the animal in peace and in war. They shared with other Indians the belief in their usefulness in battle, which had been disproved long ago by Alexander who had defeated Porus by drawing them out with his cavalry. Military minds being rigid, the elephant continued to be, often disastrously for its side, in the forefront of battle until the advent of the gun put them in their true place, in the rear with the commissariat. Retired from the wars, the elephant has remained a ceremonial animal, and a symbol of status. It continues to be the former, but few can afford to maintain it as a status symbol. Even its usefulness as a work horse in the forests has been taken over by machines. It remains the only reliable mode of transport however, in the flood areas of the rivers of the Gangetic plains in U.P. and Bihar in the monsoon. Today it is an endangered species, rapidly losing its habitat either to cultivation or to change in the habitat composition through forestry operations. The once continuous habitat of historic times is now broken up, and communicating forest corridors continue to disappear.

The present day status of elephants in the wild, in relation to man, has been well expressed by Krishnan, when he says :

"It has often been said that of no wild animal are forest–living men so afraid as of the elephant, and this is understandable, because of the unpredictable response of chance–met elephants in forests. Few seem to realise, however, that the aggression of elephants towards men, in areas where men have invaded elephant country is almost invariably motivated initially; by human hostility that the shooting of elephants is something that has to be done expertly, if it has to be done at all, and that the wounding of the animals may lead only to further trouble. Almost invariably a proscribed rogue (i.e. an animal that has killed a man or a few men, and which has, therefore, been proclaimed a rogue) carries gunshot wounds, probably received in the course of raiding a sugarcane plantation or other crops, which have suddenly sprung up in what used to be primeval forest. For some reason, gunshot wounds do not heal easily in elephants, though other animals recover from them. They are apt to form festering sores, usually maggot–ridden, that cause considerable pain and handicap to the animal, for years persisting.

The impact on elephants of human invasions of their territory is of special interest and significance. Most other diurnal animals retreat from their homes before human invasions of the deep forests, or else turn into fugitive creatures of the night, hiding by day in cover because men are active in the forests then. The elephant is not entirely, or even almost entirely, diurnal in its activity, but it seems to be the only wild animal with a sufficient sense of territory (in the face of any intrusion into its old home) and sufficient resentment of being disturbed and harried by men, to turn hostile towards men as a consequence. In forests where they are little disturbed, the normal reaction of elephants to human presence is flight. A big herd I was following at a distance, with the wind blowing from the animals to me, turned round suddenly and came towards me (and the cover of tree forests) at their fastest pace, running helter–skelter over uneven open ground; a little while later, what had alarmed them (by scent) came into view, a small boy of about 8 herding a buffalo cow. A tusker about to emerge from a thorn bush turned back and retreated into the dense cover, on hearing the sound of a man cutting wood with an axe. Many instances of the natural tendency of wild elephants to bolt from the presence of men are on record. They are even able to associate cattle with men, and usually flee from cattle, unless they are sure that there are no herdsmen with the beasts.

Where they have been much disturbed and harried by men, their reaction to humanity undergoes a change. Flight is still the commonest reaction, but they may become more assertive and indulge in demonstrations and even attacks. An interesting response of theirs, when elephants have to cross a road in a forest they stay close to the road to drink or feed, is to pull down a few culms of giant bamboo from a roadside clump, or a sapling across the path to constitute a road–block."

What Krishnan writes, regarding the elephant's reaction to the need to cross a road, has been well studied by BNHS scientists at Mudumalai where a highway has to be crossed by elephants desiring a drink in the river on the other side of the road. The behaviour change is abrupt. Herds, which do not react to human presence one kilometre from the road inside the forest, become tense and prone to charge as they near the road. The need to cross the road to drink every day apparently causes a high stress situation.

"Krishnan (20) states that in assessing these responses and aggressiveness to men, it should be remembered that elephants are long–lived animals, with a clear topographical comprehension of their stamping grounds, and that their resentment of intrusion, such as man–made structures, into their territory, and their proclivity to destroy such structures is something that can even be anticipated. It is said that on occasion their hostility to men takes the form of flinging stones (by the trunk) at the intruders, a less wildly improbable response than it might seem to those not familiar with elephants. Tame elephants sometimes demonstrate their dislike of being annoyed by picking up and throwing a stone at a man – this is well known, and it is common knowledge among men in elephant camps that some tame elephants are more prone to this action than others. I have personally experienced resentment of my attempt to get close to a herd (in which there were young calves) by the leading cow of the herd getting on to a path above me, and sweeping down stones and debris at me from above with her trunk.

The more usual manifestation of resentment of human intrusion is a demonstration or a charge. Even in an area like the Moyar block of the Mudumalai sanctuary however, where what was long known as a favourite haunt of wild elephants has been invaded by a hydro–electric project, canals, clearings for the powerlines, human settlements, agriculture and plantations; and where the human population has increased enormously and thousands of cattle are herded every day in the forests, what is astonishing is not the occasional aggression of the wild elephants but their acceptance of man–made intrusions and their tolerance of humanity. Almost every year a few people are killed by elephants in and around the Mudumalai Sanctuary (the entire area must be considered as one natural wildlife unit, though politically demarcated between three States), but these killings occur in the course of chance encounters between men and elephants inside the forests, and not at human settlements invaded by the elephants; incidentally, not only adult bulls, but cows and even teenagers, are responsible for many of these attacks, which are caused by panic as often as by deliberate hostility.

A consequence of the invasion of elephant forests by man is that with their territory much reduced in extent and with constant disturbance from humanity, small herds moving into the area leave it in a panic (especially when seasonal conditions are unfavourable to them) and move near the surrounding human settlements. Further, the raising of crops in the immediate vicinity of forests leads to crop–raiding by elephants. The methods at present in use against such crop–raiding elephants are mainly firing crackers to scare them off, the digging of elephant proof ditches around the fields (a laborious and costly method), and, of course, the use of firearms, often inexpertly and from too far away, usually resulting in the elephants turning hostile to the men. Since elephants are most sensitive to smells, it would be of interest to both wildlife protection and agriculture in India, if some non–volatile liquid, with as smell unaccepatable to elephants, could be sprayed in a twenty–foot wide belt around crops. Such a scheme, naturally, involves experimental work by research chemists to ascertain which liquid would repel elephants (camp elephants) and at the same time not harm men or crops through accidental contact but, though I have repeatedly made the suggestion to those who might be able to act on it, the response to my suggestion, so far, has been entirely one of 'no–enthusiasm'.

An incidental consequence of the human occupation and invasion of elephant forests is the rumour, published from time to time in the popular press, that there is an alarming increase in the number of elephants, which has been noticed by forest officials, who saw calves with herds where formerly they had seen none. Naturally, more elephants are seen with the deeper penetration of officials and others into the forests. As for the sudden sight of calves, presumably there were calves even in the past, for there to be calves now, and no further comment is necessary beyond this passage from 'Thirteen Years Among the Wild Beasts of India' by G.P. Sanderson: 'When an alarm occurs in a herd the young ones immediately vanish under their mothers, and are then seldom seen again. A herd containing a large number of calves would be supposed under these circumstances by the uninitiated to consist entirely of full–grown elephants."

13.1 Encounters

Everyone who has spent time in elephant-holding jungles have had an exciting encounter with elephants at some time or another. R.C. Morris (85, 86), who lived almost his whole life on a coffee estate in the midst of elephant infested jungles, relates some encounters he had with elephants in the Billigirirangan Hills in Karnataka.

Event I

"A party of four were in camp— two men and two ladies. Soon after nightfall, a herd of elephants started trumpeting near camp, and shortly after this the herd entered the shola the camp was in from the western side, surrounded the camp on three sides, commenced to demonstrate, and things looked decidedly nasty. The Sholagas (jungle tribe, excellent trackers) feverishly made a ring of fires round the camp with all available firewood, and shots were fired. Every now and then an elephant would crash through the jungle with a shrill trumpet, to within a few yards of the ring of fires, to be met with shouts and yells and a volley of shots. It was a weird and wild scene, the glare of the fires round the camp lighting up the figures of the two sportsmen standing with shotguns at the ready and loaded rifles at hand for any elephant that might break through the ring of fires, the two women standing behind trees, and the Sholagas running from fire to fire, waving fire–brands, banging kerosene tins, and yelling vociferously. There was not a tree in the vicinity that an elephant could not knock down with ease. Beyond the light shed by the fires was inky blackness, and from here issued terrifying roars, trumpets, and a medley of other sounds and crashes from the elephants. Every now and then the whole herd seemed to advance, and once or twice it looked as if they would charge through the camp en bloc. It was during one of these attacks that one of the women, in an extremity of fear, climbed a small tree which was little more than a sapling (even so, how she managed it she could not say later) which bent over, and deposited her gently into the small stream that flowed past the camp! It was a succession of advances and retreats, sometimes by the whole herd, at others by elephants singly, or in twos and threes. One tusker, bolder than the rest, very nearly broke through the ring, and the rifles were quickly seized, but he turned and went back into the darkness just in time. After fully three hours of this, the whole herd finally retreated, but could be heard venting their rage on trees in the vicinity. and Then a series of trumpets and thuds gave one the impression that two tuskers were fighting; this turned out to be correct on the following morning. Still later, the noise subsided, except for low grumbling like the rumblings of a distant thunderstorm. There was, however, no sleep for the party in camp; there was the possibility of the elephants returning to the attack, which fortunately did not occur. The morning dawned on a scene of destruction for about 200 yards to the south, east and north of the camp where the jungle had been smashed up and trodden down by the elephants for several hours. Sholagas reported that the elephants were still within a half–mile of camp, and the two men went out with their rifles, and watched a Homeric fight between two tuskers – a battle of the Giants. One was a bit smaller than its adversary, but had larger tusks, and distinctly had the advantage, finally defeating its opponent, chasing it away through the jungle, followed by the rest of the herd. A broken piece of tusk was later picked up. Thus ended an extraordinary incident. It was supposed that the elephants found the camp on their path, and decided to try to oust the intruders, but it is possible that the two tuskers had already commenced their battle and were in an in pleasant frame of mind, becoming infuriated when they discovered a camp pitched (unknowingly), on the elephant path and led them on to attack. It is stated that African elephants have been known to do this but, in connection with Indian elephants, a case such as this is very rare.

The ladies decided that they had their fill of shikar experiences for the time being, and were escorted back to the Estate by one of the men. On their way back they encountered a cow elephant (with a calf) which demonstrated at them, and seemed to be in two minds as to whether to charge them or not, luckily she decided not to.

Event II

M. and his sister were out in camp some years ago; the latter had elected to remain in camp one morning, while the former went out for a stalk. A rogue elephant, described as the

Dodsampagai Rogue, was known to be wandering somewhere in the vicinity. At 10 am., while M.'s sister was reading at the door of her tent, a wild shriek from the chokra made her start up, and she was horrified to see that a large tusker had stalked quietly into the camp; she then felt her Miniature .22 Rifle thrust into her hand by the chokra from inside the tent, and heard his agonised whispers of 'Shoot, Missie, shoot!' Finding that she was not yielding to his entreaties in this respect, he skimmed up a tree alongside the tent in a marvellous fashion. All this time the tusker stood still, taking everything in, but luckily decided not to attack. It turned and walked out of camp as slowly and quietly as it had come in, and made for the narrow strip of shola which was known to be its usual habitat. At midday M. and his trackers, when returning from the morning stalk, and passing this shola (incidentally giving it their wind) were startled by a short sharp trumpet, and out charged the Dodsampagai Rogue. M. was carrying a .500 Express Modified Cordite Rifle, and had just time to fire at the charging rogue's head, which made it swerve and present his broadside. A second shot fired behind the shoulder was a lucky one, and got the elephant in the region of the heart; rushing on for another 200 yards or so, he collapsed dead. Thus were avenged the deaths of Dod Toddy Mada and his son Jeddia, two Sholagas who had walked right into the rogue on a misty monsoon day near the same spot a year before, and were killed torn limb from limb.

Event III

M., his wife, and a friend were in camp, and had retired to bed. After midnight M. was woken up by his wife who said, 'I am sure there is an elephant in camp' (the same old camp). `Rats!' was the unfeeling and sleepy reply, but hardly was this spoken when M.'s Irish Terrier, which was sleeping at the door of the hut, rushed out barking furiously, and then came a shrill trumpet and crashing noise as an elephant careered out of camp with the dog after it. For a few moments pandemonium reigned, shouts and yells from the camp sholagas, and shots from M. and his friend, helped to speed the uninvited and undesired departing intruder! It turned out that this elephant was one of a herd feeding nearby, and had wandered in the direction of the camp finding itself in it before it knew where it was!

Event IV

M., his wife and the same friend decided to visit Bellagulla for bear. It became dark when the party were within a mile of camp, and M. stopped at a nulla to light a lantern, resting the .375 Mauser Rifle he had been carrying against a rock. Absent–mindedly he picked up the lantern and the party moved on along the path, leaving the rifle behind! When, within 200 yards of camp, shouts from Sholagas up trees warned them that the Bellagulla rogue had temporarily taken possession of camp and, to make matters worse, 'Peter' the Irish Terrier scented the elephant and, probably remembering how he chased an elephant out of camp on a previous occasion, rushed in and bayed the rogue! There followed a devil of a to do, and a nasty situation for the group, as it was pitch dark and the rogue could be heard kicking up the dickens of a rumpus, 'Peter' barking wildly, and the elephant trumpeting, but not retreating. Soon 'Peter' realized that he was up against a different proposition altogether, and raced back to M. and the others, followed, however, by the now infuriated tusker. Shots were fired into the air, and the Sholagas yelled and tried to light the grass, which was however too green to burn. Luckily the elephant turned aside when just short of the party and they reached camp without further trouble. Seizing his .450 H.V. Rifle when they first heard the elephant, M. had not had occasion to think about the .375 Mauser, and it was not until camp had been reached that he remembered it left in the nullah. It was decided to send for the rifle in the morning. This was done and, when they returned from the morning stalk, M.'s rifle, or what remained of it, was lying in front of the hut. It was literally smashed to

M Krishnan

Herd of 20 elephants in a bay. Grown cow crossing the log, Periyar.

M Krishnan

Herd of 20 elephants in a bay. Calf attempting to get over the log. Note
Cow leading another young round the obstacle, Periyar.

M Krishnan

4 cows and a young calf in Kollakumalikatte - note Duckweed.

A big cow suckling her calf.

M Kris

E. P. Gee

A Khedda under construction

E.P. Gee

Wild elephants stockaded

Kunkies moving in to rope the captives

E. P. Gee

A young captured elephant under training

Training in Progress

A Makhna in riverine Grasslands, Kaziranga

smithereens. The woodwork was matchwood, and the barrel, breech, and bolt were hopelessly damaged. The rogue had apparently gone along the path that the party had taken to camp, and, scenting human taint on the rifle in passing, had given vent to its rage by smashing it to pieces on the rocks. Not satisfied with this, proceeding further, the rogue had come on a cow, which M. had tied up for tiger, and kicked the wretched animal to death! M. and his friend vowed they would finish the rogue at the earliest opportunity, this soon came, the rogue was marked down, and laid low – an enormous elephant, 10' in height at the shoulder, with a large single 6' tusk.

Event V

M. was shikaring at Bailur, a good spot in the old days, and one morning was walking down a fireline with a Sholaga tracker, when round a corner ahead a call was heard which, the Sholaga insisted, was a bear. Advancing forward rapidly, M. and the Sholaga came face to face with a tusker which immediately charged. The tracker lost his head and must have achieved well nigh a record for a half–mile sprint down the fireline with a heavy rifle on his shoulder, omitting in his hurry to pass it to M. There followed a few intensely exciting moments racing from bamboo clump to clump with the elephant in close pursuit. The elephant soon tired of this, however, and made off much to M.'s relief. What followed when the Sholaga having viewed the elephant's departure from a safe distance returned, jauntily carrying the rifle, and congratulated M. on his escape, need not be recounted.

Event VI

On a hot day some years ago, M. and his sister, companions in shikar, were resting on a patch of sheet rock on the bank of a stream waiting for the tiffin basket to come down from camp, when they saw a cow elephant and two small calves pass across in front of them on the opposite bank of the stream. The Sholaga tracker was very emphatic that the elephant could not cross to their side of the stream, the banks being very steep for two or three miles down. Thus reassured, they lay down and slept, and so did the tracker. After they had been dozing for about an hour, a loud crack awoke them and, slowly turning his head, M. saw the cow and her two calves towering over them barely 30 feet away. Shades of unholy pachyderms! Of all the nasty situations, this was the worst. M.'s sister pluckily did not move, but the sholaga whispered incessantly, petrified with terror, 'Shoot, shoot!' and nearly gave them away. Luckily he had the sense not to get up, and was hidden from the elephants by a boulder. The rifles were unloaded (it was mid–day, very hot, the jungle burnt clean, and ordinarily there was little possibility of any game being seen till later); it would have been a fatal move to try and load them at such close quarters. After standing motionless, a calf on either side, the cow and her calves advanced and passed close to M., within a few paces, and slid down the steep bank into the stream passing below the sheet rock up the stream, so close to us that the back of the nearest calf could have been touched with an outstretched rifle. They then climbed up the bank on the opposite side, and soon disappeared from view. The tracker was quietly crying with relief! On a previous occasion, when sent to the camp with a message in the moonlight, he had come face to face with an elephant and, rooted to the spot, emitted a series of the most ghastly shrieks imaginable. Luckily the elephant was not inclined to do him any harm, although encountered at such close quarters and, watching him for a minute or two, turned away into the jungle.

Event VII

M. had wounded a boar, in a valley covered with thick decidu-ous forest, and followed it up into a gully in which grew several large clumps of bamboo. Here the pig was found lying on its side at its last gasp, and was given a finishing shot. The results were startling: crashes to the left and right, and a tusker came in view on M.'s left front, with a solitary bull bison on his right! Game paths running on either side converged and met behind bamboos to the front, and on these paths the two huge animals rushed, and met! There was a terrible thud, preceded by a short trumpet from the elephant, the a bellow from the bison, followed by a crash and a struggle in the bamboo, then the elephant appeared to the right moving rapidly away. Advancing cautiously, M. and his men saw the bull bison, a magnificent specimen, lying, against a clump of bamboos, breathing heavily, with a horrible wound in its near side, undoubtedly caused by the elephant's off–tusk. The tusk had penetrated one of the bull's lungs, and a hissing noise sounded from the wound as the poor brute breathed. A bullet in a vital soon put it out of its distress. Thus closed a extraordinary occurrence, one which M. can be said to have been in a way responsible for, as it was his shot, (magnified by the gully) that roused the tusker and the bull, and in their flight the elephant, alarmed and angry, saw the bison approaching along the other path and deliberately rammed the old bull, probably attributing to it the cause of the disturbance. The elephant later met M.'s tiffin coolly, who said he had just escaped with his life up a tree as the elephant had chased him, and to prove this he showed M. the contents of the tiffin basket –– a mass of broken crockery and glass mixed with food, and no beer to drink!

Event VIII

M., his wife, and children were motoring up the ghat road one evening, returning from a trip to the Nilgiris, when round a corner they came on a herd of elephants. M. jumped out with his rifle, while his wife reversed back and out of sight. M. stood watching the elephants move slowly off the road into the jungle below, when round the corner the car came buzzing again, another elephant had apparently made its presence known behind them!! In the meantime, the last of the herd had moved into the jungle, and the car rushed past them, much to their consternation and surprise. On another occasion, motoring up the road at night, an elephant trumpeted just off the road as the car passed it, and was heard to rush swiftly through the grass, whether after the car or not it was difficult to tell for certain. Elephants were all over the place; M. and his wife expected to meet one round every corner, and suddenly, when within half a mile of the first Estate, the expected happened. An elephant stood on the roadside, facing the headlights of the car so close that their only chance lay in attempting to rush past it, and this they did, M.'s wife driving, with M. holding his rifle levelled on the elephant. The elephant neither moved nor gave any signs of ruffled feelings; it was the local Government Timber Elephant.

Elephant on road ways

An incident recently occurred on the Ghat Road leading down from the Billigirirangan Hills.

A single cart–bull had been trotting in front of a car travelling from the Estate down the Ghat for some way. Eventually the car was stopped and H., a visitor to Honnametti, got out and ran after the bull in the hopes of turning it off the road. On rounding the corner an extraordinary sight met his eyes:– An elephant group – a bull, 2 cows and a calf, had just come on to the road and, as the cart–bull trotted up to the party, the 2 cows put their heads together and without hesitation pushed the cart–bull off the road down into the long grass below. Luckily it was not much of a drop, and the cart–bull appeared to suffer no harm!

13.2 Elephant Capture
13.2.1 Pit Traps

The capture of elephants goes back in the mists of time, first as prey and later, once the taming process had been learnt, as a method of replenishing stocks of tame elephants and for selling the surplus. The pit method is obviously the oldest as it was primitive man's way of subduing and killing an animal much more powerful than he was. The Khedda or stockade is a much later refinement.

The pit traps, described by Evans (17) in 1896 as used by Burmans, are the same as have been used in elephant habitat elsewhere in the world, though the purpose was diametrically opposite. The Burmans used the traps to kill elephants, as thousands of years ago their forebearers may have used them while hunting elephants. Evans says :

"The people sometimes catch a 'rogue' or other destructive beast by means of pitfalls. These are made in the following manner:– The point selected for digging a pit is on one of their well–known tracks to certain water or cultivation, and usually at a spot where the grass or jungle is very thick. The pit having been dug, all traces of fresh earth are removed, and the mouth is then carefully concealed with bamboos, elephant grass, etc. After this plenty of fresh droppings are procured, and these are thrown over the grass. The ruse tends to throw an animal off his guard, and so he falls into the trap. The men then destroy the animal with spears or a gun. Karens now and again capture one or two with the aid of tame elephants."

In South India, particularly in the states of Tamil Nadu and Kerala, the pit-fall method was the method of choice and was used till very recently. H.B. Bryant (75) describes the method and discusses the results. He writes:

"Out of a total of 17 captures 12 are now living. It may be remarked, moreover, that the casualties took place amongst the first three years' captures when the attendants, who are local hillmen, called Mulcers, were entirely inexperienced concerning elephants. During the last two years, I have increased the bed of brushwood considerably, and made it a rule to have the bed reach to within 4 feet of the top of the pit. The results speak for themselves; not a single animal has since been injured in the face, although two of the latest captures were the largest animals caught since operations were commenced.

The removal of a capture to the kraals, which are within two or three miles from the pits, is a very simple matter, provided everything is in readiness beforehand. The size of the animal's neck is estimated, and a peg is put in the rope so as to prevent the noose going smaller than the estimated neck–size. This noose is then thrown over the elephant's neck and pulled tight to the peg, the end of the rope being bound round a neighbouring tree. Next, one of the elephant's hind legs is noosed, and the end of this rope, too, is for the time being bound round a neighbouring tree. The neck rope at the peg then has to be tied with twine or fibre to prevent the noose being loosened by the elephant. This operation is, taking it all round, the most risky one connected with the capture. But, if proper care is taken there is nothing to fear.

The pit is then filled up by means of billets of wood being thrown in, and as the animal rises nearer the surface of the ground, the two ropes fastening him are pulled tighter around the trees. Eventually he gets out of the pit somewhat fatigued; the ropes which secure him are then fastened to two tame elephants, and the animals are marched in a single file (the captured, one being, of course, in the middle) to the kraal where all the ropes are removed. He is watered three times a day and soon made tame by kindness, given sugarcane, etc. Somewhat large animals are generally in the kraal 3 months before they can be taken out, the little ones of 4 ft. or 5.5 feet high, however, I have removed within three weeks of capture.

The work of capturing elephants is an exceedingly interesting one, and only needs care and constant supervision to render it successful. Certainly the more one has to do with these animals the more one is bound to recognise what intelligent, useful beasts they are. Having left the South Coimbatore District, I much regret that, for some time at least, I shall have no connection with this kind of work entrusted to forest officers".

13.2.2 Mela-Shikars

In the North-east of India, the methods of capture used were the Mela-Shikar, by which elephants were chased and noosed, and the Khedda, in which elephants were driven into a prepared stockade. The latter method was also in use in Mysore (Karnataka) state. Both methods are described by A.J.W. Milroy (65) who was responsible for making the method of capture and training of elephants, humane. Milroy writes:

"Elephants are caught in Assam by two methods. Mela Shikar and Kheddah. The former consists of pursuing the wild herds with tame elephants carrying nooses, and this method, together with pitting (now illegal), has been practised from very ancient times.

Three or four koonkies, as the tame elephants are called, usually operate together at mela shikar, and it is considered desirable that one of the elephants should be a big male of known courage in case any of the wild elephants prove aggressive. Each koonkie has 3 attendants, the phandi, who sits on the neck and throws the phand (or noose), the lohitiya, who hangs on behind and prods the koonkie near the root of the tail when speed is required, and the kumla, who remains in camp and is responsible for feeding the koonkie.

The catching gear consists only of the jute phand, which is attached to the koonkie's girth.

The koonkies can often work their way undetected into the middle of a herd when it is feeding in open order, provided the locality has not been much hunted recently, but the wild elephants soon become exceedingly wary, and will then fly both farther and faster from the smell of a tame elephant than they will from man.

In such a case there is no alternative but to pursue, and try to cut off and noose those calves which cannot keep the pace and fall behind. The whole performance, with the screaming of the elephants and the smashing of the jungle, is very noisy and terrifying, as may be imagined, but serious accidents are uncommon, as a matter of fact, and such damage as befalls the men is usually caused by thorns and branches of trees tearing and bruising them.

Female elephants, whose calves have been noosed, will sometimes attempt a rescue, but good koonkies will always square up to the attacker and drive her away.

The big males of a herd seem to prefer keeping to themselves some little distance apart and, when danger threatens, are among the first to seek safety in flight, provided the koonkies do not get in their way. An elephant in musth constitutes more of a problem, and the phandis draw off if there is any danger of coming into conflict with a male that is under this dangerous influence.

Phandis necessarily vary greatly in skill, but it commonly happens, even in the case of the most expert, that the noose does not get home properly on the wild elephant's neck, and it is then necessary to call for a phand to be thrown from a second koonkie.

Quite a big elephant can be caught by this method, but in that case the first noose scarcely serves more than to brake the headlong pace of the terrified beast, and assistance has to be summoned at once to prevent escape.

The phands may be two inches or more in diameter, but even these ropes are not always heavy enough to take the strain, and the writer has known a big makhna (tuskless male) break 7 ropes in succession before he could be finally secured.

Mela shikar leads to a number of the wild elephants being unavoidably strangled, and it is fortunate that this form of death is instantaneous, on account of the structure of the elephant's wind-pipe.

The koonkie proceeds to put on the brake as soon as the phand is round the wild elephant's neck, and then the tug-of-war begins, the wild animal doing all it knows to escape from the unaccustomed restraint. It is the phandi's concern to shorten the rope gradually until the captive is secured alongside his own animal, and he can only do this by seizing such opportunities as occur between bouts of pulling and struggling. The noose has to be tied by a small piece of rope to prevent it slipping up and throttling the elephant and it happens occasionally that the noosed elephant gets so hopelessly wound round trees that the phand tightens and death ensues.

13.2.3 Kheddah
Kheddahs in Assam are worked on a less pretentious scale than those organised in Mysore, or formerly practised by the now

defunct Kheddah Department, and no attempt is now made to surround herds with a large number of men, and then force them into a hastily erected stockade.

Stockades in Assam are built either across main elephant paths, or else in the vicinity of salt–licks, which the elephants visit of their own accord from time to time.

In most districts in Assam the herds are found to travel from one feeding ground to another by certain well–worn paths. Wherever the ground is favourable they can wander, maybe several miles, from the main paths, but it generally happens that sooner or later steep hills or boggy ground compel them to return to their fixed paths, which follow the safest and easiest lines across country with unerring accuracy, representing, as they do, the result of the accumulated wisdom and experience of countless generations of travelling elephants.

The most favourable stockade sites are in ravines, through which the driven elephants must pass, unless they have the courage to break back through the beaters.

It is necessary that a stockade should not be too obvious to the approaching animals, so it must be built in thick tree forest, where camouflaging can be successful.

Very rocky ground is avoided because of the difficulty in sinking the posts to the requisite depth, and it would obviously be impossible to build sufficiently strongly on marshy soil. Stockades vary in shape according to the locality, but are generally more or less oval or oblong, about a cricket pitch wide and a few yards more in length.

A gate at each end is necessary, where elephants can be driven from either direction, and the gates have to be built across the path itself; a skillful band of hunters, who know their work thoroughly, often prefer to build their stockade across a subsidiary path, trusting to their own skilful management to deflect the driven elephants (from whichever direction they may come), from the main on to the subsidiary path; this arrangement saves labour as it obviates the necessity of constructing more than one gate.

The best site for a gate is clearly where the path passes between two trees, because the trees can then be utilized as door–posts and, more important, because there is no artificial narrowing of the path, the elephant being accustomed to squeeze between the two trees at this spot.

Drop–gates used to be employed, but these are cumbrous to lift up, and heavy swing doors, 10 to 12 feet high, made after the pattern of an ordinary English five–barred gate, are now used.

The doors open inwards and, before a drive commences, the door, through which the herd must enter, is opened and kept in position by a long rope, leading to a machan concealed in some convenient tree outside the stockade. A slash with a knife cuts the rope and releases the gate which, hung so as to swing to of its own accord, has its pace accelerated by means of a spring, consisting of a rope tied to the top of a bent–over sapling, which tends to straighten itself as soon as the watcher in the machan has released the gate.

The old fashioned stockade consisted of stout posts, 18 or 19 feet long, sunk in the ground to a depth of 5 feet with a spacing of about 3 feet, and horizontal logs were packed in between to a height of 13 or 14 feet; but such massive structures have proved unnecessary, involving very heavy labour, as the timber must be carried from distance, in order not to disturb the forest close by.

Nowadays, vertical posts, 17 or 18 feet long, are buried 5 feet in the ground, about 5 feet apart, with 3 rows of horizontal beams are tied on outside, one row near ground level, one at breast height, and the third near the top: the whole structure is strengthened by struts from the ground to the 3 rows of horizontal beams.

The spaces between the upright posts are filled by vertical poles (3 inches in diameter are sufficient), which merely rest on the ground and are kept in position by being tied to the inside of the 3–rows of beams.

Another method is to bury rather smaller posts every foot, the interstices being filled in with poles.

A well built stockade may look extraordinarily flimsy, but there is plenty of give in it, and it is adequately protected from direct assault by a V shaped ditch, seven feet wide and five feet deep.

It is not customary in Assam to tackle old and big males, which may happen to be caught, because it has been found that the koonkies (if any can be found with sufficient courage and strength for the job) may be severely damaged in the encounter, and also because mature males often lose heart and practically refuse to live in captivity, so it is not necessary to build stockades strong enough to retain the biggest elephants.

It so happens that the masters of a herd seldom get caught, except when in musth, because they selfishly try to break away when danger arises, and the beaters are only too thankful to let them through, but these goondas, as rogues are called, are not really very troublesome so long as they are caught with a herd. They have to be shot, not from fear that they would break out, but because they damage smaller members of the herd, and are, as has been explained, of doubtful commercial value.

Solitary rogues often wander into stockades at night, and occasionally the watcher in the gate–machan makes a mistake in the dark underestimating the size and age of the elephant, closes the door; then the fun begins. Determination on the part of the men may suffice to keep a makhna in, but a tusker seeing red is an awesome beast, and can walk through a stockade at any spot he likes despite the ditch, or and more commonly, he just puts his tusks under the door and heaves it over his back.

V-shaped funnels or wings extend out from the gateposts, so that all elephants which are taking a course parallel to the path may be directed to the entrance.

The final act of preparation (excluding religious observances) consists of camouflaging the stockade. Living tree–ferns and orchids are fastened on to the doors and door–posts, and branches of trees are stuck in the ground to conceal the funnel.

Care is taken during of construction work to preserve intact the jungle growing in the middle of the enclosure, and branches and creepers are hung over the sides of the stockade to mask a distinctive outline.

The ditch is effectively hidden by fresh branches placed across it higgledy–piggledy.

A super–camouflager will sometimes take the trouble to fashion little tracks through the jungle in the middle, the idea being that the elephants which enter first will waste time following these tracks, and so enable the men to hustle in the laggards.

One of the outstanding advantages of the present–day stockade is that the elephants can see through it. Very few herd animals are game enough to try and rush the ditch and palisade in the face of a man armed with a torch and spear, at night when the elephants are more restive, the encircling fires are visible and command respect.

The weak point is the gate, a moveable structure without any part buried in the ground, and with no protecting ditch. The obvious place of attack, because it bars the exit along the well–known path. The dear old elephant however, is not very worldly wise, and it is found that the gate can appear to the elephants the strongest part of the whole contraption merely by fitting it with sticks and branches, so that the beasts cannot see through it.

Driving is best done late in the afternoon and evening, when the elephants are on the move themselves, and the beaters like to time their drives so that the elephants are entrapped just before dark, when deficiencies in the concealment of the stockade may not be noticed.

Elephants like to rest in thick cover during the heat of the day, and inclined to be pig–headed and circle round if driven while the sun is still high; after dark they become much more aggressive and may effectively resist pursuit

A drive may be a lengthy business extending over several days and nights, but in that case the earlier stages, when the herd is still far from the stockade, consist merely in the men keeping a long way behind the elephants, so that they will move quietly in the desired direction without stampeding, any attempts to take divergent paths being frustrated by men sent forward to block the way.

The real excitement begins about 3 O'clock on the last afternoon, when pressure is first put upon the elephants.

The beaters as a rule number from 7 to 12, save in exceptional circumstances; crowds of men and excessive noise are regarded as signs of unskillful work.

The beaters are divided into two parties, which follow on either flank of the herd, the men keeping in single file, a formation which permits them to get through the undergrowth without straggling, and to form line if the elephants stand up to them.

The principal difficulties are caused by goondas trying to break out of the drive, and by mothers of weary calves.

No impediment is offered to the flight of a goonda unless smaller fry are following him, when it becomes necessary either to force back the goonda, or to nip in behind him and head back the others, a very delicate task.

Mothers will charge back time and again in order to let their calves get on, and they frequently spoil drives by holding back the beaters so much that the leading elephants, with no one behind to hustle them, discover the approaches to the stockade;

217

they will then leave the path and, if ground permits, make a big circuit at their leisure round the stockade. All the succeeding elephants follow in the footsteps of the leaders, as they know they would never have branched off like this without some good reason.

Herds will sometimes absolutely refuse to be driven any further, and one is tempted to believe that in these cases the herd must have passed through the unfinished enclosure at night when it was in course of erection, or been made wise in some other way.

Guns are fired only in the last resort, and when elephants are deliberately heading in the wrong direction; the sound of a gun is so terrifying that the herd may panic and scatter pellmell through the forest, completely beyond further control. Not even guns, however, will stop a herd that has made up its mind to break back, and the beaters are saved from extermination only by their uncanny powers of distinguishing between bluff and the real thing on the elephants' part, and their amazing ability to make themselves scarce as the elephants thunder through them.

If they keep on getting round in front of the herd, persistence on the men's part may eventually cause the elephants' determination to evaporate, and they will then allow themselves to be driven all the way back.

The diverging paths near the stockade are blocked by men in machans, these stops descending and joining in the passing hunt when their work is done, and there are also stops at the ends of the wings, in case the elephants come along very wide of the real path.

Once the herd has entered the funnel, a gun is fired and every one behind the elephants proceeds to make all the noise he can. The sudden irruption of sound stampedes the animals, but escape should not be possible if the men running along outside the wings resist any attempt at a breakthrough.

218

It is not always possible to impound all the members of a herd which straggles into the stockade in extended order, because the elephants which first enter, sooner or later realize the position and try to retreat. It is amazing, however, that they should take as long as they do to appreciate the situation; the elephants bustle in at the door and hurry across to the far side of the stockade, but the sight of the ditch with the palisade beyond seems to bemuse them, and it is only after some moments' contemplation that they slowly turn and begin to wander back.

The door must be shut, whatever elephants there may still be outside, before the animals inside make a rush for the exit. The writer has seen elephants which had been excluded because the gate could no longer be kept open, barge the gate open, before it had been tied, and join their companions within, but as a rule the excluded elephants make a mad rush for one of the wings and burst their way through.

There is a certain amount of danger to the beaters from these escaping elephants, but it is quite certain that no elephant would then waste time hunting a man if it could possibly get away past him.

Methods of great finesse must be employed to catch elephants in stockades built near salt licks.

The herds visit the salt–licks during the night–time only, and at irregular intervals, so it is necessary for the men to be always on watch from late afternoon until dawn.

Two men are stationed in the gate machan, and the rest are distributed in high machans in the forest on the far side of the lick in such a manner that the elephants can tread their accustomed paths without getting any scent of man.

As soon as the elephants have reached the lick and are busy taking their medicine, the beaters descend from the machans and hasten to their appointed stations by especially cut paths, which are kept scrupulously clean and free from leaves.

When sufficient time has elapsed for all to reach their stations, torches are suddenly lit and the elephants driven towards the stockade; it sometimes happens that they simply rush straight into it, but more often they are less obliging, and skill and bravery are required to prevent their escaping along any of the numerous game trails which radiate from the lick. It is a matter of the greatest difficulty for anyone not accustomed to night work to appreciate what is happening, but a correct diagnosis of all the different crashes in the jungle must be made by the men, as it may be necessary to let small batches go rather than run the risk of frightening the main portion of the herd.

The noise alone is sufficient to terrify an ordinary mortal, and the close proximity of the big beasts is alarming, but accidents seldom occur so long as the men use their torches boldly.

The salt–licks are very frequently visited by solitary rogues, and it is found that these are often the advance guard of a herd. There is always the chance of a herd coming early in the morning, if a goonda has been at the lick the previous evening, or of the herd coming the next evening, after an early morning visit by a goonda.

It may be presumed from this that elephants pursue an ordered routine when undisturbed, and that a herd will follow the regular round of drinking and, feeding at the accustomed places, and lying up in the usual retreats, once started on one of its regular routes.

The goondas are, of course, not molested while at a lick, but a whiff of human smell will occasionally set a goonda to squeal-ing in anger and charging aimlessly about.

The men's machans have to be built in big trees, as a suspicious elephant will prospect the locality carefully, and may even be bold enough to try and tear down the machans.

The writer remembers how on one splendid moonlight night a large tusker crept up noiselessly beneath his machan and stood there puzzling as to the source of this poisoning of the night air; at last his trunk reached the ladder and told him that a man had gone up it not so very long before. The ladder was soon made into mincemeat but the tree stood firm, and the huge beast soon rolled off in a very grumpy frame of mind. The next obstacle which he encountered was the outside of the stockade, which provided him with a little healthy exercise, and finally he played spillikins with one of the wings before wandering off in high dudgeon. The amazing part of the story is that the two gate-men slept through the whole performance, and were greatly astonished when dawn arrived and they saw the destruction all around them.

At one lick, which we stockaded, there dwelt a very old and evil-tempered makhna, which soon came to learn all about the sites of the various machans, so provokingly out of his reach. One night, abandoning his accustomed path, he entered the stockade unwittingly and, being short-sighted, tumbled into the ditch on the far side. This thoroughly frightened him and he essayed to retreat at his best speed, but again his sight failed him and he tumbled into the ditch by the door.

The episode was too much for his nerves, and we never saw him again.

Elephants will certainly do quite unaccountable things at times; a goonda that walked into a stockade one night bit the cane which was holding the gate open, and consequently imprisoned himself inside the stockade. He had to do a lot of damage before he could punch a hole big enough to allow himself to escape through the palisade.

Elephants very seldom break out of a stockade, and when they do it is generally due to the presence of a big tusker, which unmindful of the spears and firebrands succeeds in bursting his way through and escaping with all his herd.

It is quite clear that the elephants would have no difficulty in getting out, if only they had the sense to rush pell–mell at the stockade and use their weight against it, but that is not their way. They are exceedingly timid animals, and spend most of their time in the stockade huddled up in the centre, milling round and round, each trying to secure an inside berth. The scrimmages are painful to watch because one fears for the small beasts, but these remain safely beneath their mothers and seldom come to any harm.

As an illustration of how timid elephants are may be shown from the story of a herd which was nearly reduced to panic by the entry of two very small fowls into the stockade. The religious ceremonies which are performed on the completion of a stockade include the releasing of two fowls, which from motives of economy are usually quite small chickens. These chickens exist in the neighbourhood of the stockade until some wild cat comes along and carries them off. On one occasion the diminutive pair sauntered into the stockade through a gap, looking for food amongst the debris on the ground, and threw the small elephants of the herd into the wildest confusion until angry charges from the bigger animals expelled them from the enclosure.

Single elephants will continually charge out from the scrum in the middle, but their charges end in precisely the same way as the rushes which a dog will make at a cat; the brakes are put on before the ditch is reached, and after a few kicks into space with the fore–feet the elephant retires.

Elephants are more restless at night, but a shout from a man and a wave of a torch are generally sufficient to maintain discipline.

Different countries have different methods for getting the wild elephants out, in Chittagong, for example, the koonkies enter the stockade backwards, the phandis being armed with long spears to keep off any inquisitive wild elephant that comes too close with evil intent. Men descend from the koonkies and operating beneath them dexterously manage to bind the legs of the wild elephants, which can then be taken out easily.

More direct and spectacular methods are employed in Assam, the koonkies entering head first and dragging out the reluctant wild elephants without any preliminary hobbling.

The koonkies are arranged in single file with the biggest animal, preferably a tusker, in front. The wild elephants smell the koonkies from afar, and the first intimation of the koonkie's approach is conveyed to those watching the stockade by the uplifted trunks and visible uneasiness of the herd. The elephants generally retreat towards the far side of the stockade and their attention is distracted there by fodder being thrown to them.

The bands tying the gate are loosened and, while men pull on ropes, the leading koonkie butts the gate open and stalks in with the remaining koonkies crowding after it.

It is advisable that the gate be opened with reasonable speed. The writer has seen a big female charge at a gate which stuck after being opened a little way, and she banged it shut with such force in the face of the koonkie on the other side that his morale was seriously affected.

It is even more advisable that the gate should shut quickly after the last koonkie has entered. On one occasion the leading koonkie swung the gate open, so violently as to unhinge it and prevent its being closed. In the subsequent confusion the men lost their heads and the koonkies were seized with panic, although there were only a few small females to deal with, and the whole mob, wild and tame, barged out through the open door amidst the groans and tears of the stockade men.

Wild elephants never combine to overwhelm the koonkies; one or two of the bigger beasts may look a little aggressive, but the koonkies go straight up to them and start hustling the herd round and round with the same confidence as a few disciplined men will show when dealing with an unruly but leaderless mob. No great violence is necessary and there is no excuse for damaging the wild elephants.

It used to be the custom in Assam to delay putting the koonkies in until the wild elephants had been weakened by thirst and hunger, but such cruelty is entirely unnecessary and has been discouraged by Government of fixing a time limit, within which the stockade must be cleared, or else the catch set free.

After five minutes or so the animals are allowed to settle down, and the men untie their nooses and get to work; the noosing is often a tiresome job, especially in the case of small elephants, which will insist upon running under their mothers; this makes it difficult to shorten the rope and tie the noose properly to prevent it getting any tighter, and unless this is done there is always the danger of strangling.

It is necessary for the koonkies to kneel down when the noose on a very small elephant is being tied, otherwise the man cannot reach it.

An elephant may require one, two, or even three koonkies to manage it; in the latter case the third noose is generally tied to a hind leg and is very effective in checking headlong progress.

The noosed animals resent being detached from their companions and have to be hauled to the door. There is a danger, when the koonkies have not managed to noose the whole catch, of the un-noosed elephants following the procession out, so the biggest koonkie is detailed to act as rear-guard, and he turns round and looks very fierce if the rest of the herd show signs of following.

Once outside the door (and the getting outside may be a regular case of pull devil, pull baker), the pace quickens up, and the koonkies have to use all their strength to prevent their captives from pulling them off the track into the forest. The passage from the stockade to the camp is usually rather a rough one for all concerned.

The new elephants are tied up for the first night by the hind legs to one tree and by a long rope from the neck to another tree, as high up as possible, to prevent the elephants' catching the rope and biting through it. It is necessary to have a koonkie on each side when the hind legs are being fastened, in order to obscure the elephant's view and prevent its frantic kicks from being properly aimed.

An elephant tied in this way can throw itself on the ground and exert all its weight in trying to break the ropes on the hind legs, and it is highly desirable that it should thus tire itself out as much as possible because, in the succeeding marches to the training camp, the koonkies have to carry the men's kit as well as lead the captives, and if the koonkies are few one koonkie may have to take two wild elephants.

A barbaric device to keep big elephants quiet on the march was to cut the back of the neck with a knife so that the noose could be fastened into the wound causing pain to discourage struggling. Government is now taking every precaution to discourage this sort of treatment. It is not difficult to detect a neck that has been deliberately cut, but the phahdis can obtain much the same result by sprinkling damp sand under the noose, which quickly eats through the skin in a more natural looking manner. The Black List now awaits the men who cannot bring their elephants in without a clean neck.

Tying the hind legs takes considerable time, so after the first night it is customary to fasten the elephants short by the neck to a tree, in such a way that they can run round and round the tree from which the bark has been removed in order to facilitate the rope slipping round without fraying.

Training is the next episode in the elephant's career on its road to a life of domesticity and usefulness.

Keeping an elephant tied up tight by the head, and spearing it for every misdemeanour has hitherto been considered the correct way to train an elephant, but the writer has been conducting experiments for the last five years, first on a small and later on a very extensive scale, and has been able to prove that a more rational method of treatment yields better results in every way.

In the first place the training casualties, which have been known to be as high as 48 per cent, have been reduced to less than 1 per cent, and in the second place it has been found that elephants, which are decently treated settle down to their work in an incredibly short space of time, and are more easily and effectively trained then those which have been maltreated and have had their spirits broken.

The elephants, of course, seek every opportunity during the first few days of their captivity to attack any human being who goes near them, but their lack of success, coupled with the heartiness with which the retaliatory stick is laid on, soon convinces them of the futility of their attempts, and their desire for a quiet and inoffensive life asserts itself so strongly that they abandon further resistance.

The stick they have to get sometimes is adequate punishment for these kindly beasts, though it cannot possibly hurt their thick skins.

The use of the spear is to be deprecated, not only because the wounds inflicted may set up septicemia, but also because fear of the pain distracts the elephant and prevents it concentrating on its task, thereby delaying the completion of its education.

An elephant has to be tied up fore and aft by its legs in the training depot, except when taken out for training; it is unnecessary to tie it up tight by the head (save during the evening performance), and, indeed, it is dangerous to do so as it may cause a bad neck wound, leading eventually to its death.

Rope harness is attached to the elephant for the benefit of the man who has to mount it.

The "evening performance" is a great show.

Eight or ten men approach the elephant after dark and, after its neck has been tied closely to a post, a man seizes its tail and the mahout springs onto its back.

One man in front waves a torch in its face, and the others surround it, keeping well out of reach of the trunk, and proceed to scrub it with wisps of grass; all to the accompaniment of appropriate songs.

The frightened animal bellows, shakes, throws itself on to the ground, lunges at everyone with its trunk and tries to catch the irritating torch, but all in vain, it is well lambasted with sticks and the torch proves itself to be a beastly hot thing to hold.

The treatment is continued for a week or so, until the elephant makes no resistance and the men can rub its face without being attacked.

The actual training takes place morning and evening.

The elephant is taken out between two koonkies, to which it is attached by very short nooses.

The mahout is already on one of the koonkies and leaps on to the new elephant when all is ready. The animal may shake a little, in which case the mahout must hold on very tightly, while the mahouts on the koonkies hit the elephant over the head, and the men on the ground in front and behind beat it with sticks. Shaking is a most dangerous vice and has to be stopped at all costs; it is lucky that very few elephants take to it.

It must be remembered that an elephant has generally lost a good deal of its pep by this time. It has been through a rough and tumble in the stockade, may have had several days' march with inadequate food, has been tied on the stretch by all four legs (to prevent it getting a real good rest), and has experienced the terrifying performance at night, so, take it all round, the poor beast cannot be in its best shaking form.

The man on the ground in front is a source of much irritation to the new elephant, but it cannot get at him and he can safely prod its trunk with his stick or bamboo, while the mahout hammers it, whenever it tries to rush forward.

The man behind, who sings the whole time in a horribly strident tone, is safe from being kicked because the action of the hind legs is limited by ropes, but he punishes all attempts at kicking, and the elephant has to learn to tolerate him.

When the mahout feels securely fixed, the order to proceed is shouted out, the koonkies go forward and the elephant gets a prod behind each ear from a sharpened bamboo.

The order to stop is shouted, the koonkies stop, and the mahout leans forward and catches his beast a good clout between the eyes.

The order to go back is followed by the mahout digging the point into the elephant's forehead and pulling, while the two koonkies pull the captive back a few steps.

A full–grown female requires two koonkies for 4 or 5 days, after that one koonkie drops behind and, if the elephant behaves, goes about its business. The remaining koonkie will be needed for another 4 days, but after that a man on the ground with a leading rope will suffice, until the animal can be taken out by its rider in the company of other old and new elephants.

Progress has meanwhile been made in the depot; the elephant will allow itself to be tied up without attempting to kick, and it will feed nicely from the hand.

An elephant should be ready for removal to the purchaser's home from within 14 to 21 days after the commencement of training, according to its size, though they are still far from being trained.

A full grown female should be bringing in a few stalks of fodder after a fortnight and after 4 or 5 weeks should be fit for loading with almost a full feed.

Elephants are easiest taught to kneel down by being stretched out fore and aft, and then prodded behind the withers with a sharp bamboo, while the word of command is shouted, and men haul on the front leg ropes till the elephant has to sink down to the ground.

Runaway elephants may forget everything else, but never seem to forget how to kneel down.

All the other accomplishments are gradually taught, and the elephant should be safe to shoot from at the end of 4 or 5 months, though still by no means absolutely trustworthy.

13.3 Care and Management of Captive Elephants

`The Care and Management of Captive Elephants' by G.H. Evans still continues to be standard reference, though methods of maintenance have progressed considerably since the publication. In this section, what Evans (17) and others had written in the Journal are reproduced. According to Evans the points of a healthy elephant are :

"The animal is in constant motion, with the ears flapping, and the tail and trunk swinging to and fro. The skin is almost black, and the bristles covering the body are firm to the touch; the light–coloured spots on the head and trunk are of a pinkish colour; the eye is bright and clear, pulse from 48 to 50 per minute; mucous membranes of mouth, etc., are of a beautiful pink colour; the back is free from scars; a moist secretion exudes around and above the nails, and is easily seen by throwing a little dust on the parts; the pads are hard, and free from tenderness; any signs of the latter may readily be detected, as the tender patches are smooth and a yellowish–pink colour. If the appetite is good, the animal sleeps for a few hours every night, and on waking commences to feed.

Signs of ill–health are general languor, the skin looks greyish in colour, as do the spots on the head and trunk; the mucous membranes are pale or deep red, with or without dark blotches on the palate; pulse is abnormal, appetite is lost; the animal does not take proper rest; eyes are dull, and there is frequently a copious flow of tears; there is usually fever, and the animal may be out of condition. As with other things, when buying elephants the purchaser should not be in a hurry, as his bargain may not afterwards prove to be all he desired. A little time should be taken to ascertain the idiosyncrasies of the beast about to be bought. The manner in which the keeper goes about his charge should be noted. Some animals are very full of tricks and, if not approached to their liking, may attack a new keeper or, if timid, be scared for ever. The animal should be marched about, and the pads carefully inspected after exercise; it is a common thing to fill up holes in the pads with stopping.

Burmans look upon elephants with certain habits with super-stitions dread; such creatures may be bought at very moderate figures. An elephant showing a peculiar general restlessness of the body, somewhat after the manner of a bear, is much dreaded, as also is a creature that has the habit of swinging his trunk only to the right and left.

The height of elephants is measured in cubits. The cubit is about twenty inches.

Powers of Endurance: Though such enormous creatures, they are constitutionally delicate. I fear that, through lack of appreciation of this fact, these animals have not received the amount of attention they justly deserve; and owing to the popular opinion that they are very strong, they have been too highly tasked. A great deal of the ill–health and mortality amongst elephants may well be ascribed to this cause. It cannot be too forcibly impressed, on those entrusted with the care of public animals, that untiring and vigilant superintendence over the attendants is the means, above all others, for the proper preservation of the efficiency of the animals committed to their charge. They must remember that men usually employed with transport, if left to themselves are, from general indolence, carelessness, or from a desire to avoid the fatigue and hardships of a campaign, quite liable to render their animals unserviceable; ample supervision enables the carrying out of systematic checks against carelessness, and more particularly checks to malpractices. A little. neglect will often deprive a force of the valuable services of many animals".

This is as valid today as it was when it was written a hundred years ago.

Usefulness

In the past elephants had been extensively used in forestry practices, and in Burma was and continues to be vital for timber extraction. Evans (17), describing conditions in the late 19th century states:

"In a country like Burma the great value of these creatures can readily be appreciated, large areas being covered with dense impenetrable jungle, immense marshy tracts, steep hills and deep ravines; added to which the whole country is intersected by rivers, large and small. In the absence of waterways in such a place, elephants are more than useful – they are indispensable; they can with ease penetrate the dense and path-less jungle, their great size and weight causes them to leave a very fair track as they move along; they can cross wide rivers, ford fast–running streams, carry men and baggage across swamps and heavy marshes penetrable to no other kind of transport animal. The value of an animal possessed of such strength and docility for transport purposes cannot be over–estimated.

In Burma, elephants are largely employed in the timber trade; in fact, the great commerce carried on in this line may be said to depend almost entirely on elephant–labour. The timber being scattered over wide areas of country without roads or slips, the logs have to be dragged by elephants through the jungle, over ridges, down ravines, and finally pushed into the flowing streams, where, owing to then immense strength, elephant can stand in the strong current and sort the timber for rafting, clear it when the logs get jammed, and push them back into the water when stranded. In the large timber yards in Rangoon, Moulmain, etc., they have to haul the logs out of the river, bring them up to the sawbench and, after they are heaped, the elephants remove and stack them as neatly as if done by human hands, and in all these operations they are cheap and most efficient. It is quite one of the sights in Burma to see the timberyard animals at work".

The elephant still remains the most environment friendly transport for the wild and remote parts of the country, and its use as a transport animal will be one way of saving this endangered species.

Training of Calves
Gordon Hundley (37) writing generally on the breeding of domesticated elephants, gives a brief note on the birth and training of the calves.

Should a female be known to be pregnant, she is allowed light work and a longish rest before the calf is expected but, in some cases, calves have appeared unexpectedly while the mother was grazing or even during work. Usually they are born while the mother is roaming loose, and soon after birth the little one can stand and stagger. A few hours after birth he can walk. Calves measured shortly after birth averaged two feet ten inches. This measurement is from the ground to the shoulder.

It is curious, but true, that a calf usually adopts a foster mother, who assists the dam in protecting and caring for the calf. Should the foster mother be pregnant, she must be moved or the calf will render the coming of her own calf a hungry one. The departure of the foster mother will be borne with anger and her return welcomed with pleasure by the little one.

Calves soon learn to pluck grasses and, although they will suckle up to three or more years, a continually increasing amount of green fodder is taken. Some believe that suckling is by the trunk, but it is not so. The trunk is curled above the forehead while suckling.

The training of the calf usually begins when he is about five years old, but Karen who are the most expert elephant man, have been seen with trained youngsters which could not have been more than four years old. The little beast is taught to allow himself to be fettered and loosed, to squat down and to rise, then a small saddle is placed upon his back and as time passes a small load is carried. Their early years are spent carrying loads until they grow sufficiently to permit the dragging of small logs. From this, they develop into working elephants, which spend their lives in the extraction of timber, the royalty and duty on which places many lacs of rupees into the coffers of Burma.

The Sgau Karens have handled elephants for generations, and numbers of calves have been born to their herds. It is common to meet men who compare their ages with those of their working elephants, and it is sometimes easier to judge the elephant's age than the man's. Numbers of calves born in the herds of elephants employed and owned by large timber working firms are to be seen nowadays, born and bred, trained, worked and growing old in captivity.

At times calves are amusing and at others most exasperating: they are however always interesting ".

Chapter 14

HUNTING

Elephant hunting was considered the apex among blood sports from the dangers involved. In India only bulls were permitted to be shot and these had to be proscribed as 'Rogues' after they had killed people. All the episodes included describe conditions in the country more than half a century ago, for elephant hunting as a sport fell out of favour about the middle of the century. Elephants are still proscribed and shot but it is usually considered a control measure, and no one writes about it. In India, hunting elephants is no longer a sport. Elephant photography however, which could be equally dangerous is a flourishing hobby among those who have knowledge and the courage to attempt it.

W.S. Thom (18) writes of the status of big game hunting as it was in the past and of the methods and excitement of hunting elephants. His remarks apply to conditions in Burma (Myanmar) more than sixty years ago. The methods he describes however for getting near wild elephants and keeping oneself away from danger are equally applicable today.

"Big game shooting nowadays is, I am afraid, very much decried. People look askance upon anyone who may happen to have shot a few more animals than other people, and refer to them as butchers. The filming and photography of wild animals in their natural state is now all to the fore. In my day, however, one could not go in for that sort of thing unless one had a big banking account, as cameras for that kind of work 25 and 30 years ago (this was written in 1932) cost a mint of money. Cameras have, however, now been perfected to such a pitch, that this kind of hobby can be indulged in more easily, whilst they are not quite so expensive.

In the heyday and first flush of my shikar days sportsmen did not think so much of game preservation as they do now.

There were no game preserves or game licences when I came to Burma in 1886, and many sportsmen did not worry so much regarding the numbers of animals shot by them, provided the animals could be considered warrantable trophies, and nearly every sportsman tried to beat his neighbour so far as the size of the head or the length and weight of a pair of tusks were concerned whilst he had also to consider the question of recouping himself for the expenses incurred and the cost of his weapons and ammunition. Nowadays, all that sort of thing is gone. A man who slaughters game for the sheer love of shooting and bagging animals is no longer tolerated. There is no doubt of course that we all to some extent inherit in our breasts the savage instincts of our forefathers. A great deal has been written and is still being written and done on the subject of big game preservation everywhere; but so far as I can see little or nothing can be done to stay the final destruction of all big game, not only in this Province but in India and Africa. The spread of civilization, the motor car, the modern high–powered rifle, new roads, the woodman's axe, the Arms Act and Rules, electric contrivances for night shooting, poaching by people of the country and the fact that the Forest Department is understaffed, are all factors which are now slowly but surely tending to bring about the steady diminution of game. It is of course admitted that the necessities of civilization must come first in the scheme of things, and the preservation of fauna must take second place.

I am entirely in agreement with Major C. Court–Treatt, author of `Out of the Beaten Track', when he says, 'assuming that the purpose of all sport is the attainment of adventure and the exercise of skill, I dare to maintain that elephant hunting can legitimately be regarded as the greatest of all sports; and, since only the elephant hunter is qualified to dispute it, my assertion is not likely to meet with any great volume of dissent. Adventure there is in plenty, and hard work too; and the hunter needs to be highly skilled in the habits and anatomy of the animal before he can be enrolled into the spiritual membership of elephant hunters'.

I fancy I have encountered, in my wanderings in the jungles of Burma during the last 45 years, more big game than has fallen to the lot of most sportsmen. I trust also I may be pardoned for remarking that my knowledge of the elephant, its habits, and its haunts, and how to track it, where to fire at it, and the kind of weapon to use, is perhaps as good as that of any other European sportsman in the East. The best time of the year for tracking elephants is during the rains, when the ground is soft and their tracks are more easily followed, especially when they are feeding in bamboo jungle. As a rule the animals possessing the best tusks are solitary, but a monster with very fine tusks is sometimes found leading a herd or on the outskirts of a herd. I found it much easier to follow up the tracks of a solitary tusker elephant, than to stalk into a herd with the object of picking out the animal with the best tusks. As often as not, a slant of one's wind or scent is obtained by some member of the herd, usually a female, or a young tusker, when a warning is given, and the whole herd either slips quickly and quietly away, or stampedes, without giving the hunter a chance for a shot. Woe betide the sportsman if the stampede is in his direction, as sometimes happens, if he cannot get behind a decent sized tree or bamboo clump in time. The danger of a stampede is that he is liable to be confronted by some infuriated cow elephant with a calf or some bull possessing small tusks or some cantankerous 'muckna' or tuskless male. On these occasions he may have to shoot in self–defence, when the usual report will have to be made to the Forest Department, which will probably fine him, and if a tusker, annexe the tusks. The easiest way out of the difficulty where a herd of elephants in a panic stampedes towards you, is to stand perfectly still behind a tree, or bamboo clump, as their sight is far from good, and take the risk of their passing you without having seen you; or, if they do happen to see you, there is always a chance that they will hurry on all the more quickly to avoid you. On the other hand, I have known herds of elephants to charge deliberately in a body towards the sportsman on scenting him, without having been disturbed in any other way, but they were generally herds that had been harassed a great deal by being frequently fired on by persons armed with inferior weapons. The danger is then very great, and unless the sportsman's nerves are in good order and he has also had long experience with elephants, he should contrive to get out of their way as quickly as possible either by climbing a tree or by making a clean bolt for it. There is no mistaking the sounds emitted by a herd of elephants that means business as it comes charging, shrieking and trumpeting along. A succession of angry screams and trumpetings will be emitted first, which will convey the warning and the sounds of thumping feet and the breaking of branches will then follow. The sportsman's Burman hunters, if they have not already made themselves scarce by ascending the nearest trees, as they are sometimes inclined to do, should be able to warn him of the danger and advise him what to do and which direction to take. Elephant shooting is easy enough if you have good eyesight, are fleet of foot, know how to shoot straight, and above all are using a good rifle. The latter is as important as all the rest put together. When charging, an elephant, on being wounded, comes tearing along at a great pace, faster indeed than most people would give it credit for being able to travel, and when the animal has really got into his stride he can overtake the fastest runner in the world after the first hundred yards or so, but he trusts to his keen sense of smell more than anything else to overtake his enemy – man. To escape from a charging elephant, it is not safe for a hunter to run in a straight line for any distance, for he has a better chance of eluding the animal by going off at right angles, especially if he is running up wind, that is to say, if his scent is being carried towards the approaching elephant. The screams of an infuriated, wounded, charging elephant are terrifying, and awe inspiring in the extreme, and woe betide the hunter, who trips and falls, or is overtaken, for he would be pounded into pulp and every bone in his body would be broken. An elephant usually seizes a human being with his trunk and dashes him to the ground or against his own knees, and then flings him away into the air or strikes him a terrible blow with his tusk. Sometimes he kicks his victim with his forefeet, or, after seizing him with his trunk, throws him to the ground and kneels upon him, if he does not drive his tusks through his body. In nearly every case fatal injury is inflicted.

An elephant cannot take all four feet off the ground in a jump, like a horse, to negotiate say an eleven or twelve foot ditch. A man escaping from a charging elephant can therefore jump over to the other side, for it would not be possible for any elephant to negotiate it in its stride. In other words, an elephant cannot cross a deep ditch that is beyond the compass of its stride. It would, of course, be possible for the elephant following a man under these conditions to go down into the nullah and up the other bank, but that would give the hunter time to escape. The hunter should also see, in the event of his getting behind the trunk of a tree or bamboo clump to escape from a charging elephant, that it is large and thick enough to withstand the impact of an elephant's charge, for an elephant is able to knock down any ordinary sized tree and will go through a fair sized clump of bamboos as if it were like paper.

The secret of success in elephant shooting is to get as close as possible to the animal and make sure of the first shot, if possible, into the brain. When a clear view of the brain is not possible, a shot behind the shoulder to reach heart or lung should be taken. If both lungs are perforated by a heavy bullet propelled by a big charge of cordite, say 100 grains from a .577 cordite rifle, the animal will usually not survive, but he will have to be followed for several miles, in the case of the lung shot, before he is rendered helpless by internal haemorrhage. Sanderson, the author of the work "Thirteen Years Amongst the Wild Beasts of India", says – 'the head shot is the poetry and the body shot the prose of elephant shooting'. An elephant's brain can be found by (1) shooting a little above the bump from in front; (2) and (3) by shots fired in the temple hollows on either side of the head from left or right half front; (4) by a direct shot at right angles from the side into either ear hole; or (5) by a shot from a little behind the ear when the ear is thrown forward. Then there is (6) the heart shot. The heart, shaped like a small rugby football, lies low down between the shoulders. This shot should be taken from a little behind, when the animal moves a foreleg forward, at the height of the elbow-joint of the leg. Some sportsmen, in order to make absolutely certain of bagging an elephant with really fine tusks, rely entirely on the lung and heart shots, for, in a head shot, unless the brain is reached by the bullet, the animal will not die, as there are no big arteries in an elephant's head and he will usually get clean away if he does not turn and charge. An elephant, when followed and approached after a shot or two through both lungs, if he is disabled will be found generally standing stockstill, with blood pouring out of his trunk which will generally be up in the air, and then he can be easily finished off. It is only when an elephant dies, or is at the point of death, that he lies down and, as often as not, when shot through the brain, he collapses on to his knees and remains in that position without toppling over. If an elephant should enter a stream and drink water after he has received, say a couple of shots through the lungs, he will become more quickly disabled. I have known solitary tuskers with only one tusk, when shot through the brain, to topple over on to the ground on the tusk side. Burman hunters emphatically state that elephants with two tusks, when shot through the brain, will fall to the ground on the side which carries the heavier tusk.

Elephants have been known to plug up with mud the bullet wounds received in their bodies in order to keep them from becoming fly–blown. It is also well known that elephants indulge in mud baths and plaster themselves all over with mud in order to protect their sensitive skins against the attacks of gad–flies and even mosquitoes towards the beginning of the rainy season, in April, May, and June. At this season all large dangerous game become more irritable from the stings of insect pests. The brain of an Asiatic elephant is more easily reached by the bump shot from in front, than is the case with the African species."

Elephant shoot on the Baragur Hills

R.C. Morris (87, 88) was a coffee planter in the Biligirirangan Hills, and a very well known big game hunter sportsman, naturalist. Later in his life he became a wildlife conservation enthusiast. In the following episodes he describes the hunting of proscribed rogues in the Baragur Hill ranges of Coimbatore Dt., in Tamil Nadu.

"Three solitary tuskers having been proscribed on the Baragurs, the morning of February 28, 1926, found three of us, Major R.E. Wright, I.M.S., Mr. P. Saunders, (both of Madras), and myself at Hassanur (North Coimbatore) full of enthusiasm to go after the proscribed rogues. A delay occurred at Hassanur as the top two leaves of my Ford front springs had, we found, snapped and new leaves had to be substituted, which I luckily had with me (the roads round this part of the district being so vile, I find it pays to carry nearly all the spare parts of a Ford with me!). We left Hassanur at 2 p.m. and travelled along sixty miles of a perfectly terrible 'road', the last fifteen miles being across fields and along a cart track through the jungle, arriving eventually at the forest bungalow we had decided should be our first stop, at 7 p.m. Here we were delighted to find our good servants (who had been sent on in advance) had prepared everything for our arrival, and we were not sorry to tumble into our cots after drinks and an early dinner. We were up before dawn and, having arranged for our kit to be brought along on pack bulls, we left after a meal at daylight for the second stage of our journey. Nine miles of track (even worse than the day before) took us to the foot of the northern end of the Baragurs; leaving the car here in the bamboo jungle we ascended six miles of steep paved road–way that led from the foot of the hills to Madeswaran Mallai. There stands a famous and very sacred temple, pilgrimages to which, from the surrounding country–side, take place monthly. We had our trackers with us and we were more than pleased to arrive at a shady nalla, about a mile from the temple itself, where we threw ourselves down for a well–earned rest. The climb had been a most exhausting one, the path being steep, the sun blazing hot, and the paving stones hard. The shikaris went off to mark down the first elephant. We had arranged that Wright should take the first elephant we came across, Saunders the second, and I the third. The bamboos were all in seed, and hundreds of jungle–fowl were feeding on the bamboo rice, and after a rest we amused ourselves stalking them. At about 5 pm the trackers returned with the news that they had marked down one of the three rogues, not half a mile from where we then were. We were not long in getting to the place where the men had seen the tusker, and we found him with his back turned to us standing among some clumps of bamboos bordering a patch of open ground. We crept up to within about twenty yards of him; he then got our wind (the wind was all over the place) and his trunk slowly came round, followed by his ponderous body, until he faced us. That he spotted us was quite certain as he curled his trunk up and looked as if he meant business. Wright fired supported by our rifles which, however, were not necessary as Wright's shot aimed at the bump above the trunk, found its mark, and the tusker collapsed stone dead. The tusks were very curved and massive, the left tusk being more than a foot shorter than the right. The elephant was a very old one and had not one single hair on the end of its tail. The right tusk measured 6'3". (weight 64 lbs.) and the left tusk 5' (weight 54 lbs.). In quite a short time, crowds of the inhabitants of Madeswaran Mallai (a village adjoining the temple) came to view the fallen elephant and rejoiced at its downfall, as for five or six years they had had a thin time of it with three rogues roaming through the jungle surrounding their village. Another elephant was reported to be in the vicinity, but the light was too bad to make any move other than to the bungalow at Madeswaran Mallai. Needless to state, we were very elated at our success that evening; everything had gone well so far and 'according to plan'. We left early next morning for the spot where we were told the second elephant was last seen, but there was no sign of him; he had evidently been scared off by the shooting. At about 10 am however, news came in that the elephant was at a place known as Kokubarai some six or seven miles away, and that the third

241

tusker (a fellow with crossed tusks) was also there. This was great news, and we travelled as fast as we could up hill and down dale over a rough and stony path, and reached the shola which one of the elephants was said to be in at noon. Sure enough, as we walked quietly along the path bordering the shola, Saunders taking the lead, the tusker came out on the path in front of us, and started to trek along the path, tail on. He soon left the path, and went off at a fair pace along the hillside; we were hard put to it to keep him in sight. Eventually he slowed down somewhat, and we managed to get above him, hoping for a side shot. This we found difficult for some time; in and then came our chance. The elephant turned about, and started to retrace his steps, then paused. Saunders got in an excellent earshot, supported by Wright, and the tusker rolled over dead with a tremendous crash. His tusks were a perfect pair, and each measured (and weighed) the same (length 5'4", weight 35 lbs.). By this time we were fairly tired, and wished we could bag the third tusker without another long trek. Little did we realize then that our wishes were to be fulfilled. We were now about twelve miles from our camp, and it was a boiling hot day. The third cross–tusked rogue was said to be a fiend, by far the worst of the three, and this was proved true. A man, who had been sent to keep in touch with the tusker from a safe distance, came back with the news that the tusker was standing in a small shola about two miles off. This was not so bad; we felt we could do another two miles anyhow! The elephant had gone along a path that skirted the hillside, and along this path we followed, my tracker Bomma in front carrying my rifle, I next, a local Lingayat third carrying Saunders' rifle, Saunders fourth, another tracker carrying Wright's rifle came fifth, and Wright brought up the rear. We hadn't advanced more than a mile, and were just passing through a patch of infernally thick undergrowth, when Bomma, who had climbed a log that had fallen across the path, suddenly turned round, thrust the rifle into my hands with the word 'the elephant is coming', and retired to the rear. I had visions of the rogue charging along the path and bursting in upon us while we were in the thick stuff, and realized our only chance was to get out of the patch by getting up above the path. To do this it was necessary to retreat a few yards, in my haste I forgot Saunders was close behind me, and turning round I knocked him off his feet! I told him to get up and above the path as fast as he could and, hastening a few steps further, found myself clear of the thick patch and face to face with Wright who, being last, hadn't been able to take in the situation and couldn't understand why everybody was scattering. He had, however, seized hold of his rifle. 'Up above the path, quick' I whispered, and we both scrambled up through longish grass, keeping our eyes on the path expecting every second, to see the tusker appear. I saw Saunders had managed to get slightly higher than we were, and that he was endeavouring to climb up the side of a rock the top of which was flat and level with the hillside. It didn't occur to me then that Saunders had no rifle, and that only our two trackers were with us. The next moment a shrill trumpet rang in my ears, and looking up I saw the cross–tusked rogue bearing down upon us. As I looked he paused for a second, and I realized that I had to shoot quickly and shoot to kill. The elephant was within five yards of me and still closer to Saunders who, however, flung himself backwards into a crevice of the rock. I flung up my rifle, took quick aim at the bump above the trunk and fired, and I heard Wright fire immediately afterwards. The tusker pitched forward, the tips of its tusks about six feet from me, we both fired once more to make sure that he wouldn't rise again, but we need not have done so as the elephant was quite dead; both our bullets had entered its brain. It is hardly necessary for me to say that, from first to last, the whole affair took a mere fraction of the time it has taken me to write this. When we had sufficiently composed ourselves to take things in, we realized that Saunders was rifleless and that his rifle bearer was not on the spot. He was discovered some way off with Saunders' rifle still on his shoulder. He had bolted back with it directly he heard Bomma tell me the elephant was coming. I yelled to him to bring the rifle, and never did I see a man more visibly ashamed of himself than he was when he rejoined us. The rifle was taken roughly from him by one of our trusty trackers, and he was told to clear out in no uncertain terms. Saunders' feelings can be well imagined when he found himself without a rifle and the elephant literally almost on top of him; for a second it had actually placed one of its feet on the rock Saunders was busily climbing! We mounted the rock and Bomma pointed out the spot ahead of us where he had first seen the elephant. It was stationary and facing us when he caught sight of it, he said, and had started moving rapidly towards us, presumably on seeing Bomma. The spot indicated by Bomma, and verified by the other tracker, was on examination of the tracks quite fifty yards from where it was shot, so that the elephant had covered this stretch in very quick time. The old fellow who had brought us news of the whereabouts of this tusker was very emphatic in his statements that he had last seen the tusker a mile further on. The Sholagas declared that our shooting had 'drawn' this rogue, and that it had retraced it steps. It was quite evident that the rogue had been getting our wind as we approached him (this was impossible to avoid as it was blowing in all directions, had paused, and then moved forward rapidly on seeing Bomma, but why not along the path we were then on? It is my firm belief that the elephant, seeing Bomma disappear, had divined our intentions (or rather his intentions) and raced along the hill–side above the path to cut him off and, suddenly coming on a group of us, made the pause that proved fatal to him. That his pause was only momentary, and he would have been among us the next moment, is absolutely certain, for we were far too close to him. The aftermath was all the more pleasurable, in that the affair had been so full of incident and thrills. The tusks were a splendid pair, the right one 7'7.5" (weighing 68 lbs) and the left 7'4.5" (weighing 63 lbs). There had certainly been a humorous side to the affair; our intense desire to escape from what we considered a death–trap having led us right under the feet of the elephant as it were. We were by now very weary and hot, and felt we could not face the trek back to our camp. We therefore walked back about four miles to a cool evergreen shola and decided to sleep the night there. We sent a man for our servants and kit; our pack bulls were still in camp, and we rested till they turned up at about 10 pm. It was very pleasant dining and sleeping on our cots that night, on the open hillside just above the shola. We decided to end up our shoot by motoring southwards through the Baragurs to a place named Tattakerai, where another rogue elephant had been proscribed our intention being to have a go at this one also. We accordingly, next morning, sent off our kit and servants by a short–cut down to a forest bungalow at Geriki–Kandi, on the Kollegal–Bhavani road, and tramped down with our shikaris to our car. After mending a leak in the hose–pipe, we started off and were once again motoring along dreadful tracks and byeways where no car had ever before been seen or heard. A five–mile shortcut which we took across fields from one village to another, in order to avoid an alternative route of fifteen miles, was a positive nightmare; how the Ford Car stood it beats me, and my respect for a Ford was increased a thousandfold on the completion of this journey. The track was good in parts, but where it was bad it was generally 'horrid', the car having either to climb a series of outcrops of rock or dive into wash–outs and miniature gullies. The tyres were a mass of prickly–pear thorns, and we were very soon mending puncture after puncture. On arriving at Geriki–Kandi, where we intended to sleep the night, we spent a hot and beastly hour or more mending inner tubes. We decided to push on to Tattakerai to make enquiries about the rogue, and to return to Geriki–Kandi after doing this. We climbed seven miles of a steep and poisonous ghat, and were glad to reach Tattakerai, which is situated on the summit of the Baragurs (4,000') and comparatively cool, the heat at Geriki–Kandi being unbearable. The Forest Ranger had informed us that the rogue had not been heard of for three months but, on making further enquiries at a village named Oosimallai, a mile along the road from Tattakerai, we learned that the rogue visited the fields there nightly. This was cheering; we left our trackers there, and motored back down the ghat to Geriki–Kandi. On our arrival we found our servants and kit had arrived, and we were very soon in our cots outside the bungalow. We left at 5 am next morning, giving instructions for our kit to follow us, and arrived at Tattakerai at 6 am and at Oosimallai at little later. Here, we left the car, and struck off into the jungle with our trackers and two local sholagas. We did not have to go far before we came on fresh tracks of the elephant, and a little later we heard him breaking bamboos. Two of our shikaris were sent to locate him; they unfortunately 'jumped' a herd of bison which crashed into the jungle and disturbed the elephant, causing him to move off into some very thick stuff. On inspection we found that we would gain nothing by following him up into this cover, as it was far too dense. We then climbed a rock on the hillside overlooking the cover, in the hope of being able to locate the elephant. One of our trackers penetrated the cover below us for a short distance, in order to climb a tree to get a better view, but with no better success. Soon after his return the elephant moved up to where this man had been, and evidently smelt him, as he trumpeted shrilly and kicked the ground repeatedly. This showed that the elephant was inclined to be vicious, and. we decided to throw stones in the hopes of drawing him out. Our plan very nearly succeeded as, on hearing the first stone fall, the rogue trumpeted again and charged to the spot where the stone fell. This went on for some time, our stones being hurled nearer and nearer to the edge of the cover. We got the elephant to within about ten yards of the edge of the cover, but nearer than this he would not come; he finally retired some way in, and would not move for stones or taps on trees, so we decided to leave him in peace till the afternoon, in the hope of his coming out to feed in the open jungle. In the meantime, we discovered a way into the outskirts of the cover from down below, and took up our position in a favourable place waiting for him to come out. But this he would not do and, as the light was getting very bad, we decided to try to move him by the use of stones again. Stones were, therefore, hurled into the cover from above, which only resulted in the elephant's leaving cover and that jungle in the opposite direction with a scream. He had evidently decided that the jungle was bewitched! We returned to the bungalow at Tattakerai and decided to have one more try for the rogue before closing our shoot. We left next morning for the same spot, hoping to find that the elephant had returned, and we sent two of our trackers in another direction. They soon marked down the rogue and, if one of them had brought us word of this, we would in all probability have added a fourth elephant to our bag, as they found him in wide open jungle. They, however, stupidly sent a local Lingayat to fetch us, and the man, for reasons known only to himself (probably after some heavy thinking), took us down into a deep and hot valley saying the elephant was making his way down the valley, instead of guiding us back to where our men were keeping in touch with the rogue. We walked up the valley for five or six miles; when we reached the head of the valley, and saw no sign of the elephant's having been there at all, we were considerably peeved. Even from there it took us quite another half hour to reach our trackers. This delay of nearly three hours lost us the tusker as, by the time we were on its tracks, it had gone into thick cover. We cautiously followed it up, this being our last chance as we had to leave the next day. We finally caught a glimpse of the elephant's head half–turned towards us, giving only an eyeshot. This was taken, but either the elephant moved, or the aim was not quite correct, the shot failed to bring him down and the elephant crashed off. We never saw him again, although we followed him up for a considerable distance. We had to leave next morning, but we left one of our trackers, a good man who, with a local, was to try and mark the elephant down, as I hoped to return later to finish him off. We left at 7 am motoring through the Baragur hills, through Baragur and Tamarakerai, down the narrow ghat to the plains on the east, and back up to Hassanur, and so ended a most enjoyable and successful shoot, having lasted a week crammed with all the pleasures and thrills of the chase one could desire. We left the extraction of the tusks, and the amputation and cleaning out of the forefeet of the elephants, to my two skinners who had experience of this before, and they did their job very well. The tracker, left at Tattakerai to follow up the tusker, returned several days later with the information that he could find no trace of it as tracks here mixed up with those of a herd. He believed the elephant was going strong, and none the worse for the knock it had received.

On the 3rd of February 1929, Lt. Col. G.E. Taliens, D.S.O., of the Lancashire Fusiliers, and Major F.S. Gillespie, R.A.M.C., both of Wellington, Nilgiris, and I set out to bag three rogue elephants that had been proscribed in the Baragur Hills, and had been marked down in the Madeswaranmalai Reserve, in the northern part of the hills. Our shikaries and skinners had all gone on a day ahead, with instructions to engage pack bulls at Cowdally for our kit. Arriving at Cowdally we found the bulls awaiting us and, leaving instructions that these were to come up to Sengady Bungalow on the hills, we carried on hoping to reach there before dark. Our transport up to this point included a Chevrolet, carrying ourselves and our servants, and a Ford van containing our saman. Arriving at the foot of the Ghat four miles from Sengady, we halted for the Ford to catch us up. After waiting for some time, with no sign of the Ford, it was decided to motor back along the narrow road to find out what was holding it up. We did not proceed far before we met one of the men who had been travelling in the Ford with the driver and learnt from him that one of the back wheels had collapsed and the Ford was lying in the road three or four miles back. It was dark by the time we reached the spot, found that the van had luckily not turned over, but that the bolts holding the spokes at the hub had sheared off, with the result that the spokes had all come out, but otherwise undamaged. The van was unloaded, and pushed to the side of the road. The driver, with one of the trackers whom we had picked up at Cowdally, was sent to the nearest village to enlist the services of a blacksmith; in the meantime we sat down on the road and had some grub which the servants quickly prepared for us. Luckily the pack bulls turned up and we were able to leave for Sengady in the Chevrolet, (with our trackers standing on the running boards) leaving instructions for the servants to load up and follow with the pack bulls by a short–cut. The remaining four miles to Sengady were not easy, the road being narrow, the surface none too good, and the gradient steep. We eventually reached the thatched Forest Rest House there however, without further trouble, were glad to stretch ourselves out on the floor, and soon fell asleep. Our servants and pack bulls arrived just before dawn, and breakfast was soon served, followed by our departure for Ponnachi, which entailed a ten mile walk. The car was left at Sengady in charge of the local Forest subordinates. Ponnachi was reached by midday, and the rest of the day was spent in getting fresh khubbar of the Ponnachi rogue. An early start was made on the following morning for the village of Marrur, where locals were engaged, and the thick bamboo jungle scoured by our trackers and locals, in couples, for fresh traces of the rogue while we sat down to await their return. After an hour's wait two men came back with the news that they had marked down an elephant which was probably the rogue; at the same time we received khubbar of an elephant in another direction. As our head tracker had sent for us, we decided to make for the spot where he was said to be watching the elephant. This turned out to be false news, however, as there, was more than one elephant there and we could definitely see part of the herd grazing out in the open on the western face of Ponnachi Beta, the northernmost hill of the Baragurs, rising nearly 5,000 ft. in elevation. While we were watching the herd through our glasses one of their number dislodged a boulder and it rolled down the hillside into the jungle with terrific crashes, terrifying the remainder of the herd below and causing them to move off rapidly trumpeting shrilly. We also saw a herd of bison passing through the thick bamboos above us, and two of our trackers saw bear. We then retraced our steps, and lost no time in getting to the place where the other elephant had been marked down only to find that he had retired into thick cover as the sun was now well up. Considerable time was lost by the false khubbar we had received. We had difficulty in getting through the extremely thick bamboo above the elephant and, although we crawled down to within a few yards of the animal, the cover was so dense that it hid it entirely from view. It was decided, therefore, to wait for the elephant to come out of the cover late in the afternoon and, our tiffin having arrived, we retired further up the hillside for our meal. A little later we received word that the elephant had moved further down towards a nullah in which there was water, and directly our meal was finished we decided to follow it, but found to our annoyance that the elephant had evidently got our wind and vanished. The ground was very hard, the trackers were unable to make out the direction in which the elephant had gone, and the hunt finally had to be given up.

On our return to Ponnachi Bungalow, a council of war was held and, as our time was limited, it was decided to make for Madeswaranmalai that night after dinner, especially as we had received news that the other two rogues had been marked down there. After our meal was over the pack bulls were loaded up, and we started on a tiring ten mile tramp, aided by the light of four petrol lanterns. Our pace was naturally limited to that of the pack bulls and we did not reach the spot where we proposed to camp till 2.30 am, thoroughly tired and glad to turn in, which we did without delay directly our camp cots were unloaded and prepared for us out in the open. A monthly pilgrimage to the well-known temple at Madeswaranmalai occurs, and early next morning batches of pilgrims arrived, having climbed the stone paved path which we had toiled up the previous night. Our trackers had been sent out early in the morning to pick up fresh tracks of the rogues, and were told to meet us at a certain spot. We had barely reached the place when word was brought to us that one of the rogues, a crossed tusker, had been marked down. This turned out to be false khubbar, however, as the man who brought us the news heard langurs crashing in the bamboos and had taken it for granted that it was the elephant. Soon after this however we received definite news that the crossed tusker had been seen and was being watched, and we were guided to the place. After a heavy climb we arrived at the spot where the elephant had been seen, and found that it had moved into thick cover. The wind was very treacherous and, on following the tracks of the elephant through thick evergreen cover, we were warned by a shrill trumpet and a crash ahead of us that the elephant had got our wind, and was getting annoyed. This brought us to a halt, and we decided to give the elephant time to move off into more open jungle. On taking up the tracks a little later, we found that the elephant had crossed fairly open ground towards thick jungle, and on proceeding a few yards further we again heard a crash which caused us to leap for our rifles, which had been handed to our shikaries on reaching the open ground. The rogue was now in a patch of extremely thick cover, and we decided to get to the other side of the patch to cut it off in case the elephant intended going straight through it. By the time we had worked our way to the further side of the cover the elephant had cooled down a bit and we heard it breaking bamboos quite close to us. A long wait followed in the hope of seeing the elephant break cover in our direction and, as it was evident that it had no intention of doing this for some time, a local Forest subordinate with a few men offered to try to drive it towards us. It was decided that this was the wisest course to adopt, and we stationed ourselves in the best place we could find, covering its most probable line of approach. The men, however, started beating in the wrong direction and the rogue, after expressing its annoyance by crashing about in the cover for a minute or two, suddenly showed itself below us working its way through thick undergrowth across our front. Major Gillespie, who had won the toss for first shot, decided to take the ear–shot. It was a difficult shot as very little of the elephant could be seen, and it was moving off at a good pace. The elephant fell heavily on receiving our shots (Gillespie's shot was followed by one from me), but got up again and disappeared from view with a shrill trumpet and staggering from side to side. A few seconds later we heard another trumpet and raced in that direction as hard as we could, came on to the upper reaches of the paved Pilgrim's pathway, and found ourselves at the place where it was all too evident the elephant had crossed, for a scene of wild confusion met our eyes, broken chatties, clothes hung up on bushes, other articles dropped here and there, and one or two frightened pilgrims with scratches on their arms and legs appearing from their hiding places. It transpired that the elephant had crossed the path just when a batch of pilgrims had been coming up it. It had luckily heard the pilgrims and given vent to the second trumpet that we had heard before bursting out on the path, thus giving time for the pilgrims to scatter, which they did so successfully that actually only two of them saw the elephant cross, the others having disappeared into the surrounding jungle like lightning, dropping everything they possessed. The line of the elephant's flight could be easily seen as, apart from the path it had made for itself through the cover in its onrush, there was a broad and continuous trail of blood. Here we halted for a drink and for our trackers to collect. It was not long, however, before, to our surprise, we heard the elephant puffing and groaning up on the hillside behind us, proving that it had turned back and recrossed the paved path. It did not take us long to get up to it, and we found the elephant moving slowly and painfully in dense bamboo cover; it was evident that it was hard hit. The elephant soon moved down to the edge of a stream, and we cautiously approached it by another paved path, one of the features of these jungles. Suddenly the elephant got our wind and was immediately an embodiment of devilish fury. It whipped round and came back, crashing through the bamboos to within a few yards of us, and then halted with curled trunk, uncertain of our exact position. The Forest Guard with us lost his head, and started wailing 'climb trees'. Major Gillespie and I fired almost simultaneously, and the elephant dropped dead.

Up to now we had not had a good view of its tusks and we were, therefore, astonished and delighted to find that the rogue carried an enormous pair of tusks which were crossed near the tips. I realised at once that the tusks were a record for South India, and that Major Gillespie was to be congratulated on his magnificent trophy. By a strange coincidence the elephant died a few yards from the spot where we had arranged to camp for the night and had, in fact, as could be seen from the broad trail of blood, crossed our actual camping ground. Our pack bulls and servants arrived on the spot with our kit a few minutes later. Had they turned up fifteen minutes earlier, they would have run straight into the wounded rogue with possibly disastrous results.

At about 11 pm, that night, after we had turned in, two of our trackers went down to the stream to fetch water and found another elephant beside the dead one; needless to say, they hastily retreated. To our surprise, next morning we found that the intruder had dragged the dead elephant, from where it had fallen, further towards the stream. This was most interesting, as I had known of three cases previously of elephants shifting dead tuskers that had been shot, evidently with the idea of helping them to rise. Forest subordinates soon arrived on the spot to 'take measurements of the tusks and fore–feet. Instructions were given to our skinners to remove the tusks and both fore–feet and the tail which, however, was devoid of its much prized hairs, and we set out after the second rogue which was supposed to be near by.

It soon became evident, however, that the previous day is firing had disturbed the other rogue and it had, in fact, been seen trekking down the deep Yerekygorge dividing Madeswaranmalai from Ponnachi Betta. Four trackers were sent in advance to mark down the rogue, while we followed by another route. The temperature down in the gorge when we finally got down was very different. The heat was intense and there was very little shade. We followed the tracks of an elephant or two, until we met two of our trackers coming back up the valley, and were informed by them that they were not the tracks of the rogue whose tracks they had seen further up the valley. We retraced our steps, and later came on our other two trackers who had been up the side of the gorge following the tracks of the rogue, which led them back again into the main valley where, for the time being the tracks were lost. We sat down in the coolest place we could find, while the trackers looked round for fresh tracks of the rogue which they soon found leading up the valley. We followed these tracks till midday, and then proceeded to a spot where we had arranged for the servants and camp kit to meet us; here we had our lunch and a rest, while the trackers went on ahead. It was late in the afternoon, when word was brought to us that the tracks had led to thick bamboo cover, where the trackers thought the elephant was probably standing. This was good news, but we were doomed to disappointment as, after searching the whole of the head of the valley, we could find no traces of the elephant nor could we see where the tracks led. We decided to renew our search for the rogue the next morning and returned to the river bed where we were to camp. Our water, from two or three pools in the sand, was none too good and had to be well boiled.

Until noon the following day our hunt for the rogue proved fruitless and we were delighted to receive news at about 2 pm that the rogue had been marked down in a deep ravine higher up the slopes of Madeswaranmalai, and it was apparent that the brute had not wasted its time in the hot and steamy gorge but climbed back to its old haunts. This necessitated a very arduous climb in the hottest part of the day, and we were considerably hot and exhausted by the time we reached the spot where our good tracker was watching the elephant from the opposite side of the ravine. The wind was blowing up, so we had to cross at the head of the valley and work our way round to the other side above the elephant, so as not to give it our wind. We then had to work our way carefully down towards the elephant, and this was not easy as the steep slope was covered with loose stones, several of which we dislodged and with difficulty prevented from rolling down the slope, thus giving ourselves away. We finally took up a good position, but the elephant was feeding in such thick cover that, although we were within a few yards of it, its head could not be seen at all. There was nothing for it but to wait in the hope that the elephant would move into a better position, and we realised with anxiety that the sun had set and that only half an hour's good shooting light could be relied upon. Suddenly the wind changed, the elephant stopped feeding, and its trunk could be seen 'taking the wind'. After a moment's hesitation the elephant swung round giving us a magnificent view of its head. Col. Tallents, taking careful aim, gave the elephant the right barrel of his .577 cordite rifle, followed by one from Major Gillespie. It was obvious that both bullets found their marks in the elephant's brain, and that the shots from my rifle were unnecessary, as the elephant collapsed on receiving the first two bullets. I say 'shots' from my rifle as, although I intended to fire only one barrel, both barrels went off simultaneously on my pressing the front trigger. The shock, both to my feelings and to my shoulder, was considerable, as the recoil of .450 cordite rifle, with both barrels going off at the same time, is something to be remembered. The elephant proved to be a magnificent specimen, larger in body than Major Gillespie's crossed tusker. Its tusks were not so long as those of Major Gillespie's rogue, but were very thick. News was sent up to the skinner, and we wended our way back down the bed of the rocky ravine to the valley below. This took us two or three hours, the going was extremely bad and tiring, as the mantle of the petrol lantern had collapsed, and we had to light our way with bamboo torches renewed every half hour. We finally reached our camp at about 9 pm, tired but well pleased with our good luck.

We found that news had, in the meantime, come in that the third rogue had been marked down at Ponnachi near the village of Marrur; it seemed likely that we should emulate the exploit of the three elephant hunters who had killed three rogues on Madeswaranmalai in 1926 in two days. I was a member of the party on that memorable trip, and had the luck to bag a magnificent crossed tusker which had made an unprovoked attack on us. We set out early on the following morning to climb up to Ponnachi, and although we started out in very good time it was hot and muggy, which made the climb out of the gorge tiring and uncomfortable, and we were very glad to sit down at last in the shade near the village of Marrur at the foot of Ponnachi Betta (hill). The villages of Ponnachi and Marrur are blessed with a few scattered coconut palms, and we were soon quenching our thirst with green coconuts. After a rest, we moved on to the village of Marrur, and here we waited under the shade of a tamarind tree for fresh news of the rogue marked down on the previous day. It was not till 3 pm that our head tracker, who had gone out after the elephant with two locals, returned with the news that the elephant had left the cover it had been last seen in, and had trekked northwards along the eastern slope of Ponnachi Betta towering above us, and had gone down to the Cauvery river which, miles away, flowed down a deep valley to the North and North–east of Ponnachi Betta. The news was disappointing, especially to me, as this was to be my elephant. We returned to Ponnachi Bungalow and, after discussion, it was decided to spend the next day in a long tramp the whole way round Ponnachi Betta, as there was just a possibility that, by doing so, we might come upon the rogue working its way back up the valley to the West of Ponnachi Betta. We started out early next morning, and tramped to the south–western foot of Ponnachi Betta then along its western slopes. For a time the going was good, but the ground later got worse as the grass was long and the slope covered with loose stones, and we frequently had to pass through tangled masses of dead bamboo; it was noon before we found ourselves at the northern end of Ponnachi Betta overlooking the Cauvery river which could be seen below us like a silvery streak on a wide expanse of sand, showing that there was very little water in the river. On our way we had seen a cow elephant and calf on the opposite side of the valley. We found that there were no other elephants in the valley and it seemed likely that the cow and the calf separated from the portion of the herd that had scattered when a boulder dislocated by the rest of the herd grazing above rolled down on them a few days before. Working our way to the north–eastern side of the hill, we sat down for lunch while Bommah, our head tracker, and two locals descended to the valley at the eastern foot to take up the elephant tracks, and were asked to follow directly we had finished our meal as Bommah was certain of picking up the tracks down in the valley. Here again the going was exceedingly bad, and the temperature down the valley much higher than up the hillside, in fact it was like a furnace, and to our disgust we found that Bommah could find no trace whatever, of the elephant. We learnt from herdsmen, who were grazing their cattle in the valley that they were quite sure no elephant had come down the valley within the last few days. Curses were now showered on Bommah's head, as it was apparent that he had simply taken it for granted that the elephant had descended the eastern slopes of Ponnachi Betta, believing the assurances to this effect from the two locals who were with him.

We now had to climb up to the top of Ponnachi Betta, which meant climbing from 1,000 feet to nearly 5,000 feet, and a very steep climb at that. There was no time to waste, so we started on the high ascent, and the higher we climbed the further away the summit seemed to be; to make things more difficult and uncomfortable for us, a large part of the climb was through grass far above our heads. Eventually, we found ourselves at a .spring not far below the ridge, and here we refreshed ourselves before tackling the last bit which finally brought us to the top of the mountain. The panoramic view from the top of this hill was amazing, certainly the best I have ever seen. To the west and south–west could be seen the Nilgiris and the Billigiriran-gan, to the south of us stretched the Baragurs, on the northernmost and highest peak of which we now stood, and to the north lay seemingly endless stretches of small valleys and foothills; to the east could be seen long stretches of the Cauvery, until it disappeared from view round a ridge, and beyond it the plains up to the Shevaroys, the Kowlimallais, and the Pacchaimallais, and to the south–east an endless stretch of plains. The sun had set and we had to hurry, especially as we had no lantern with us, and we were faced with a walk of about eight miles in darkness back to the Ponnachi Bungalow, including a descent down the western side of the hill along a rough and stony path. We passed through the evergreen shola of Ponnachi from north to south, and by the time we had reached its southernmost limit it was quite dark. By luck we found a length of dry bamboo and, using this as a torch, we slowly made our way downhill, picking up on our way another piece of bamboo which served as a torch, too, when the first one had burnt out; this lasted us till we reached thick bamboo jungle near the foot of the hill with ample material for torches, and we eventually reached Ponnachi Bungalow at midnight. Early the next morning our kit was all packed up and loaded on the pack bulls. We let the bulls get ahead of us, and then started on our eight mile tramp down to the cars. We finally reached the Estate late in the afternoon.

The Ponnachi rogue did not live long after this, as Mr. A. S. Vernay and I went after it again recently, marching on its tracks for two days from Ponnachi down into the valley where we had left the cars and up to Madeswaranmalai. We finally came up to the rogue in thickish cover, not far from where we had come on Gillespie's elephant. The tusker was in high grass, and not in a good position when Vernay decided to take his shot. The first two shots missed the brain, the elephant charged, and was brought down with the fourth shot.

Thus died the last elephant proscribed for the present on the Baragur Hills. Another was shot by Lt. Col. R.E. Wright, C.I.E., I.M.S., of Madras, just before Christmas near Tattakerai on the Baragur Hills, this elephant and a man–eater being the chief objects of our trip at the time. The tusks of this elephant weighed 40 lbs. each, and their length 6'2" each."

Wild Elephants in Assam

J.E. Hall (89), writing of his experience in shooting a proscribed rogue in Assam, seems to have lived largely on whisky with an occasional catfish speared by his tracker for breakfast, while his gurkha companion apparently lived exclusively on whisky! Hall also participated in Mela Shikar and everyone, except the elephants, seem to have had a good time.

Hall writes:

"A few years ago the shooting of elephants, except for an occasional 'Proscribed Rogue', was totally prohibited. Such rogues, when very occasionally proclaimed, were soon destroyed by local sportsmen, long before any 'bandobust' could be made by an outsider. The steadily increasing popularity of the motor–car has, however, ousted the elephant from favour, and the present demand from Rajas and wealthy Indians for these useful beasts is very small in comparison to former years. With little or no organised Kedah–catching operations and strict protection, wild elephants have so much increased in numbers, that in certain areas they are a menace to cultivators, and as a result have to be controlled.

Early in 1938, several 'Rogues' were proscribed in various parts of Assam, and I made up my mind rather suddenly to have a try at shooting some of these. Having arrived at a place called Ranigodam, near where a Rogue had been reported, I installed myself in the local DakBungalow. This is where I came up – hard – against the Assamese villager. Not a man, cart, or service of any description was to be hired or bought. Payment was no consideration, they just would not face the work. Quite possibly some of the 'Mahaldars', or lessees of elephant catching, who were operating in that area, engineered this boycott. They probably reasoned that, if I started shooting bull elephants, their operations would be spoilt by the wild elephants retiring back into tribal territory. Nor could I hire tame elephants, they were all engaged in Mela–Shikar. I was now in despair; the immediate prospects of success were very remote. At this very unpleasant moment, the D.F.O's ranger came to the rescue. A very quiet and reserved young man, his suggestion was that I shift my camp to a village called Chakardah, about 6 miles away, where I could get into touch with a retired pensioner of the Assam Rifles, a Gurkha called Balbahadur, who had the reputation of being a famous shikari.

We decided on action, it took 8 hours to raise a bullock cart from the villagers, yet when it was produced the hire demanded was reasonable enough. This I personally paid into the village headman's hands, and he seemed surprised to get it. It afterwards transpired that the Mahaldars had let out a rumour to the effect that I was requisitioning men and carts without payment, being a military officer. What a libel on the unfortunate military! Later on when they realised that I was not interfering with their business the Mahaldars became friendly.

Having set out in pouring rain, I arrived like a drowned rat to find Chakardah most depressing. It was a fairly large village nestling at the foot of dense jungle–clad hills, with a large swampy lake as foreground, and a few paddy fields scattered about. We managed to get shelter in the forest guard's chowki, a single–roomed hut, that bore evidence of a recent attempt by a wild elephant to pull it down. It was quite isolated, having as its solitary neighbour Balbahadur's shack. The swampy lake was filled with resident species of wild duck, paddy birds, and cranes, whilst all day long herds of semi–domesticated buffaloes grazed in the swamp grass tended by Gurkhali herdsmen. Balbahadur soon entered into an agreement with me, and in no time produced an Assamese tracker named Kuttru, and another nondescript assistant. Kuttru, I may say, was an excellent tracker, who never lost a trail, in spite of the fact that the tracks we were following were crossed and confused continually by those of herd elephants. Up and down the bamboo covered hills, through Taraban swamps, Ringal cane thickets, lantana; it was all the same to him. He would lead you right up to an elephant, and say 'Maro'. I once asked him if he ever felt afraid, and his reply was most amusing and to the point. I give it verbatim. 'You have come to shoot elephants, not I, so long as you don't run, I won't; if you do, I'll go home. The last Babu–Saheb who came after elephants ran away, after wounding an elephant, and we were nearly all killed. If it comes to running, rest assured I can run and climb trees much faster than you, and in any case my business is finished when I take you up to the elephant'. When not tracking, his chief amusement was to wade into the swamp in the pouring rain, and spear fish. He caught an enormous number of a sort of mudfish, which he carefully dried for future consumption. I once tried a couple fried and they were very tasty, so that he had to provide a couple for my breakfast whenever we were not out tracking.

Balbahadur, on the other hand, was a taciturn individual, who seldom spoke unless directly addressed, was slightly deaf and absolutely fearless. He never backed a step when facing elephants, and I veritably believe would rather have been killed than lose Izat by showing fear. His chief relaxation, I may say was drinking large pegs of my whisky, neat. Every performance being followed by frightful grimaces, with the explanation that whisky kept the fever out of his stomach. He had a head, and could down half a bottle without showing any effect. On one trail we lived on whisky and tea for nearly two days, most of the time in pouring rain, and were never really dry. His prescription must be right as I never had fever, to which I am rather prone in jungles.

A couple of blank days were spent in trying to pick up the Rogue, which, had however, disappeared after demolishing a couple of cooly huts at a nearby tea–garden, following up this exploit by chasing two Nepali sawyers who were cutting timber in the forest.

He then wound up by eating all their provisions, including some rice tied in a red cloth, cloth and all. Confirmation of this feat was forthcoming when his droppings were found. These were plentifully garnished with scraps of red rag.

During the course of my wanderings on this shoot, I came across a 'Mithun'; a type of hybrid Gaur found in Assam. He gave an easy shot as he fed on some short grass on the opposite side of a ravine, about 80 to 100 yards away. I could have bagged him easily but, having no license for game in this area, very reluctantly had to let him go, as to–date I have never bagged a 'Mithun'. I also saw a Red Serow, a rare animal, but this particular brute raced downhill into a dense Ringal cane thicket. Several times we came across pig, sambhar, kallij pheasant, jungli moorgi, and once one misty morning walked into a tiger on his kill – a village cow. I should have shot him, as he was actually on village land but, not knowing this at the time, was not chancing the forfeiture of my elephant license by being accused of poaching. Both Balbahadur and Kuttru urged me to shoot this tiger, though we were all on foot within a few yards, and they had the pleasure of saying 'I told you so', when we heard from the Ranger that this beast was a nuisance, having killed several buffaloes engaged in timber dragging, and that I should have shot him, as permission had been obtained for his destruction.

Eventually, during the course of our wanderings, we came across a village of Garo tribesmen, high up in the hills. These were not the really wild type, rather semi–civilised fellows, and they gave us khubbar of two solitary elephants in the jungle. They were quite willing to work for me, and wanted us to visit their village. This suited my purpose admirably, as it solved the problem of transport; I was also tired of Chakardah and its everlasting swamp. To settle the business I tramped straight on to their village just as I was, and we celebrated our arrival by getting our hosts to throw a feast of roast pig and rice beer. Of course I had to pay for these festivities, which waxed loud and long. My shikaris enjoyed themselves, but had the sense to send out a party of men early next morning to bring in my kit, and servant. This party returned with everything by 11 am Good marching, as the total distance involved was 14 miles up hill and down dale, through heavy forest.

The next afternoon we picked up the tracks of an enormous solitary elephant, the print of whose forefoot circumference measured 65", or a computed height of 10'10". The tracks were about a day old, and we followed them till nightfall through the most impossible places, up and downhill almost vertically, in regular giant staircases of elephant tracks, through Tara–ban swamps, up to our waists in stinking mud and water, through dense rattan–cane thickets, that dug millions of vicious barbs into one, and tore clothes and skin to shreds. Periodically we stopped to scrape off leeches as fat as my little finger from gorging our blood. I invariably burnt these dreadful pests. This devil–ridden elephant never seemed to stop; his tracks showed that he was moving fast. That night we all went to sleep on the banks of a brawling, tumbling stream that looked beautifully fishable. No fires were allowed, and we huddled together, cold and hungry. Towards midnight we heard the trumpeting of a herd of wild elephants, away to the south–west; later a single elephant rushed madly up the valley we were sleeping in, most probably after catching our wind. What with mosquitoes, cold, hunger and excitement, I hardly slept a wink. Towards morning I dozed fitfully, and woke to find that Balbahadur had made some tea, and that Kuttru and Bangte, the Garo Headman, had gone on ahead tracking.

After a hasty wash, followed by some whisky–tea, we pushed on and, some hours later we contacted Kuttru, who was a case of 'nerves'. It appears that he and Bangte, whilst following the elephant, had been most viciously charged. I had my doubts, but these were allayed when we came to the scene of action. We could see where the elephant had circled back to a bamboo clump, from where he had charged the two men from not more than 15 yards away. The tracks of his charge were deeply imprinted on the soft soil, as his direction was downhill.

He had then crossed a swamp, and ascended the opposite hill which was covered with dense bamboo thickets. Kuttru with a most ridiculous looking dah in his hand, took up the tracks but, as these were now so clear, I took the lead. The wind was wrong, and the advance was made with great caution. I may state that I smoked continually, this being the easiest way of testing the breeze in these dense damp forests, where sand, a wet finger, or fluff are all useless. The elephant, as we found later, had crossed the ridge and circled back along the top of a spur running west. We must actually have passed him within 60 yards, but much below his line of scent or smell. On topping the ridge, I was following up the racks, when Kuttru, who has the eyes of a hawk, spotted the elephant 40 yards away, behind a dense bamboo clump on our right. The beast was perfectly motionless. To get a shot at this distance was impossible, there were far too many interlacing bamboos, and besides the elephant's quarters and tail were towards us. He looked a monster, reddish brown in colour, quite unlike the usual black tame ones. I got pucca stag fever, my hands shaking with excitement; Kuttru looked at me in a very superior and pitying way, and I mentally promised to box his ears when the show was over. Balbahadur quite frankly suggested that I sit down and recover my nerves, whilst he had a crack at the elephant. Recovering myself, I got them behind a bamboo clump, whilst the Garos made themselves scarce. I then crept up behind the bamboo clump, till only this separated the elephant from me. He seemed very suspicious, and kept swinging his head and trunk from side to side, apparently to catch the wind. I then saw for the first time that he was a makhna, or tuskless male. I had no qualms about shooting him, owing to the condition of my license. How long I waited I don't know, probably not more than a minute. I then discovered that Kuttru had crept up to me without a sound; he suggested in a whisper that I step to the right of the clump and as the elephant swung round to face me, let him have it. I did so and stood up; without a sound the elephant swung towards me and I let drive midway between his ear and temple. With a great scream he came round, but fell on to his knees and, whilst he was struggling to rise, I rushed up and fired just above the bump between his eyes. He heeled clean over, and I had bagged my first elephant. Besides the natural exultation I felt, I must admit pangs of regret at having destroyed so magnificent a beast. Measured between uprights, as he lay, from the top of his shoulder to the sole of his forefoot, he taped 10'2"; the circumference of his right forefoot in death was 62". In my opinion he stood about 10'5" in height (vertical) at the shoulders, and this measurement was later confirmed by his rubbing marks on various trees. His tushes were both broken off short at the gum but, for a makhna were still exceptionally long and thick. When his carcase was seen by the Mahouts engaged in Mela–Shikar, they said that he was the biggest elephant seen in these parts for years, and was known as a notorious crop raider, who occasionally chased people about, but he was not a man–killer, and had been living solitary for many years. They estimated his age as between 80 and 100 The ears were very ragged, and showed a great amount of turnover. The bulk of the body was enormous. In a couple of days, no–one could go within a mile of the place due to the terrible stench.

The next few days were devoted to observing wild elephants and their ways, whilst scouts were sent out to hunt up the recent tracks of the other solitary elephant – the Rogue. One morning, as were on our way to a salt lick situated in a narrow valley, where we hoped to see elephant and with luck Mithun, we heard a herd approaching in the opposite direction. We rushed a little way uphill, sat tight, and were soon rewarded by seeing 8 cows and 3 calves walking along in Indian file, not more than 50 yards distant. The moment the leading cow crossed our tracks, she stopped dead and tested the wind; in no time her trunk swung in our direction, and every other elephant followed suit, including the tiny calves. Right about–wheel, canter, seemed to be their next orders, and they shuffled away uphill as fast as they could go, with a tremendous crashing. The whole movement was executed as if on a parade ground, and we all had a good laugh at the gravity of the little fellows. Another afternoon, Kuttru, the valiant, led me right up to two young tuskers, that had temporarily left a herd. The larger of the two was about 8'6" in height with light tusks; Kuttru called him a Khuru–Dantal. The other was not above 6', with tiny tusks just protruding from his jaw. The bloodthirsty tracker wanted me to shoot both. I got within 5 yards of them, and climbed a tree to get some snapshots. It was delightful to see how they caressed each other with their trunks, and how the smaller copied every movement of his elder brother, even to rubbing his forehead on the same tree.

Eventually Balbahadur, who originally had lagged behind, came blundering upon the scene, when the elephants rushed off downhill. They just bounded down like dirty, black, rubber balls, the smaller of the two coming an awful cropper over a log in the grass. He looked such a clown with his head on the ground and his hind legs stubbing the grass, that I sat and roared, sending the herd that was in the valley crashing away at a great pace.

One day, when following up a solitary Ganesh or single–tusked elephant, we ran slap bang into a herd, which he had suddenly joined. The place was a sort of natural ampitheatre; a flat, tree covered hollow, surrounded by high bamboo–covered hills, with steep sides. The herd was all around us, split up into what appeared to be family groups, all resting under the shade of the trees. The two nearest groups were all cows and calves, then a solitary makhna, not, however, anything as large as the one I had shot. Not far from him, and close to a group headed by an immense old cow, stood the 'Ganesh'. Unluckily for me as, had I caught him up when solitary, I was justified in shooting him, for he was a known crop–raider but, within the shelter of a herd, he was in sanctuary and inviolate. His one tusk was every bit of 65 lbs. if not more, as thick as my thigh and projecting 4 feet from his jaw, stained the colour of nicotine, with the point rounded and blunt. Out of his head, it would have gone to 6' in length. Balbahadur, as usual, got us all into trouble. Close to where he crouched, about 15 yards to my left, was a pinky–grey calf; the little chap could not have been more than a few weeks old, and he was trying to pull down a creeper with his tiny trunk. Balbahadur spotted this prodigy, and crept to within a yard of it. He had a shawl in his hands, and seemed to be trying to tie its hind legs together, in an effort to capture it. At this moment the old cow spotted him and, with an unearthly scream, charged headlong at him. "Pandemonium" is the wrong word to describe the next few moments. The entire herd, consisting of some 40 animals, rushed everywhere screaming; bamboo clumps were scattered, the individual stems cracking like rifle shots. The whole place was like an inferno only, instead of comparatively benign devils, there were dozens of infuriated and frightened elephants. I hardly know what happened to the rest, I saw Kuttru and the Garo shin up the hillside and Balbahadur dodge behind a bamboo clump. I ran across to him and was nearly trampled by a couple of runaway cows. The mukhna was screaming just the other side of our clump, so we faded silently away up the opposite hillside to

Kuttru and the rest. The Ganesh had disappeared and, by the time we had rejoined forces, the herd who were still in possession of the arena started filing away. We counted 33 animals, but others had already made good their escape. Later on we heard from the Mahouts that they had captured 2 young elephants from that herd a few days previously, one of them being a young tusker whose dam was the old and vicious cow. She and the mukhna had then turned on the koonkees, or catching elephants, and severely pummelled a valuable female, whilst the rest showed such a pugnacious disposition, that they decided to leave this herd alone. One of the Mahaldars offered me Rs.500/- to catch the calf we had seen, as it was supposed to be an albino and very valuable. He also offered to lend two koonkees and his Mahouts, phandees or noosers, and pay all expenses. His Mahouts were, however, a miserable opium eating lot, and he a great sharper, so that nothing came of his proposal. On the other hand, some Gurkha Mahouts and phandees in the service of another Mahaldar were a desperate gang. I did one hunt with this lot as a paying guest, and they did show sport. Having closed up to a herd, they rushed in, cutting out two half–grown young with their koonkees. There were two of us in this particular case, and we followed that calf through swamp and bamboo, along the valley. My companion koonkee did the actual noosing, as she was a leggy and fast female. My mount was a much slower mukhna who, however, came up in time to help in the final roping and tie–up. I finished that little jaunt more dead than alive with not a square inch of skin on the inside of my legs. You must know that these koonkees are not fitted with pads, only ropes, and one has to hang on with hands, teeth and toes; falls to rival those experienced in pig–sticking are frequent. I paid the promised 'bakshish' to my Mahout, and was thankful to get off his elephant alive, and with no bones broken. Any more sport of this description would have meant a lengthy stay in hospital for me. I may add that my part in the hunt was to beat my mount with a thick stick over the rump, to make him move faster, as I had misplaced the charkatta, only two being carried per Koonkee in this Mela–Shikar. You may guess that I did nothing of the sort being too busy hanging on for dear life. Whilst our pair of koonkees was successful, another lot had a fearful time, one of the phandees being swept off his mount by a trailing creeper, making his koonkee useless for further catching; the other had to cut loose the calf they had noosed, as he was too big for their very light female, and who, mount – a and besides dragging her along, very nearly choked himself in the noose as a result. Altogether a very successful hunt, and the Mahouts considered me very lucky and wanted to take me out again, but one experience sufficed. All good things end, however, and I returned to Chakardah on my way home. On my very last night in the jungle, the Rogue, who had protected his hide so well that we never once caught a glimpse of him in spite of continual hunting, staged a grand Finale, which ended in his enriching me with his beautiful symmetrical tusks. I had finished packing my kit and rifles and, after the first hot bath, for many days, had turned in amidst the unwanted luxury of warm blankets, clean sheets, and silk pyjamas. I was asleep almost before my head touched the pillow, and was in the middle of a vivid dream, wherein a monster elephant with long curly tusks, absolutely impervious to all bullets, was chasing me; a fearful scream from an elephant made me wide awake. Balbahadur rushed to my hut from his own, and shouted "elephant"; meanwhile the screaming and noise went on, added to which were loud shouts and wails from the village where Mahaldars had picketed their koonkees. I developed some latent energy that I consider is unparalleled. Within half a minute, I was rushing to the scene of tumult in my pyjamas and slippers, with the heavy rifle in my hands and the last 7 cartridges I possessed. To get there, I had to wade through the swamp, and cross some 400 yards of flooded paddy field. In the process, I lost my slippers, lost my bearings, and landed up to the armpits in a bog. Some of the Mahouts rapidly came on the scene with a lantern and extricated me. While rushing me along to their lines, they gasped out their story. This (summed up) was to the effect that a solitary bull dantal or tusker had been seen, during the day following one of their koonkees – a makhna. The latter had been showing signs of 'musth', and as a result had been securely chained up that evening. Towards nightfall he started showing great restlessness. About midnight, an elephant trumpeted in the jungle nearby, to which the makhna answered and, about a quarter of an hour later when they were all asleep, the wild tusker crossed through the outlying part of the village, and came into their lines. The first intimation they had of his presence was when he attacked the tame makhna. The screams of the latter awoke them in fright, as they noticed that he was bleeding from a shoulder wound inflicted by the rogue. In spite of their shouts and the waving of lighted firebrands, the Rogue, who had backed away at their first approach, again charged the unfortunate makhna, driving one of his tusks into the base of the latter's trunk. Eventually the tusker knocked down the makhna, not a difficult task as the latter's forelegs were shackled by chains. By this time the entire village was in the utmost confusion; men, women, and children ran about screaming that their last day had come. The makhna continued his terrible screams, as the wild tusker pummelled and kicked him. The moment I arrived was very nearly my last; in pitch blackness, under a steady drizzle of rain, a horde of frantic men, women and children laid hold of me. At this moment, a mahout came running up with a firebrand and the tusker, who previously had not been visible under the shade of the trees, stepped forward into the circle of light about 50 yards away. In the mad stampede that immediately ensued, I was swept into a ditch by the solid wave of humanity that rushed back; with fists, legs and gun–stock I had to fight my way clear, otherwise I should have been suffocated. As this ditch was practically an offal pit for a nearby cattle pen, my odoriferous condition can be better imagined than described. Eventually, with myself standing guard over the tusker, Balbahadur, my orderly, and the Mahouts, drove the panic–stricken villagers into the comparative safety of the cattle–pen, thereby clearing the field for action.

Supported by Balbahadur flashing the electric torch on to the tusker's head and carrying my second rifle, we started the attack. The tusker faced us and came on; when he was about 10 yards, away I let drive into the spot where I judged the bump of his forehead was placed. He swayed to the shot and recoiled backwards then, recovering himself rushed us without a sound; Balbahadur dragged me back into a Lantana bush. As the elephant passed I fired on his ear, but hit him in the centre of his neck, as by this time I was firing in the dark; the blasted torch having been dropped in the confusion. He screamed loudly at the shot, and appeared to be half paralyzed, as he started moving in a blind sort of a way very slowly uphill. I ran alongside in the thick Lantana, and fired three times at his head, trying to brain him, but could not get the correct spot in the dark. Fumbling in my pocket I discovered that I had only one cartridge left, one having dropped in the confusion at the ditch. The elephant was now standing in a dense clump of Lantana, so I ran right up to him and fired into his ear from about three yards. He dropped like a stone without a sound, just missing crushing me, as he had been on higher ground than myself. I escaped literally by inches. As it was, I fled after taking the shot, as by this time my nerves were in shreds. The first to come up to me with a smoke was Balbahadur, who had been close behind, and I stopped to recover as much of my courage as I could. The rest of the crowd soon followed, and we jauntily announced the death of the Rogue. A 'stripped–to–the–skin bath' followed at the elephant lines, and I put on some clean clothes, but was much too excited to sleep immediately. We sat up with the Mahouts, gossiping and yawning, drinking copiously of tea laced with whisky. They were fulsome in their praises, stating that they had never before met any Saheb before, brave enough to shoot a goonda–dantal by night. I did not edify them by saying that, in actual truth, funk had dried up my throat to such an extent that I was left with a raging and apparently insatiable thirst.

Next morning, after cutting out the tusks, I decided that, as the carcase was within a hundred yards of the nearest huts, it was absolutely necessary to bury it, to prevent an epidemic when it rotted. The villagers absolutely refused to do this, in spite of my offering whatever wages they demanded. They said that it was too much labour, and in any case the carcase would soon rot. Luckily the Forest Ranger came that morning, and he soon impressed some Garos and Cacharees who did the job. It was terribly tedious; whilst the coolies dug an immense pit, I with Balbahadur had to cut up the carcase. We were at it till 4 pm The above incident is typical of the attitude of Assamese Mikiri villages.

They just will not do any manual labour unconnected with their daily lives, whether paid or not. To the men who had sweated all day, I paid the agreed amount of Rs.25/– plus as much country–grog as they wanted, and they were very contented. They fully deserved every pice of that money. Late that evening, the Ranger boated me back across the swamp up to the main road, where I soon caught a bus back to Gauhati.

I forgot to add that, in cutting out the right tusk, we found a Martini–Henry slug embedded in the skull. This had traversed the tusk and entered into the bone of the skull, splitting the tusk for about 18" of its length inside the socket. The pulp of the tusk was in a diseased condition, smelling horrible and, in my opinion, probably the sole reason why this animal turned into a Rogue. He must have been wounded by either a crop watcher or shikari, and subsequently been in agony for the rest of his life. The tusks are a beautifully matched pair, with sharp pointed ends."

Hunting Rogue Elephants in Burma and South India

Phythiam Adams (90) narrates his experiences over many years in the hunting of elephants, from Burma as a beginner to south India as a very experienced shikari. He writes his "Jungle Memories" commencing with:

"The first time that I encountered elephants in the jungle was in North Canara in 1909, while I was in camp at Dandeli, trying for bison or anything else which might turn up. On 8th May I was working through the jungle with my shikari, Raya Gowda, towards Pardhana, where I proposed to halt for a week or more, and at about 8.30 am heard elephants trumpeting. There had been a lot of rain and, as we were moving silently towards them, I saw a yellow animal dash away through the clumps of bamboos about 40 yards off – possibly it was a tiger with designs on an elephant calf, but the thick carpet of leaves left no pugs marks. I went on and found a number of cows but no tusker, so withdrew and worked further round, nearly running on top of a big cow. I saw her before my shikari did, looming above the bamboos about 50 yards away – she looked like a huge, wet, grey rock in the rain, and at first I was uncertain what it was. But, as we got closer, my shikari spotted her, and hurried me back behind a big tree, when with my glasses I could see a calf lying down close by. We withdrew quietly, and further on came across a youngster blowing sand over his back; – he spotted us, and bolted with a great crashing of bamboos, and the rest followed him. This herd, which had only recently entered the district, was later proscribed on account of the damage they did, but at the time I had no permit, and examined them simply out of curiosity. The lesson I learnt was that with slow and silent progress, and due regard to the wind, it is possible to work close to individual animals, and in and out of a herd, without being detected".

The Magyigon Rogues

"In 1913 while stationed with my regiment at Rangoon, I obtained 60 days privilege leave and, after a 3 weeks shoot at Paungde in the Prome District, in the course of which I bagged some good heads of thamin (including a magnificent one of the rare spatulated type with 14 points), I decided to try the Arakan Yomas for rhino. I reached Thayetmyo on 3rd June, and started my march towards Midon, but at my second halt met the D.S.P., who incidentally at first mistook me for a notorious character known as the 'White dacoit'! He advised me to give up all idea of working the Arakan Yomas in the monsoon, but to try the Pegu Yomas on the east of the Irrawaddy, where there were excellent chances of elephant, bison and tsine. I already had a permit for one elephant, and when I passed through Thayetmyo on my way back the Deputy Commissioner asked me if possible to deal with three rogues, which were giving trouble at a place called Magyigon. He strongly advised me to use only solid bullets, as another sportsman had recently fired no less than 28 softnosed at an elephant without success, though it was eventually recovered. Four marches brought me to the village in spite of delays occasioned by floods and a broken axle of one of the carts, and the rest of the day was spent in settling in at the very comfortable forest bungalow, and discussing shikar prospects with the local moksos (shikaris). They told me that there were 3 rogues in the vicinity, of which the most notorious was named 'Bedin'. Only a short time before, he had played havoc in the village gardens, and had even tried to push over one of the great teak posts which supported the Rest House. The second rogue was said to have short but thick tusks, while the third was a 'hine', or tuskless male.

Next morning I started off at 5.30 am and an hour later found fresh tracks of elephant – at first, only the indentation of one toe–nail, which I should not have recognised without the tracker's assurance. He was positive from its depth that the animal was a tusker and, shortly afterwards, when complete footprints were visible, identified them as belonging to 'Bedin'. At 7.30 am. I saw a very fine tusker standing in rather open bamboo jungle, flapping his ears but otherwise motionless – I think now that he probably suspected our approach. There were no big trees under cover of which I could work up, but I managed to reach an antheap in the open about 50 yards from him without being detected. I knew that one should get as close as possible before firing, but further approach seemed impossible, so I rested my .400 H.V. Jeffery on the antheap and fired a solid bullet at his ear hole. At that range I could not distinguish the exact spot, as the ear was flapping to and from, and the bullet failed to reach the brain. He swung round with a roar and came straight towards me for 20 yards while I tried to make myself as small as possible behind the ant–heap – then went downhill on my right like a runaway locomotive. I got in two more shots with the .400 and two from the 10 bore (which my orderly ran up and handed to me) firing for the spine, as he went up the opposite side of the 'choung' but, though badly hit, he carried on. I followed as fast as possible, but he soon outdistanced us, and we had to slow down when the track entered some very thick cover. After following the trail through the two patches of 10 foot–high 'kine' grass, where visibility was limited to about 6 feet, I refused to enter any more, but skirted them and picked up the tracks again on the far side. In one place the trail led up a watercourse with precipitous banks about 10 feet high, ending in an almost perpendicular sheet of rock up which I could not have believed that any elephant could climb; but he had, and at the top had swung round, and waited some time on the top of the bank. Fortunately, he had gone on again before we arrived, or he would have had us at a serious disadvantage. At 11.30 am. I sighted him moving slowly ahead of us and hurrying forward, caught a glimpse of his tusks in a thicket 40 yards away from where he had halted. I could not get a shot at his head which was covered by a mass of dead stuff, and I did not then appreciate the value of a body shot. But when he moved on about 5 minutes later, I ran up alongside and fired up at his ear–hole, with as little result as my first shot, and with a bellow he made off again. We followed till 1.30 pm and then, on the advice of the trackers, gave it up and returned to the bungalow.

My trackers were not happy about the killing power of the .400 and implored me to rely in future on my double 10 bore. I knew, of course that there was nothing wrong with the rifle, and that my bad shooting was to blame, but to humour them I took my 10 bore, and a .303 carbine as a second weapon, when we started out next morning. By 7.15 am we had picked up the overnight tracks and, at the request of the trackers, we halted to do puja to the jungle Nats. The rifles and dahs were placed on a cloth under a tree, with incense, and cheroots, and prayers were offered for our success. On previous occasions, a similar ceremony had produced a quick result, but on this day its action was delayed. We followed the trail steadily, hour, after hour, but could not come up with the rogue, though we found the place where he had slept. At last at 1.30 pm, I heard bamboos being broken ahead of us, and saw there were now tracks of two elephants – I thought one of them was my wounded animal, but later found that he had branched off. Moving towards the sound, I saw two elephants feeding – one of them a small tusker, but the other a good deal larger with short though thick tusks, and the trackers told me that, he was one of the rogues. They also intimated that now they had brought me within sight, the rest of the operation devolved on me, and without making any bones about it climbed up trees to await the result. The jungle was very open but I managed to work up to a small clump of bamboos 20 yards from the rogue. Here, I left my orderly with my spare rifle and, being determined to make no mistake about it this time, walked out across the open until I was within 10 yards of his backside (which seemed close enough to slap!), and then, as his head swung round, fired a conical bullet from my 10 bore at the earhole. He dropped to the shot and never moved again but, as the small tusker came up to investigate and seemed inclined to give trouble, we withdrew about 100 yards. A shot in the air drove the survivor off, and the trackers now came down from their trees, but would not approach the fallen tusker, till I had fired a shot with my .303 into his body, which I remember quaked like a jelly. He was 9'3" at the shoulder, with a good average pair of tusks but nothing like Bedin's – there were a number of dead horse–flies stuck to the skin of his back, evidently squashed by the branch I saw him plying when we first sighted him. We had scarcely finished taking measurements when some 40 Burmans – men, women, and children – turned up. They had followed us all day, at a discreet distance, for the sake of the meat, as they were confident that I should bag an elephant, and had closed in on hearing the shots. They got busy at once, some building small huts of split bamboo to smoke the meat in, and baskets of the same material to carry it back, while others started to cut up the carcass. The Burman is an artist with his dah, and it was most interesting to watch the use of it. But time was passing and we had to get back to camp which I now learnt was 4 hours away. It was not till then that I realised how tired I was – we had been on the go for 2 days, and had covered an immense distance over very bad country, through heavy jungle with tangled undergrowth and fallen trees, swamps and thorny cane brakes, uphill and down, and much of the time in pouring rain – added to which was the mental strain of following a wounded animal for so many hours. By the time we reached the bungalow at 7 pm we were about all in, trackers and orderly included, and personally I have never felt so tired before or since – Was it worth it? Of course it was – every time! For the next 2 days I could get nothing done about Bedin as the whole village had gone out to the dead elephant, were gorging themselves on the meat, and smoking what they could not eat, but as soon as that was over I renewed the search for the wounded animal. I sent trackers out to distant jungles, and for the next week was out all day looking for tracks, but apparently he had cleared right off, and we never saw him again, nor did I hear his fate till 7 years later. It was in 1920 that, while travelling down to Rangoon on the Night Mail, I got into conversation with another passenger, and learnt that he had come across Bedin by chance some time after I had left Magyigon, and bagged him. He told me that, though very emaciated, the rogue appeared to have recovered from his wounds. I forgot the weight of the tusks, but they were a very fine pair, much above average.

The mistake I made over this elephant was taking the head shot in the first place, instead of firing at the heart. I had, at the time, no practical experience of elephant shooting, but had studied the diagrams in Sanderson's book, and had come to the conclusion that the head shot was the one to take. So it is if you are close enough, but you have to be very close indeed to make out the ear–hole, and at 50 yards it would have been a fluke if I had found the brain. Far better would it have been if I had fired at the heart, in the first place and during the follow up, when I had a clear view of his side but could not make out his head. Later on I heard of a sportsman who had been very successful with elephants, and his method was to fire both barrels of his H.V. rifle at the heart, and then return to camp – the elephant was almost invariably found dead next day, within half a mile.

So much has been written about headshots, that many sportsmen have come to believe it is the only way in which an elephant can be shot, but this idea, which probably dates back to the old days of black powder rifles, is a mistaken one. A heart shot is not to be despised – if well placed it is equally fatal, although the effect may not be so immediate. Major Evans in "Big Game shooting in Upper Burma" puts it aptly when he says that the head shot is the poetry and the body shot the prose of elephant shooting.

The Taiping Tusker

How difficult it is to get a shot at an elephant from the back of another is well illustrated by an experience I had while shooting near the Taiping river north of Bhamo in 1914. In the lines at the Fort were 9 Commissariat elephants which had once belonged to King Thibaw and had been captured during the 3rd Burma War. We were allowed to hire these for shikar, when not otherwise required, for the ridiculously small sum of Rs.1/– each per diem. In June, I engaged two and marched to Teinthaw on the Mole Chaung, when I heard there was a good solitary bull bison. On the 3rd morning I was out on 'Luxmee' to try and bag a hogdeer for the pot and while working a swampy plain of 10 feet high grass, heard an elephant trumpet – we could just see his back above the grass, about 10 yards away. I had a permit for two elephants, so moved up to view his tusks, and within 30 yards could not take them out clearly. He went off, and kept moving in a circle of about 400 yards diameter, but would not leave the grass, so from my elephant I climbed a tree, and then had a good view of him as he came straight towards us (probably attracted by my mount) and halted 40 yards away. I could see that his tusks were smaller than the ones I had obtained the previous year but, even had I wished to fire, it would have been impossible to get in a fatal shot, as his body was hidden by the grass, and a frontal shot at his head from above was out of the question – so we left him to it and came away. Later I heard that he was a rogue and had killed 3 men, but he certainly showed no signs of ill–feeling towards us. He had once belonged to the Wunthoo Sawbwa, so my mahout told me, and had been turned loose when that chief fled to China in 1891 after his abortive rebellion.

The Yinmabin Rogue

The year 1920 found me at Meiktila, in Upper Burma, in command of the 2/80th C.I. I had my hands pretty full with the command of the station in addition, and the custody of 5,00 unfortunate Turkish prisoners still awaiting repatriation, but found time for an occasional weekend run up the Kalaw Ghat to Yinmabin, which was an excellent shooting centre. On my first visit there, I was told of a rogue which, only the week before, had killed an old woman gathering sticks in the forest and, according to my mokso, had torn her arms and legs off. I applied for and was granted a permit to shoot this animal, but my opportunities were limited, and it was some months before

I came across him. As is usually the case he was solitary, but at times joined a herd, from which he had no difficulty in driving away the hine (tuskless male) normally in charge. Each time I met the herd it was, therefore, necessary to comb it out; very exciting work it was dodging from tree to tree, and, of course, all the time keeping the wind, but it was not until 10th November that I found the rogue with them. We first met the hine by himself, half a mile before we came up with the herd, so guessed our luck was in. There were about 20 of them spread out more or less in a semicircle and, by working from tree to tree, I managed to get into the middle undetected within 35 yards of the rogue. He was partly hidden by two big cows, and I had to wait some minutes before they cleared him; luckily, no puff of wind gave me away, as there were elephants on three sides of me. It was too far for a certain head shot so, as soon as I got the chance, I fired a solid bullet from my .405 Winchester at his shoulder. He rushed away, followed by most of the herd, but a young tusker bolted on the other side of the tree behind which I was sheltering, with his trunk up trying the wind. I fired a shot in the air and he halted, and I then heard an extraordinary wheezing noise in the direction the rogue had taken, rather like a platoon doing deep breathing exercises. I ran forward, and found him on the ground trying to rise. Here was a problem of which shikar books take no account – how to finish off an elephant which is lying down. I went up to within a few yards of it and, kneeling down to get the correct angle, fired at his heart, but his struggles continued. So I ran round behind him and put a bullet into the base of the skull; that settled the matter, and incidentally taught me a very useful shot. My first bullet had gone too high and smashed his shoulder, so once he was down he could not get up again. I think his lungs must have been pierced, too; an elephant's heart is rather low down and I did not allow for this.

The Cradle Tusker

It was in December 1931, while I was living in Mysore City, that I first heard of this rogue. He was in the habit of visiting the fields near Areipalaiyam village in North Coimbatore at certain seasons, but most of his time was spent in Mysore territory where he could not be pursued. He had been proscribed in Coimbatore for a good many years, and was credited with the deaths of 8 villagers, had been fired at on several occasions but escaped serious injury, and finally derived his name from his curved tusks which were reported to be a magnificent pair. Such was the description of this notorious rogue, and he seemed to me an animal very well worth trying for.

I camped at Areipalaiyam, in January 1932, to study the ground and to obtain first hand local information, and soon realised that it was going to be a big job, as the rogue's visits were so uncertain and of such short duration. Further trips in May and July also drew blanks, and it was obvious that without timely information of his movements I should have little chance of intercepting him. My good friend M, who owns an estate not far away, very kindly lent me the services of two of his trackers, and promised to let me know when the rogue next crossed the Coimbatore boundary. The expected wire arrived on 1st November, and dusk of the following day found me installed in the Areipalaiyam forest bungalow with the comforting news that the Cradle Tusker was in the vicinity and that at last I should be able to try conclusions with him. Soon after dawn on the following day I went down to the Sholaga village and picked up the trackers, and we started up the path which runs over the ridge to the Gundal Rest House. At the col, I saw for the first time the footprints of the rogue, which were simply immense when compared with those of the other two elephants which accompanied him – a tree against which he had rubbed himself also gave me some idea of his great height. The tracks led down to the Gundal Valley, so we followed, but after ravaging some fields the elephants had, so we learnt, been driven off by fire and had retreated up the Hethinibetta hill. A terrible climb of 1,500 feet followed, the path being simply a rocky track practically straight up through a tunnel of bamboos, without a breath of wind. I have seldom sweated so much, and felt it all the more as I was soft after 5 months' enforced rest due to an injured knee. About 1 pm, we topped the col where a spur runs from the main hill to join up Kortaybetta, and at once I distinctly smelled elephant, and also heard movement in the bamboo covered ravine below us. Working along the hillside, we found a convenient rock, and sat down to rest and await events. Half an hour later a small tusker appeared, and cleared off in a hurry for no obvious reason, but we could still hear at least one elephant feeding about 150 yards below us. The trackers now went to see whether an approach was possible and, shortly before 2 pm, one of them hurried back and beckoned to me urgently. I went down and saw, indistinctly through the bamboos about 80 yards away, the head and tusks of a big elephant, which the trackers assured me was the Cradle Tusker. Leaving the men behind, I advanced with my driver, George, carrying my spare rifle to a tree about 30 yards from him, and as the elephant moved forward to our right I had a clear view of his head and tusks. The latter, however, were not so long as I had been led to expect and, to make absolutely sure that there was no mistake, I beckoned one of the trackers and questioned him. He assured me that it was the Cradle Tusker – he had known the animal for years, and was positive about it. Being satisfied, as soon as he stopped moving and I had a clear view of the earhole, I fired at it, but did not allow for being on slightly higher ground so we afterwards found, that my bullet – a solid 423 – passed below the brain, and was embedded in the base of the tusk on the far side. At the shot, he swung round and rushed back a few yards, then towards us but, as we remained motionless, he was uncertain where the shot had come from, besides doubtless being a little dazed. He then turned away, and up went his trunk in the air trying to get our wind. I aimed behind his ear but as he moved still further round and exposed the base of his skull, got the head on to that and fired. At the shot, he reared up and fell over backwards with an almighty crash, against a clump of bamboos which gave way under him with much splintering and cracking, and I was on the point of running up to give him another bullet if necessary when a third elephant, which we had not previously seen, made his appearance and came hurrying towards us. He was quite a good sized beast with tusks about 3 feet long but, compared with the Cradle Tusker, looked an infant. I don't think he saw us but, as he was getting rather too close and I had no permit to shoot him, we withdrew to our rock and shouted at him, so he cleared off and allowed us to examine our prize.

In that classic `Thirteen Years among the Wild Beasts of India' Sanderson expresses the view that, 'there is little doubt that there is not an elephant 10 feet at the shoulder in India'. I only wish he could have been present to check up on the Cradle Tusker! Careful measurements between uprights at heel and shoulder gave him a height of 10'6", and this was confirmed by the foot measurements, allowance being made for loss of expansion since the animal was in a horizontal position. The size of the tusks had been greatly exaggerated, but even so they were a fine pair, taping 5'7" and 5'6.5" respectively, with a girth of 16", while their combined weight was 97 lbs. according to the Forest Dept. scales. In accordance with the rules they had to be surrendered, but were eventually returned to me by order of the Board of Revenue, after I signed a declaration that I had shot the rogue 'at close range and at great personal risk'!

On the following morning, when we returned to extract the tusks and remove the feet, we found the third tusker still in the vicinity, but 'Little Boy' soon chased him away. He had visited his dead companion during the night but had made no effort to move him, as elephants sometimes do. When skinning the rogue we found 2 bullets just under the skin of his side and foreleg, and another was deeply embedded in the forehead –

no doubt there were others, which we overlooked, as in the course of his career he had been fired at often.

Now, to analyse the shots taken, and to see what can be learned from them, I think there can be no doubt that, with such a bloody–minded animal, it was imperative to take the head shot, and this seemed to offer no difficulty. I was reasonably close, had the side of the tree to steady my rifle, and thought I had him cold, and yet I missed the brain, because I did not allow for the fact that we were not on the same level. An elephant's brain is small compared with the huge bulk of his head, and the side shot is definitely difficult, as it is not easy to make out the earhole among the wrinkles of the ear. The frontal shot is much easier, in fact, I was told on the best authority of a thugyee (village headman) in the Thayetmyo district of Burma who, with a single barrel 12 bore, and the ball cartridges supplied by Government as a protection against dacoits, accounted for a number of cow elephants in this way! For the second shot, I had to thank my experience with the Magyigon rogue as already related – it is a shot well worth knowing.

The Benne Rogue
It is over 10 years since I shot my last elephant, but the encounter was an exciting one, and the memory of it is still so fresh that reference to my diary serves only to confirm it. On 26th April 1937, a Forest Guard, accompanied by another man, was walking along the road between Masinagudi and the foot of the Sigur Ghat in the Nilgiris, when an elephant, previously proscribed, suddenly rushed out of the jungle at them and killed the guard, who had stumbled in his efforts to escape. My house is at the top of the Sigur Ghat, some 9 miles from the scene of the tragedy, but I did not receive news of it until two young officers, who had gone after the animal, looked in on their way back and gave me an account of what had occurred. It had taken them 2 days to locate the brute and, when they did come up with it, they had fired a number of shots into its head

and body but owing to lack of experience, none of these was fatal, though one shot actually floored it. That night the rogue moved along the foot of the hills, and was located on 2nd May in some very thick cover near Anaikatti, where they had to leave it.

As it happened I had already booked the forest bungalow at Anaikatti from the 4th, so when we arrived I at once sent men to track down the wounded animal, since both R. and I possessed permits to shoot it. The trackers returned in the evening with the news that they had located the rogue with another elephant at Sirur some 6 miles to the east, and that he was in a bad way, constantly lying down. Next morning on arrival at Sirur, we took up the tracks and soon found several places where the animal had lain down, but there was no blood, which rather surprised me, in view of the number of wounds he had received. Soon afterwards, we heard bamboos breaking, and the tusker's head and back appeared above the lantana about 50 yards below us. He was uneasy but not alarmed and, after 5 minutes, moved slowly uphill – we followed along the hillside above him and, as he came out of the bushes into the open, had a grand view of him not 30 yards from the rock on which we were sitting. Before firing, it was essential however to make sure that it was the rogue and, as I could see no sign of wounds (he was well plastered with mud), we went back to the river and measured his footprints, which definitely showed that he was not the proscribed animal, though his lying down so frequently rather indicated that he was sick. So we left him to it, and were sitting on a knoll having a rest before taking up the tracks of the second animal, when the latter appeared crossing the open about 1,000 yards away. He was a magnificent beast with tusks showing at least 5 feet of ivory and so curved that they reminded one of a mammoth's. They alone were sufficient to show that he was not the rogue, whose tusks were known to be short and straight and, as no other tracks could be found, we had to give it up and return to Anaikatti. We remained in camp there until the 9th but, though I had trackers out daily, no further sign of the wounded animal could be found, and it was not until several days later that I had news of him. Where he had been in the meantime is unknown, but on the night of the 14th he came on to the main road beyond Masinagudi and walked along it to Teppakadu, where the villagers heard him wheezing – no doubt from a lung wound – as he crossed the bridge over the Moyar river close to their houses. His tracks then led towards Mudumalai, so R. and I motored down there on the 16th, only to learn that the rogue had moved on towards Benne. Next morning he was definitely located near the elephant camp 8 miles away, so we at once motored there, arriving about midday, bagging en route a wild dog which I hoped would prove a lucky omen. The rogue was said to be at the foot of some low hills 2 miles away, so we set out, meeting on the way one of the trackers who had located the elephant and identified it by the wound in its side. A climb through long grass up a spur brought us well above him and, after a short halt, we then began the final approach down to the small stream where the rogue had last been seen. The jungle was thick, and there was a nasty tangle of bamboos, while big trees, which are such a comfort when working up to an elephant, were few and far between. After about 200 yards, we found a place where he had just fed on bamboos, and then suddenly saw him only some 30 yards away standing in the bed of the small stream with his head towards the steep bank on our right. After a whispered consultation, we decided to move up the bank to the left so as to be above him, which was done, and R and I then advanced down the open slope to a tree which I had marked not 20 yards away from the rogue, where our feet were about the same level as his back with the ground sloping gently towards him. He was tail towards us, idly swinging a hind leg and his tail and occasionally flapping his ears. There was no wheezing noise from the lung as reported and, since from our position we could see no wounds, I beckoned up Mada and the mahout whom we had left behind, to make certain that he was the right animal. They insisted that it was, so I got ready to shoot, as the wind was uncertain and might change at any moment. We had arranged overnight that I was to fire first at the head and R. to fire afterwards at the body. We had not anticipated an end–on shot, but there was no time to make other arrangements. Accordingly, I fired at the back of his head, though I doubted whether a shot at that angle would prove effective, then R. fired at his spine. The huge brute seemed to crumple, but suddenly whirled round with coiled trunk and in grim silence came straight for me. We both fired again and down he crashed, dead, only 15 yards away with 2 bullets in the brain. We counted no less than 9 old bullet holes, one severe 5 inches in diameter, behind the right. shoulder (too high for the heart) from which pus was dripping, and what looked like a piece of lung – we could not examine this properly as he had fallen on that side. There were 2 wounds on the bump at 3 and 6 o'clock – a big wound on the left side of the forehead and 5 more scattered about the upper part of the head. In all 14 shots had been fired into him during the encounter on 1st May and in spite of this, he had covered not less than 50 miles and probably twice that distance, and had survived for 17 days, so I don't think there can be much doubt that, if we had not encountered him, he would eventually have recovered. All of which goes to show that an elephant is not an easy animal to kill, unless hit in the right place. Measurement showed the rogue's height to be 9'4", and the tusks when extracted taped 54" and weighed 48 lbs. The rifles used on this occasion were both H.V. with solid bullets —— mine a .423 Mauser and R's a double .470, and the 4 shots must have been fired in the space of 5 seconds.

This brings to an end my experiences of shooting elephants, which, limited though they are, contain some lessons which I hope may be of use to others. To any sportsman about to hunt these animals for the first time, may I offer a few words of advice? First read Sanderson's book and after studying the diagrams of an elephant's head, compare them with a living elephant if possible, or at least with the photographs which so often appear in illustrated papers, paying particular attention to the bump and the ear–hole – you should then have no difficulty, then, in deciding where to aim when you are up against one in the jungle. But, remember, the head shot is not worth taking unless you are very close indeed, and that to get close you have to take some risks of detection – do not, therefore, despise the body shot. When you are going after a rogue, try and get another sportsmen to accompany you, and arrange with him beforehand that one should take the head and the other the body–shot – also which of you should fire first. Remember that you are dealing with a bloody–minded animal, who will certainly kill you if he gets a chance – you need, therefore, feel no compunction about firing to cripple him if you are doubtful whether a fatal shot offers. Once an elephant is down, run up and give him a finisher in the base of the skull before he can rise. Do not follow the example of the Burmese thugyee, but use a high velocity rifle of not less than .400 bore with solid bullets. Finally, before you shoot, be quite certain that the elephant in front of you is the animal for which you hold a permit. Two elephants had been shot by mistake for the Cradle Tusker before I accounted for him, and both were proscribed posthumously. It is not always that district officers are so complacent!"

The Gandamanayakanoor Tusker

The final episode is by D R D Wadia (91) he, in the forests below the High Wavy Mountains in Tamil Nadu where he shot a record tusker in 1928. Wadia writes:

"The Gandamanayakanoor Zamindari covers an area of 240 sq. miles out of which only 100 are cultivated (tea, cotton, wheat, cardamoms, etc.). The headquarters are at Gandamanayakanoor, 65 miles from Madura which, incidentally, is your last railhead. I left the H.Q. on April 1, for my first camp at Myladamparai which is 12 miles away. This place was selected because there is a tin shed there and, as it was continually raining in the evenings, the prospects of spending nights under damp canvas did not appeal to me! As things turned out, it was just as well that I did not push on into the interior. After 14 days of depressing inactivity, owing to incessant rain, I had nearly made up my mind to chuck it, and pack up for home. Signs of favourable weather, however, made me decide to chance it and push on another 20 miles to Udangal, where according to local gossip dwelt 'Record' Bison, Tiger, and a host of other game! Consequently, I got all the necessary things ready and we left on the 15th at 7 am on foot. We had hardly gone for half an hour when we happened on a lot of elephant tracks which could not have been very old. There were over 20 distinct sets of footprints of fairly large animals, as well as some of baby elephants. After searching abut for the definite tracks of a tusker, and not being satisfied, I decided to push on at a rapid pace to the next village (Kumlundhulu) 7.5 miles further, so as to circumvent the herd if possible. We were spared the trouble however as a 100 yards further fresh spoor of elephant was picked up, and this time we could hardly restrain our excitement, as among them was a set of huge footprints, which my men swore were those of a 'mighty tusker'; this was soon confirmed by the damage to the tree trunks, and a little further on the impression of a tusk in the soft mudbank of a dry nullah. Here was undoubtedly the best piece of luck we had struck so far, and we decided to track the animal forthwith. Tracking through the soft sand was easy enough, but five minutes of it brought us into very thick jungle. We were stalking along a regular elephant run and the visibility ahead was fairly good, but hardly encouraging. Another 15 minutes and we heard the elephant behind us not more than 150 yards away; we hastily tested the wind and, finding it against us, ran back 50 yards or so and waited. There was another path at right angles to the track we were following and the shikaris expected them to break cover about 30 yards in front, when I could have a good shot as they crossed the opening. All the time we could hear the herd feeding, and approaching well spread out, but we could not get a glimpse of the animals. It was hardly a comfortable situation, especially when I realized that it was rather a large herd, and that there was no means of avoiding a stampede, should it take place in our direction. We had no choice, however, so we decided on the 'wait and see' policy, frequently testing the fickle wind. We had not long to wait before a fairly large female leisurely strolled past the expected spot; she had a calf at heel. Then followed another female who half glanced towards where we crouched, then another calf. This little chap took quite a good look in our direction, but fortunately his interest was not intelligent! The fifth to cross was the 'Lord and Master' of the herd, with a natty line in 'ivory tuskings', so I let him have the right in the temple – a .470 solid. He fell on his knees, but recovered himself and, just as he was trying to stand up, I gave him the left, which I found later hit him 2" below the first shot. This crumpled him up completely and, after turning in our direction, he collapsed. All this time, which could not have been more than a few seconds, we had hardly paid any attention to his companions who were feeding around. These were alarmed on hearing the sudden reports, and a general stampede commenced. One of my men shinned up a neighbouring tree, the other whisked forward and crouched near the dead elephant, while I made for a small opening where the bushes were not so thick. I had just enough time to turn back and see five or seven elephants rushing past in Indian file within 2 yards of the spot whence I had fired, and immediately under my second shikari. I pushed through the thorny undergrowth to what I imagined was safety, when, looking down, was reminded by fresh footprints and droppings all over the place that it was not so very safe after all. I had no idea whether the whole herd had passed or whether there were more coming over but, needless to say, I beat it quickly.

Fortunately, the storm had blown over, everybody was safe, and the tusker was bagged. I shall never forget the moment when I came up to see the stout lad! As he lay there, he presented a magnificent spectacle, and seemed immense. My men were highly excited, and started tugging at his tail and slapping him in delight.

The measuring was done in under 30 minutes of the animal's being shot, and were afterwards checked by the Manager of the Estate, and another gentleman.

I sent the measurements to Rowland Wards, and they are published in the new edition of their Records. I am told that the correct method of measuring an elephant is to take the height at the highest point, i.e. to the slight ridge they have on their spine — please correct me if I am wrong, and Rowland Ward's best is 10'6".

[The correct method of measuring the height of an elephant according to Lieut.–Cl. G.H. Evans ('Elephants and their Diseases') is at the shoulder, as is done in horses. The height at the highest point of the back, however, would always form an interesting and useful additional record. EDS.].

Chapter 15

CONSERVATION AND FUTURE OF THE INDIAN ELEPHANT

The problems facing the Asian Elephant in India are a reflection of the state of environmental conservation in India. As a species able to live in a wide spectrum of vegetational types, the elephant acts as an indicator species of the condition of its biotic environment. A sub–optimal habitat is unable to meet the demands made on it by a herd of elephants, whose presence will result in further deterioration. Elephants in such habitats are compelled to seek sustenance elsewhere, and come into conflict with man. At the present rate of habitat loss, and degradation of existing habitats, it is doubtful if present populations can survive. One has to consider seriously the possibility that the Asian Elephant will be known as mainly a domesticated animal in the 21st century.

At the turn of the present decade, the nineties, the population of the African elephant was believed to have come down to 600,000 from the more than one million that had existed two decades before. In comparison, the Asian elephant with an esti-mated population of approximately 34,000 to 54,000 is truly endangered. The population decline of the Asian elephant, however, has not been as catastrophic as that of the African species; rather, a gradual erosion over the centuries, which has accelerated in the second half of the present century. The historical and present day distribution of the elephant records the continuing deterioration of the elephant's habitat. Within historic times there has been a progressive desiccation of West Asia. This deterioration is largely man–made, and the elephant has disappeared from areas where the forests have been destroyed for human needs.

The problem, facing the elephant and its ecosystem, is uncontrolled increase of human population, and demands on natural resources for the needs of this population. The example of India is illustrative. The human population of the Indian subcontinent was 251 million in 1921. In 1971 the state of India alone had a population of 547 million. Population projections estimated 734 million for 1986, 872 million for 1996, and 945 million for the year 2001. This projection assumed that the birthrate would drop to 25.7 percent in 1996–2001. Conditions in India do not support this assumption and the current population is in excess of projected figures.

In India an enormous area of prime elephant habitat has been lost since 1860 to the plantations of coffee, tea, rubber and teak which were carved out of existing forests. After 1950, hydroelectric projects ravaged elephant habitat through the submerging of forests and unscrupulous exploitation of the remnant forests. In Central India, the forests holding elephants cover the single largest deposit of iron–ore in Asia, and mining has been a continuing process since 1909. The states of North–east India, which used to be the stronghold of the elephant in India, are the areas where the main human–elephant conflict has developed. Exploding human populations have destroyed crucial elephant habitat for cultivation and plantations, extinguishing traditional migratory routes; and slash–and–burn cultivation has devastated habitats, making unlikely the survival of the elephant in some of the states.

The demand for forest produce, both for industry and fuel to support an increasing human population, has been rising rapidly. In India, firewood remains the main source of energy fuel. The demand increased from 8 million m^3 in 1967 to 24 m. m^3 in 1976. The firewood position in India's energy resources at that point of time can be gauged from the fact that, in 1970, India used 51.35 million tons of coal, 15.31 million tons of oil, and 122.76 million tons of firewood – twice the amount of coal and oil (Anon, 1978). The situation has now further deteriorated.

The elephant occurs in states which have the highest human density per square kilometre; Kerala (549), West Bengal (509), Bihar (324), Tamil Nadu (317) and Uttar Pradesh (300). The elephant is unlikely to be exterminated, but it will be much reduced in numbers, restricted to a few national parks, and perhaps, finally, seen only as a domesticated animal.

The conservation Action Plan of the Asian Elephant Specialist Group of the World Conservation Union (IUCN) estimated the total population of the Asian elephant between 3 and 54 thousand, with the minimum country population between 50 to 60 in Nepal, and the maximum between 17 to 22 thousand in India. India, currently, has the largest surviving population of the Asian elephant, approximately 50% of the total world population of the species. The problems that the elephant faces in India are broadly the problems that it faces, or will face, in other areas of its homelands in south–east Asia. The Indian population is discontinuously distributed in four major geographical zones: a south Indian population (c. 6000 – 8000) in the forests of the Western Ghat Hills in the States of Karnataka, Tamil Nadu and Kerala; a central Indian population (c. 2000) in the forests of Orissa, Bihar and south West Bengal, a northern population in Western Uttar Pradesh close to Nepal, and a North–eastern population (c. 9000–12000) in the States of West Bengal, Assam, Arunachal Pradesh, Nagaland, Manipur, Tripura, Mizoram and Meghalaya.

The status of the elephant in adjoining countries is equally bleak. Nepal, which has the lowest country population (c. 50–90), has lost over 80% of its elephant habitat to human settlement. Bhutan (60–150), though it still has substantial forest cover, is influenced by conditions in adjoining India as the population is shared with India. Bangladesh (c. 200–350) is rapidly losing its elephant habitat to development programmes, and the population is likely to diminish rapidly. The Myanmar population (c. 2000-10000), the second largest, has a reasonably undisturbed habitat and prospects of long term survival. Its present status however, needs further study. The elephant continues to be used in the extraction of Myanmar's timber wealth. In Thailand, in spite of the elephants having been a protected species since the 18th century, over–exploitation of the habitat, and the pressure of human population, has made the species highly vulnerable. Cambodia (c. 2000), noted in the past for its abundant elephant population, has suffered disastrous environmental loss from the thirty years of war which ravaged the country and its forests. As in the neighbouring countries of the Indo–Chinese Peninsula, namely Vietnam (c. 500–1000) and Laos (c. 2000), precise information on the status of the environment and of wildlife, including the elephant, is not available. The elephant population of China (c. 300) is restricted to an insignificant area in Yunnan province bordering Myanmar and Laos, where forests still exist. In Sri Lanka (c. 2700–3000), where there was an ancient tradition of protection dating back to the 12th century, there was a major loss in the population during the colonial period, until the species was given protection late in the present century.

Presently, large–scale development programmes have destroyed the elephants' habitat, and there is no future for the elephant except in a few protected areas. The Malaysian elephant (c. 1300–3000) has, like the Sri Lankan elephant, became a victim of development programmes, and occurs in small groups often pocketed in unsuitable habitats. There seems to be no hope for elephant survival outside protected areas. The elephants of Indonesia (Sumatra 2800–4000), and the possibly feral population of Kalimantan, Borneo (100–500), suffer from the same type of human population pressure which affects elephants throughout the range of the species, and there seems to be little chance of survival outside limited protected areas.

The loss of habitat to cultivation is the main area of conflict between man and elephant, and will, in the long run be the major cause for the extinction of the elephant over most of its range. Some examples may illustrate this point. The district of North Kanara, the northern–most range of the elephant population in south India, was largely under forest cover but, with the eradication of malaria, now has extensive enclaves of cultivation fragmenting the existing forest area. The majority of elephant herds were pocketed in small islands of forests surrounded by cultivation and, in course of time, destroyed. In north Bengal, in a period of four years, during the seventies of this century (1974–78), the population was reduced from 250 to 100 through control shooting, poaching and capture. Since 1967, vast areas of standing forests have been brought under cultivation, destroying elephant habitat, and blocking migration routes essential for the health of both the elephant and its habitat. The situation has not improved over the years, and about 186 elephants remain a problem population subject to severe human–elephant conflict.

This, then, is the scenario which faces us regarding the conservation of the elephant. Again, taking India as an example, conservation has been practised off and on over many centuries. I quote from an article published in the *Journal of the Bombay Natural History Society* in 1949 by a hunter–sportsman, who wrote, "So far back as the days of Ashoka Maurya (273–242 B.C.), the killing of an elephant was punished by death, and even now the shooting of one without a permit may involve a fine of Rs.500. But it would be a great mistake to imagine that elephants have always been protected. Prior to 1873, when the Madras Elephant Preservation Act became Law, these grand but destructive animals were classed as vermin, and a government reward of Rs.50 was paid on each one brought to bag, without distinction of sex or age. In spite of the inadequate weapons of those days, so many were killed that the government became apprehensive lest the supply of elephants for commissariat and forest work be seriously affected, and consequently passed the Act in question, under which it became an offence to shoot any elephant without special permission."

Today, the elephant is on Schedule 1 of the Indian Wildlife Protection Act, and also on CITES list of completely protected species. Whether this is an advantage, however, in the management of the elephant in India is a question that has to be examined. In the country with the largest population of elephants, special attention to their conservation commenced with the formation of the Asian Elephant Specialist Group of the IUCN in 1976.

The status survey that was made between the years 1976–80, and reported in the document published in 1980, has not been repeated in similar detail in India, the trend turning to research on identified areas of prime elephant habitat, by scientists of the Centre for Ecological Sciences, the Bombay Natural History Society and Wildlife Institute of India. The sustained interest in the conservation of the Asian elephant fostered by IUCN and Indian institutions such as the Bombay Natural History Society, Wildlife Institute of India and Centre for Ecological Sciences, promoted the Government of India to plan the organization of a PROJECT ELEPHANT similar in principle to PROJECT TIGER. A task force was established to spell out the problems facing the elephant and to frame a long–term conservation programme for the elephant in India under a specially funded initiative, namely the PROJECT ELEPHANT. The objectives were defined as:

– ensuring the long–term survival of identified large populations,

– evolving management plans for the smaller populations, mainly with a view to reducing man–elephant

297

confrontations and ensuring their survival pending further review of the ground situation.

Elephant Reserves were conceived, to:

– ensure the long–term survival of identified large populations: the target in the first phase was to protect habitats and existing ranges;

– link up already fragmented portions by established corridors wherever possible, and protecting corridors at present under threat;

– improve the quality of the habitat wherever necessary by attempting ecosystem restoration and other measures; keeping the main objectives of range protection in view; and

– attend to the socio–economic problems associated with this, especially the problem of elephant depredation, loss of employment, and problems arising out of restrictions on use of forest produce by the human populations living on the fringe.

The Committee appointed by the Government of India identified the major problems facing the Indian population as loss and fragmentation of habitats, loss of habitat quality or range degradation, and the inability of such areas to support existing elephant populations, loss of forest lands to meet the needs of increasing human population. The conservation strategy recommended by the Committee has as its goal (a) ensuring that each elephant–holding state maintains one or two natural viable populations of elephant, (b) ensure that the local communities in the environs of such areas are not adversely affected, (c) ensure that individual problem elephants do not negate conservation efforts aimed at the whole population.

The Project is now in operation, with a much lower level of public awareness than Project Tiger. This is a key point, which needs attention. It is also funded at a much lower level than project Tiger. Similar exercises in conservation are in operation, or have been proposed, in Sri Lanka, Myanmar, Malaysia and China.

A basic tool for elephant management is research on its ecology. Curiously enough, even though the elephant has been a part of human history in India from time immemorial and treatises such as Palakapyas Hastayurveda' (Treatment of Elephants) have been written in the past, scientific enquiry into the ecology of the elephant in India was not undertaken until the late seventies of this century. The elephant has, however, been the subject of serious scientific enquiry in countries adjoining India, particularly Sri Lanka and Malaysia. Nevertheless, there is an abundance of natural history notes published in the *Journal of the Bombay Natural History Society'* from the time elephants' value as an adjunct to forestry practices was first recognised.

Pioneering research on the ecology of the species in India was undertaken by R. Sukumar in the late seventies, with the assistance of the Asian Elephant Group, and funded by World Wide Fund for Nature. Subsequently, research undertaken by the scientists of the Bombay Natural History Society, funded by the Fish and Wildlife Service of the U.S. Government, has brought out very interesting data on elephants and their effect on the habitat. For instance, Sivaganesan's studies on habitat utilisation have shown that over–exploitation of food does not lead to the destruction of a forest ecosystem, but the selected disappearance of the most favoured species of trees fed on by the elephants in the different habitat types. Methods of regeneration of favoured food species are required. The problems facing the wildlife manager in the conservation of the elephant have been clearly brought out by Ajay Desai (114). He showed that home ranges of herds cover areas with different levels of protection in a conservation area, and a herd or, for that matter, a population of elephants living within National Park or Wildlife Sanctuary is, therefore, not assured of complete protection throughout its range. Studies by Hemant Datye

(1993) in Dalma Wildlife Sanctuary, Bihar and Ramesh Kumar in Tamil Nadu/Karnataka, on an isolated elephant population, and peripheral elephant population respectively, have shown how desperate the situation is for populations subjected to severe biotic pressure from human encroachment. It is, therefore, necessary to ensure that there is a strong research component, not only to collect basic data but also to examine management oriented problems.

It is necessary to repeat the status surveys undertaken over two decades ago. True censi have been conducted as recently as 1993, but a comparison with earlier data has not been attempted, including habitat availability. An attempt to estimate the status of the species, throughout its range, is essential. There has been considerable difference of opinion on census methods. The method to be used will vary with ground conditions. This has to be appreciated, but there can be no difference of opinion that a status survey of the Asian Elephant population, throughout its present range, should be a continuing exercise. One of the major objectives of Project Elephant is to identify and protect complexes of contiguous national parks and sanctuaries, as a Composite Elephant Range. These should be the essential target areas for conservation of the elephant throughout its range.

An urgent requirement is to survey in depth the potential of a complex of sanctuaries as an elephant range, for the long–term survival of viable elephant populations, through precise assessment of existing elephant populations, assessing habitat status of the component sanctuaries and national parks, assessing the corridors between the protected areas and their viability; assessing the pressures from human activities and their long–term effects on protected area components of the range; assessing present human/elephant conflict areas within the range; assessing the impact of future development plans on the range as a whole. This is crucial for all identified elephant ranges as the future of the elephant depends on how best elephant and human needs can be met, in a continuously deteriorating environmental situation, throughout its distribution, owing to the uncontrolled increase in the human population, and the constituent escalating demand on natural resources.

A basic research, which will be useful in this context and which was in progress until recently in one identified elephant range, is data collection on ranging behaviour of elephant from radio–collared elephants, to assess exact home ranges; to identify crop raiders, the extent of such raids and probable causes, and to determine the extent to which collared elephants range outside protected areas. Another area for immediate consideration is the status of elephants stranded in habitats fragmented by human encroachment. There are several populations which have now been isolated from the main elephant ranges, and it is necessary to determine the minimum requirements of such pocketed populations for their continued survival. It is, therefore, necessary to assess the capacity of such habitats to hold existing populations, and the pressures on such populations with the long–term viability of the habitat for its elephant populations.

The future of non–viable populations is cause for considerable concern. Culling, as practised in Africa, is not acceptable as far as the Asian elephant is considered, at least in India. The only available alternative is capture and domestication. Apparently, in India, it is now the central government's policy to encourage the use of elephants in forestry practices as they were used in former years. It should also be possible to meet the requirements of non–governmental needs. It is essential however, that a school for the capture, management, training and maintenance of elephants, and the training of mahouts be established immediately. The expertise is available in India, and the need is urgent. Capture can now be humanely done, using immobilising and tranquilising drugs, and the most humane method of training is Kraal training, as is practised in South India. The major populations in India, and elsewhere in its distribution, are genetically isolated. It is now necessary to examine the genetic status of isolated populations, and to consider ways and means of establishing gene flow between permanently isolated populations. Relationships between clans in stable populations, among domesticated elephants, and whether domesticated elephants can be made the gene carriers between permanently isolated populations, are problems that now require serious consideration.

There is also the question of ivory poaching. Though not on as massive a scale as of the African species, the selective removal of tuskers has played havoc in the sex ratio of many populations. The elephant is an apex species, able by its size and its interaction with its habitat, particularly in its quest for food, to influence the direction of development of its biotic environment. It has been one of the causes for the process of change in its ecosystem. Such a function is no longer acceptable in an environment managed by man, where the process of change has been speeded up. As noted earlier, the range of the elephant has, through the ages, shrunk considerably. This process was accelerated however, as the industrial revolution in the latter half of the last century brought a mechanized commercial culture into the countries of its occurrence. The tools used by man in a region decide its future, and the tools of an alien culture now in use for gathering natural resources for commerce, and to meet the needs of an ever-increasing human population, have destroyed a natural slow-moving ecosystem. The elephant has become in the process too large an animal to find sustenance and living room in the shrinking world of nature.

The conservation of the Asian elephant in Asia cannot be the concern of only the forest departments and environmentalists. Conserving the elephant involves the conservation of prime wildlife habitats. This needs a multidisciplinary effort, where the local people, the administrators and land-use planners have to be involved at all levels. Conserving the elephant, therefore, means conserving the human environment, and it has to be a part of the development plans of each state of Asia as a whole. The Asian elephant is a part of the culture of man in tropical Asia. It is an integral part of the religions of the region and, one hopes, will not be sacrificed in the search for a better life for the people of the region.

REFERENCES

Journal of Bombay Natural History Society

(1)	Randhawa, M.S.	45:558-56 (1945)
(2)	Salim Ali.	31:533-61 (1927)
(3)	Burton, R.W.	50:399-400 (1951)
(4)	Molesworth, A.l..M.	23:350-351 (1914)
(5)	Shebbeare, E.O.	23:770 (1914)
(6)	Elwes, H.J.	24:355 (1915)
(7)	Betts, F.N.	47:547 (1947)
(8)	Champion, F.W.	32:127 (1928)
(9)	Singh, V.B.	75:71 (1978)
(10)	Mooney, H.F.	33:430 (1928)
(11)	U Tun Yin.	54:175-178 (1955)
(12)	Dollman, Guy.	39:619 (1931)
(13)	Pillai, N.G.	48:356-57 (1949)
(14)	Richmond, R.D.	36:494-96 (1932)
(15)	Pillai, N.G.	42:927-28 (1941)
(16)	Rensch, B. & K. W. Hardi	52:842-85 (1954)
(17)	Evans, G.H.	11:322 (1896)
(18)	Thom, W.S.	36:321 (1932)
(19)	Bruce, C.W.A.	14:151 (1901)
(20)	Krishnan, M.	69:298-321 (1972)
(21)	Flower, S.S.	11:335 (1897)
(22)	Stanford, J.K.	37:486 (1934)
(23)	Tun Yin, U.	54:178 (1956)
(24)	Stracey, P.D.	46:717 (1946)
(25)	Morris, R.C.	54:460 (1956)
(26)	John, A.W.	32:596 (1927)
(27)	Millar, G.D.L.	41:171 (1939)
(28)	Millar, G.D.L.	39:854 (1937)
(29)	Reade, L.L.	33:979 (1929)
(30)	Morris, R.C.	33:202 (1929)
(31)	Colyer, Sir Frank.	34:694 (1930)
(32)	Morris, R.C.	35:889 (1932)
(33)	Morris, R.C.	38:615 (1935)

(34)	Cameron, J.J.	31:512 (1927)
(35)	Anderson, R.K.	31:514 (1927)
(36)	Morris, R.C.	31:515 (1927)
(37)	Hundley Gordon.	28:537 (1922)
(38)	Gee, E.P.	53:135 (1955)
(39)	Aiyappan, A.	46:182-83 (1945)
(40)	Vincent, J.R.	46:183-184 (1946)
(41)	Tutein-Nollkenins, A.C.	38:183-84 (1935)
(42)	Allan, C.W.	21:239-240 (1912)
(43)	Robertson, G.C.	37:950 (1934)
(44)	Foot, A.E.	38:392 (1935)
(45)	Hubback, T.H.	40:730 (1938)
(46)	Paul De Lanney	40:323 (1938)
(47)	Gonzalez, J.	40:731 (1938)
(48)	Stockley, C.H.	31:813-14 (1926)
(49)	Macfie, D.F.	22:789-90 (1913)
(50)	Ramachandran, K.K.	81:687 (1984)
(51)	Hundley, Gordon.	37:487-88 (1934)
(52)	Lakshminarayana.	60:250-51 (1962)
(53)	Neelakantan, K.K.	61:438 (1964)
(54)	Morris, R.C.	50:93 (1952)
(55)	Morris, R.C.	39:165 (1936)
(56)	Stracey, P.D.	53:690 (1955)
(57)	Jackson, V.A.	26:285 (1918)
(58)	Nicholls, Frank.	53:585 (1955)
(59)	Macnaghten, H.	26:285 (1918)
(60)	Nicholls, Frank.	50:396-97 (1951)
(61)	Kadambi, K.	52:590-93 (1953)
(62)	Morris, R.S.	24:800 (1920)
(63)	Smythies, E.A.	41:654-55 (1939)
(64)	Reade, L.L.	35:674-75 (1931)
(65)	Milroy, A.J.W.	29:803-811 (1923)
(66)	Ghosh, S.K.	38:614-15 (1935)
(67)	Morris, R.C.	31:517-18 (1926)
(68)	Stonor, C.R.	44:588-89 (1944)
(69)	Mathew, A.P.	33:708 (1929)
(70)	Macfie, D.F.	32:214 (1928)
(71)	Simon, E.S.	46:396 (1946)
(72)	Tun Yin, U.	54:179 (1956)
(73)	Hundley, Gordon.	32:214 (1927)
(74)	Davidar, Priya.	68:819 (1971)

(75)	Bryant, H.B.	10:133 (1895)
(76)	Mooney, H.F.	30:912 (1925)
(77)	Leahy, P.B. (Mrs).	56:397 (1946)
(78)	Morris, R.C.	33:794 (1927)
(79)	Champion, F.W.	33:434 (1927)
(80)	Morris, R.C.	37:727 (1934)
(81)	Morris, R.C.	37:726 (1934)
(82)	Morris, R.C.	46:541-42 (1946)
(83)	Tutein Nolthenius, A.C.	47:154-156 (1941)
(84)	Pillai, N.G.	52:206-207 (1954)
(85)	Morris, R.C.	34:237-242 (1929)
(86)	Morris, R.C.	44:113-114 (1943)
(87)	Morris, R.C.	31:720-725 (1926)
(88)	Morris, R.C.	33:862-868 (1929)
(89)	Hall, J.E.	41:563-572 (1940)
(90)	Pythian-Adams	48:202-212 (1949)
(91)	Wadia, D.R.D.	33:434-437 (1928)
(92)	Lawrie, A.S.	32:792-793 (1928)
(93)	Low, Carmichael G.	33:707 (1928)
(94)	Gee, E.P.	49:113(1950)
(95)	Beckett, J.	36:242-243 (1932)
(96)	Choudhury, Anwaruddin	88:216-221 (1989)
(97)	Morris, R.C.	42: 658 (1941)
(98)	Hubback, Theodore.	42(3):503 (1941)
(99)	Morris, R.C.	50(3):933 (1952)
(100)	Morris, R.C.	52:206 (1953)
(101)	Haswell, F.W.	40:560 (1938)
(102)	Morris, R.C.	36:494 (1932)
(103)	Rajagopal, K....	62:549 (1968)
(104)	Tun Yin, U.	69:646-647 (1922)
(105)	Wilson, J.C.C.	28:1128-1129 (1922)
(106)	Lahiri Choudhury, D.K.	"The Indian Elephant in a changing world" in Contemporary Indian Tradition. Edited by Carla M. Borden. Smithsonian Institution, Press, Washington. (1988)

(107) N. Sivaganesan. (1995). Ecology of the Asian Elephant. Final Report. pp.20- 75. Bombay Natural History Society.

(108) Bor, N. L. 32:594 (1928)

(109) Priya Davidar 68:919 (1972)

(110) V. Krishnamurthy (1995) Reproductive pattern in captive elephants in the Tamil Nadu Forest Dept., India in "A Week with Elephants" edited by J C Daniel & H. Datye. BNHS/OUP. pp. 450-455.

(111) R. Sukumar & R. Ramesh (1995) Elephant foraging: Is Browse or Grass more important? in "A Week with Elephants" edited by J C Daniel & H. Datye. BNHS/OUP. pp. 368-374.

(112) S.S. Flower (1943). Notes on age at sexual maturity gestation period and growth of Asian elephant. *Proc. Zool.* Soc., London Ser. A: 113:21-26.

(113) Michael J. Schmidt & Khyne U. Mar (1996) Reproductive performance of captive Asian elephants in Myanmar. *Gajah* 16:23-42.

(114) Ajai Desai JBNHS : 88:145-156 (1991)